To: Rev. Bernard M...
Dep. of Religion & Religious Education
The Catholic University of America
Washington, D.C. 20017

From: John C. Kersten
P.O. Box 42
Clarksdale, Miss. 38614

Bible Catechism

VATICAN II EDITION

No! Please Don't Take This Book From Religious Education Library. Thank You.

"A Saint Joseph Edition"

BIBLE CATECHISM

Bible and Life

A MEANING FOR MAN'S EXISTENCE

BY JOHN C. KERSTEN, S. V. D.

With Bible Readings, Study Helps,
Treasury of Prayers, Practical Meditations,
and Other Valuable Features

Illustrated

Vatican II Edition

CATHOLIC BOOK PUBLISHING CO.
NEW YORK

This new Bible Catechism
is dedicated to
SAINT JOSEPH
Patron of the Universal Church.

"We cannot encourage enough all the means by which souls are brought to the Bible, the vivifying source of spiritual doctrine."
—*Pope John XXIII*

The parts from the Books of the Old and New Testaments are reproduced by license of Confraternity of Christian Doctrine, Washington, D.C. Used with its permission. All rights reserved.

PHOTO CREDITS: American Music Conference: 287; Arab Information Center: 70, 89; Authenticated News International: 64, 270, 274; H. Armstrong Roberts: 91, 123, 126, 142, 153, 159, 168, 182, 253, 266, 283; Philip Gendreau: 264; Metropolitan Museum of Art, Bequest of Michael Dreicer, 1921: 58; Museum of Fine Arts, Boston: 280; Museum of Modern Art, N. Y.: 219; Religious News Service: 95, 191, 277; The Trustees, The National Gallery, London: 85; Wide World Photos: 16, 91, 121, 155, 174, 267; Ken Wittenberg: 179.

IMPRIMI POTEST: Very Rev. Robert C. Hunter, *S.V.D.* *Superior*
NIHIL OBSTAT: J. Emile Pfister, S.J. *Censor Deputatus*
IMPRIMATUR: ✠ Joseph B. Brunini, D.D. *Bishop of Natchez-Jackson*
November 8, 1972

(T-245)

© 1973, 1967-1964 by *Catholic Book Publishing Co., N. Y.*
United States and Canada — Printed in U.S.A.

"Since God speaks in sacred Scripture through men in human fashion, the interpreter of Sacred Scripture, in order to see clearly what God wanted to communicate to us, should carefully investigate what meaning the sacred writers really intended, and what God wanted to manifest by means of their words."

"Those who search out the intention of the sacred writers must, among other things, have regard for "literary forms." For truth is proposed and expressed in a variety of ways, depending on whether a text is history of one kind or another, or whether its form is that of prophecy, poetry, or some other type of speech." "But, since holy Scripture must be read and interpreted according to the same Spirit by whom it was written, no less serious attention must be given to the content and unity of the whole of Scripture, in the meaning of the sacred texts is to be correctly brought to light."

"For all of what has been said about the way of interpreting Scripture is subject finally to the judgment of the Church, which carries out the divine commission and ministry of guarding and interpreting the word of God."

(Vatican II: *"Dogmatic Constitution on Divine Revelation"* no. 12.)

NOTE: The small numbers in the margin throughout the book refer to the Bibliographical Notes, pp. 323-330. Those provide a handy, up-to-date and extensive guide to further literature for those who wish more information, explanation or comentary on the points made by the author.

PREFACE

This is the third edition of *Bible Catechism*. The author has kept abreast of Catechetics on a world-wide scale for thirty years and has paid particular attention to the fate of that ancient book —*the* book, the Bible —during those years. It becomes ever more clear that without the Bible, present in all of Christian life and education, we might as well do away with Christianity itself (in the words of the new *General Catechetical Directory* issued for the whole Church "Sacred Scripture is the soul of catechesis"). Hence, this new and updated *Bible Catechism,* geared to upper grades in high school, study groups, prospective converts, CCD classes and teachers of religion.

Indeed, there are changes. A deeper insight, offered by professional Bible scholars, dogmatic and moral theologians, sociologists, contemporary philosophers and experts in education, made us update every edition of *Bible Catechism.*

The following observation is for fellow priests or discussion leaders who may be thinking of using this book for their students or study group.

The author considers himself as "critically progressive." However, this does not mean he upholds:

(1) disqualifying Church authority as such ("being in the game, but on your own terms");

(2) reserving for oneself the right to be a selective Christian (choosing what suits you and leaving the rest of the Christian message alone);

(3) denying the uniqueness of the Bible (placing it on one line with the sacred books of other religions or any good book);

(4) opposing any binding laws especially in the field of sex and marriage;

(5) reducing Christianity to a vague humanitarianism;

(6) doing away with *organized* religion as such.

With respect to such ideas, the author may be qualified as conservative. A fellow priest who advocates any of these beliefs should look for another book with which to instruct his students.

On the other hand, if mentally you are a pre-Vatican II priest, and believe that we should keep our intellectuals in the fold by teaching them the questions and answers of the *Baltimore Catechism* and hiding from them what sound contemporary theology is teaching, you will be shocked by the information which this book offers, and consequently you should not use it.

Indeed, theology is not necessarily the faith. Rather, it is faith searching for some understanding of the tremendous mysteries entrusted to man on his journey through the dark valley of human existence. Theologies—some good, some bad—are coming and going. But our intellectuals should know how contemporary theologians are trying to shed some light on our common faith, wording it in concepts which are familiar to man of this age and culture.

1. In being critically progressive, the author holds the following beliefs:

(1) like any other group, the people of God needs authority, though the way of exercising it should be adapted to time, place, and culture without violating its basic structure as given by the Founder;

(2) the core of Christianity is a "package deal" ("take it or leave it!"), but this core should be rediscovered by cleansing it from man-made sediments, which may have obscured it over the centuries;

(3) without denying God's guidance which is present in other sacred books in some way (they often reflect a ray of that truth which enlightens all men!), the Bible is a unique book which came into existence through a special guidance (inspiration) of Almighty God and contains a divinely revealed message, which is not found in its fullness anywhere else; but all the results of professional research should be utilized to discover man's word and through it God's word in Scripture;

(4) there are binding laws, though man should take his *informed* conscience as final authority;

(5) prayer and worship are necessary and valuable, since God is not only immanent in creation (fellowmen), but also transcends it as an Absolute "You" or Person; however, sound theology should guide our approach to the Ultimate Reality;

(6) both psychologically speaking and according to the oldest traditions, Christianity must be lived in groups or congregations, though the way these groups are organized should be adapted to circumstances of time, place, and culture; hence, Christians have the serious duty to find out which of the existing groups (Churches) is the best available, in other words, closest to what Christ, not you or I, wants His Church to be.

A final remark for the reader or student.

This book is both an invitation and a challenge.

An invitation to fellow human beings who ponder the possibility of joining us Christians in the Catholic tradition. This book shows how we follow the experience of the Hebrews in their restless search for meaning in life.

A challenge to fellow Catholics with sufficient intellectual background. This book differs from the Catechism you grew up with. And that could be the reason that it can help you when doubts and questions bother you. We know that the Hebrews faced this same situation. But they searched and in their search for meaning they were guided by God. And that is the reason why the Hebrews, Jesus of Nazareth included, challenge men of all times—as well as yourself—to join them in that search for meaning in life. By introducing you to their literature (the Bible), this meditation book will help you to interpret your own experience and existence.

The author is indebted to Miss Gladys Sturgis, Miss Helen Anderson, Mrs. K. Mosley, Miss E. Herrick, and the staff of the Catholic Book Publishing Company for their part in the preparation and production of this book.

CONTENTS

CHAPTER	PAGE
Preface	1

THE HISTORY OF SALVATION

PART I

ABRAHAM

1. Abraham Elected by God — *Our Faith* 11
2. Abraham Visited by God — *God's Loving Presence* ... 15
3. Abraham Offers His Son 18

MOSES

4. God Protects Moses 20
5. God Reveals Himself in the Burning Bush 22
6. The Departure of Israel from Egypt 26
7. The Covenant 29
8. The Public Worship of the Old Covenant — *The Sacred Liturgy* 33

DAVID

9. David, King of Israel — *The Kingdom of God* 36

THE PROPHETS OF THE OLD TESTAMENT

10. God Created Heaven and Earth 39
11. The Bible on Angels — *God's Concern for Man* 44
12. God Created Man — *God's Blueprint* 47

CHAPTER	PAGE
13. Adam and Eve Disobeyed God — *Temptation and Sin. God is All-knowing and All-just*	51
14. The Consequences of Sin for the Human Race — *Patience and Penance*	53
15. God Promised a Redeemer — *God is Merciful*	57

JOHN THE BAPTIZER

16. Saint John Introduces Christ — *The Redeemer Is Priest and Victim*	63

JESUS CHRIST

17. Jesus Christ Proclaims the Kingdom of God — *Reform Your Lives!*	67
18. Jesus of Nazareth — *Mary Conceives of the Holy Spirit*	71
19. Jesus Christ Is the Son of God	75
20. Christ a Light of Revelation to the Gentiles — *The Apostolate*	79
21. His Own Did Not Accept Him	84
22. The Suffering Servant of the Lord	87
23. A Sin Offering	90
24. The New Covenant in His Blood	94
25. The Resurrection of Our Lord — *We Shall Arise with Him*	98
26. The Ascension of Jesus Christ	102

THE HOLY SPIRIT

27. Descent of God's Spirit	105
28. The Gift of the Spirit	109
29. The Spirit too Helps Us	113
30. The Blessed Trinity	115

THE HISTORY OF SALVATION

PART II
THE CHURCH OF JESUS CHRIST

CHAPTER		PAGE
31.	The Church of Jesus Christ (Part 1) — *The New People of God*	122
32.	The Church of Jesus Christ (Part 2) — *The Unity of life with Christ*	126
33.	The Church of Jesus Christ (Part 3) — *The Ecclesiastical Office*	129
34.	The Church Our Teacher	135
35.	The Church, Custodian of Divine Tradition	139
66.	The Church Continues Christ's Priesthood	144
37.	Groping toward Unity	146
38.	The Communion of Saints (Part 1)	150
39.	The Communion of Saints (Part 2 — *Mary, Mother of the Redeemer and Our Mother*	152

CHRISTIAN INITIATION

40.	Baptism (Part 1)	159
41.	Baptism (Part 2)	165
42.	Confirmation	170
43.	Christian Virtues — *Faith, Hope and Love*	173
44.	Love of Neighbor	177
45.	Prayer	181
46.	The Sign Value of Marriage and Celibacy	187
47.	The Eucharist (Part 1)	193
48.	The Eucharist (Part 2)	199
49.	The Eucharist (Part 3)	203

SACRED SIGNS

| 50. | The Sacrament of Penance (Part 1) — *Temptation and Sin* | 207 |

51. The Sacrament of Penance (Part 2) — *Contrition,, Guilt And Forgiveness* ....
52. The Sacrament of Penance (Part 3) — *Authority to Forgive Sins* 215
53. The Sacrament of Penance (Part 4) — *Confession of Sins* 219
54. Anointing of the Sick 222
55. Holy Orders 227
56. Marriage in Christ 232
57. The Sacraments 241

ETHICS IN THE KINGDOM OF GOD

58. On Appreciation 245
59. An Informed Conscience 249
60. Conscience and the Commandments 252
61. Situation Ethics and Church Guidance 257
62. Community Worship 262
63. Situation and Respect for Life 265
64. Situation and Stewardship 269

THE LAST THINGS

65. Death, Judgment and Good Works 274
66. Punishment, Purge and Reward 279
67. The Resurrection of the Body and Life Everlasting 282
68. Celebration 286

Treasury of Prayers 290
How to Read Your Bible 296
The Growth of God's Promise 309
The General Catechetical Directory 310
Analytical Index 318
Bibliographical Notes 323

THE HISTORY OF SALVATION

"Abraham went as the Lord directed him" (Genesis 12:4)

PART I

Abraham, our father in Faith. *Moses*, the mediator of the Covenant. *David*, the king of Israel. *The Prophets*, who conveyed Israel's vision of the past, kept alive Faith in God and foretold the coming of the Messiah. *John the Baptizer*, the herald (forerunner) of our Lord. *Jesus Christ*, through Whom God revealed Himself after He had spoken "in times past" by the Prophets—Christ: our Teacher, King and High Priest. *The Holy Spirit*, Who completes the work of Jesus Christ.

ABRAHAM

I. Abraham Elected by God

Our Faith

In the traditions of a group of tribes on the east coast of the Mediterranean, we observe a growing awareness of an Ultimate Reality, which they called Yahweh, the Lord of heaven and earth. In their literature (the Bible), these people have described their God and His concern for man in their history and colorful stories and figures of speech.

A well-known character in these Hebrew traditions is Abraham, described as a native of the town of Ur (excavated in 1922) in Chaldea, while Hammurabi was king of Babylon (1800 B.C.). In the Abraham cycle of traditions (Genesis 11:27 —25:18) the Hebrews record their earliest experience of God, His care for man and man's response in Faith.

Abraham was a nomad. Some Bible scholars see him as an occasional leader of the commercial caravans which, following the route of the Fertile Crescent, maintained business between Mesopotamia and Egypt. (See Map in your Bible.)

1a. *The Lord said to Abram: "Go forth from the land of your kinsfolk and from your father's house to a land that I will show you.*
"I will make of you a great nation
and I will bless you;
I will make your name great,
so that you will be a blessing.

> *I will bless those who bless you*
> *and curse those who curse you.*
> *All the communities of the earth*
> *shall find blessing in you."*
> Abram went as the Lord directed him, and Lot went with him. Abram was seventy-five years old when he left Haran (Genesis 12:1-4).
>
> When Abram was ninety-nine years old, the Lord appeared to him and said: "I am God the Almighty. Walk in my presence and be blameless. Between you and me I will establish my covenant, and I will multiply you exceedingly."
>
> When Abram prostrated himself, God continued to speak to him: "My covenant with you is this: you are to become the father of a host of nations. No longer shall you be called Abram; your name shall be Abraham, for I am making you the father of a host of nations. I will render you exceedingly fertile; I will make nations of you; kings shall stem from you. I will maintain my covenant with you and your descendants after you throughout the ages as an everlasting pact, to be your God and the God of your descendants after you. I will give to you and to your descendants after you the land in which you are now staying, the whole land of Canaan, as a permanent possession; and I will be their God." (Genesis 17:1-8)
>
> 1b. Hoping against hope, Abraham believed and so became the father of many nations, just as it was once told him, "Numerous as this shall your descendants be." Without growing weak in faith he thought of his own body, which was as good as dead (for he was nearly a hundred years old), and of the dead womb of Sarah. Yet he never questioned or doubted God's promise; rather, he was strengthened in faith and gave glory to God, fully persuaded that God could do whatever he had promised. Thus his faith was credited to him as justice.
>
> The words, "It was credited to him," were not written with him alone in view; they were intended for us too. For our faith will be credited to us also if we believe in him who raised Jesus our Lord from the dead, the Jesus who was handed over to death for our sins and raised up for our justification (Romans 4:18-25).

2a. The Bible teaches religion. From the outset we should keep in mind that the Bible does not teach us science. Neither does it instruct us primarily about history. (There are historical inaccuracies in the Bible!) The Bible teaches us religion sometimes with the aid of parables, folklore, and allegories, and at other times with the aid of history, insofar as it was known to the sacred writer.

Usually, the sacred writers did not spend much time to find out what had actually happened so many centuries before. They utilized oral traditions and perhaps documents, as they knew them, to teach us about God, His relationship to His people and our relationship to Him. The fact that these traditions were used by the sacred writer to teach us religion does not make them any more or less historically correct. (The section on "How to Read Your Bible," p. 296, gives more details concerning this point.)

2b. Embellishments introduced. Bible scholars tell us that the accounts about Abraham and the other patriarchs of God's chosen people are basically history. They were finally edited about 300 B.C. Since Abraham lived about 1850 B.C., we can readily understand how these approximately 1500-year-old traditions might have undergone some changes. Colorful additions and embellishments were introduced! But the very core of the stories is history. Inspired by God the sacred writer used these traditions as he knew them, to teach us religious values.

3.

Abraham, as described in the Bible story, was a pagan, neither better nor worse than his fellowmen. God elected (chose) this simple Bedouin, lifted him from the darkness of paganism, and gave him the gift of Faith.

2c. Our Father in Faith. Abraham accepted God's special favor and believed in Him. He surrendered himself and his family entirely to God. That is why the Catholic Church considers Abraham as the spiritual father of all who believe in God. Of course, Abraham did not fully understand God's promises, neither did the sacred writer who edited the traditions about Abraham around the year 300 B.C. It is the New Testament which fully explains these promises to us. (Read Romans 4:18-25 under no. 1b, above; also Galatians 3: 16. 26-29, and the great discourse of Stephen in Acts 7:1-8.)

Faith, or self-surrender, was not easy for Abraham. God promised to bestow the whole land of Canaan upon him and his offspring. But as long as Abraham lived, he had to rent pasture land for his cattle from the local rulers. He remained a foreigner in the Promised Land.

God promised to make Abraham the patriarch of a great and numerous nation. Yet up until they were very old, Abraham and his wife Sarah were not blessed with offspring. But Abraham believed and was faithful to the Covenant of God.

3. Faith, that is, self-surrender, is a grace (gift) of God. God invites you and expects you to accept His invitation. God reveals Himself to you through Christ and His Church. Your Faith must follow the perfect Faith of Abraham as its pattern. It must be a wholehearted self-surrender to God and Christ in the Church He established.

4. Since the Covenant (partnership) of God with mankind is renewed in Christ, the holy people of God are no longer only the carnal offspring of Abraham. God now chooses from all nations of the world: "This means that those who believe are sons of Abraham. Because Scripture saw in advance that God's way of justifying the Gentiles would be through faith, it foretold this good news to Abraham: 'All nations shall be blessed in you.' Thus it is that all who believe are blessed along with Abraham, the man of faith" (Galatians 3:7-9).

Of course, God wills that our Faith should also be reasonable. We will discuss this later in Chapter 5, no. 2b. First, however, remember that Faith is a free gift of God which you must gratefully accept.

4. THINKING IT OVER

How did the Hebrews describe their earliest experience of God? What is the meaning of "Faith"? Why was Abraham's Faith not easy? Through Whom does God reveal Himself to us? Can you receive the gift of Faith through your own efforts, e.g., by reading books about religion? Who belong now to the people of God? Note how the calling of Abraham is related about 2,000 years later by Stephen (and recorded by St. Luke in Acts 7:1-8), and compare it with the story in Genesis found in no. 1a, above.

5. READ ATTENTIVELY

What is Faith? Faith is a grace (gift) of God that makes us surrender ourselves entirely to God, Who reveals Himself to us.

Ch. 2   Abraham Visited by God   15

6. PRAY MEDITATIVELY

"O Lord, let the light of your countenance shine upon us" (Psalm 4:7). "Show me, O Lord, your way, and lead me on a level path" (Psalm 27:11). Increase my Faith!

7. THINGS TO DO

Read: Genesis 12—23. Use this Bible Catechism often as a meditation book. Read it at least a quarter of an hour daily. To supplement this book, have the Bible and a Missal. You need them both for instruction in class and for study at home.

Read attentively the section on "How to Read Your Bible," p. 296.

2. Abraham Visited by God

God's Loving Presence

1. The men set out from there and looked down toward Sodom; Abraham was walking with them, to see them on their way. The Lord reflected: "Shall I hide from Abraham what I am about to do, now that he is to become a great and populous nation, and all the nations of the earth are to find blessing in him? Indeed, I have singled him out that he may direct his sons and his posterity to keep the way of the Lord by doing what is right and just, so that the Lord may carry into effect for Abraham the promises he made about him." Then the Lord said: "The outcry against Sodom and Gomorrah is so great, and their sin so grave, that I must go down and see whether or not their actions fully correspond to the cry against them that comes to me. I mean to find out."

While the two men walked on farther toward Sodom, the Lord remained standing before Abraham. Then Abraham drew nearer to him and said: "Will you sweep away the innocent with the guilty? Suppose there were fifty innocent people in the city; would you wipe out the place, rather than spare it for the sake of the fifty innocent people within it? Far be it from you to do such a thing, to make the innocent die with the guilty, so that the innocent and the guilty would be treated alike! Should not the judge of all the world act with justice?" The Lord replied, "If I find fifty innocent people in the city

16   Abraham Visited by God   Ch. 2

of Sodom, I will spare the whole place for their sake." Abraham spoke up again: "See how I am presuming to speak to my Lord, though I am but dust and ashes! What if there are five less than fifty innocent people? Will you destroy the whole city because of those five?" "I will not destroy it," he answered, "if I find forty-five there." But Abraham persisted, saying, "What if only forty are found there?" He replied, "I will forbear doing it for the sake of the forty." Then he said, "Let not my Lord grow impatient if I go on. What if only thirty are found there?" He replied, "I will forbear doing it if I can find but thirty there." Still he went on, "Since I have thus dared to speak to my Lord, what if there are no more than twenty?" "I will not destroy it," he answered, "for the sake of the twenty." But he still persisted, "Please, let not my Lord grow angry if I speak up this last time. What if there are at least ten there?" "For the sake of those ten," he replied, "I will not destroy it."

The Lord departed as soon as he had finished speaking with Abraham, and Abraham returned home (Genesis 18:16-33).

2a.   Faith the leitmotiv. This tradition of the Abraham cycle contains clearly folkloristic elements. What did the author/editor have in mind when he added it to Sacred Scripture? All the Abraham traditions as in Genesis 12—25 have his Faith as a *leitmotiv*. Hence, we should understand this passage as Paul explains these traditions in Romans 4:18-25. (See Chapter 1, no. 1b.)

"He sat in the entrance of his tent, while the day was growing hot"
(Genesis 18:1)

2b.   Growing awareness. We should keep in mind that the Old Testament is the history of a people's encounter with God and its response to that encounter. Gradually, Israel became more conscious of God's loving presence, just as a child gradually becomes more aware of what his parents mean to him. Scripture reflects this process of growing and often failing in understanding and response.

The lines "I [God] have chosen him" and "Abraham remained standing in the presence of the Lord" might serve as the keynote of this tradition.

3. Participation in this growing awareness. By reading the Bible we should participate in this process of growing. Gradually, you should become more conscious of God's loving presence to you. There are those who consider Christianity principally as either one or both of these: a burden or a mere device for avoiding hell and entering heaven. But Christianity is not primarily a group of commandments. It is, above all, a Gospel: "good tidings" that God is a loving Father, Who has chosen you.

Abraham, as described in this tradition, may be taken as an example of what your attitude toward God should be, especially when you are praying. (For more on prayer, see Chapter 45.)

4. THINKING IT OVER

How would you explain the Bible passage of this chapter? What is the *leitmotiv* in the cycle of traditions on Abraham? By reading the Bible (including this passage), in what process of growing should you participate? Is it right to consider religion primarily as a burden? What is the meaning of "Gospel"?

(Do not consider these questions as "examination questions for elementary school children." They are provided as a help to guide you and to support your daily meditation.)

5. PRAY MEDITATIVELY

Psalm 145.

3. Abraham Offers His Son

1. Some time after these events, God put Abraham to the test. He called to him, "Abraham!" "Ready!" he replied. Then God said: "Take your son Isaac, your only one, whom you love, and go to the land of Moriah. There you shall offer him up as a holocaust on a height that I will point out to you." Early the next morning Abraham saddled his donkey, took with him his son Isaac, and two of his servants as well, and with the wood that he had cut for the holocaust, set out for the place of which God had told him.

On the third day Abraham got sight of the place from afar. Then he said to his servants: "Both of you stay here with the donkey, while the boy and I go on over yonder. We will worship and then come back to you." Thereupon Abraham took the wood for the holocaust and laid it on his son Isaac's shoulders, while he himself carried the fire and the knife. As the two walked on together, Isaac spoke to his father Abraham: "Father!" he said. "Yes, son," he replied. Isaac continued, "Here are the fire and the wood, but where is the sheep for the holocaust?" "Son," Abraham answered, "God himself will provide the sheep for the holocaust." Then the two continued going forward.

When they came to the place of which God had told him, Abraham built an altar there and arranged the wood on it. Next he tied up his son Isaac, and put him on top of the wood on the altar. Then he reached out and took the knife to slaughter his son. But the Lord's messenger called to him from heaven, "Abraham, Abraham!" "Yes, Lord," he answered. "Do not lay your hand on the boy," said the messenger. "Do not do the least thing to him. I know now how devoted you are to God, since you did not withhold from me your own beloved son." As Abraham looked about, he spied a ram caught by its horns in the thicket. So he went and took the ram and offered it up as a holocaust in place of his son. Abraham named the site Yahweh-yireh; hence people now say, "On the mountain the Lord will see."

Again the Lord's messenger called to Abraham from heaven and said: "I swear by myself, declares the Lord, that because you acted as you did in not withholding from me your beloved son, I will bless you abundantly and make your descendants as countless as the stars of the sky and the sands of the seashore; your descendants shall take possession of the gates of their enemies, and in your descendants all the nations of the earth shall find blessing—all this because you obeyed my command."

Abraham then returned to his servants, and they set out together for Beer-sheba, where Abraham made his home (Genesis 22:1-19).

2. **Abraham is tried.** This tradition must be understood in the same way as the one in Chapter 2. "God speaking to man" is a figure of speech which is often found in the Bible. It means:

In the depth of his self man is aware of God's guidance. The point of this tradition is again Faith.

God tried Abraham, and Abraham believed even though he did not understand what God wanted. God had promised Abraham that his offspring would be as numerous as the sands on the seashore and as the stars of heaven. When he was very old, and after long years of praying, Abraham finally had a son. He was proud of his son Isaac. Yet, despite his pride and fatherly love, Abraham was willing, at the command of God, to offer his son as a sacrifice. The Faith of Abraham was indeed very strong.

3. **Facing problems.** You must be strong in Faith just as Abraham was. It may be that you will have to face problems in life which you cannot solve. Nevertheless, your Faith must be a wholehearted surrender of heart and mind to God. Often you can see only the underside of the embroidery, a tangled mass of colored threads; later, you will see the upperside, a fine needlework of flowers!

4. **THINKING IT OVER**

Which stories in Genesis 12—25 deal with the firmness of Abraham's Faith? Could you think of any event in your life that has put your Faith to a test? How did you react?

5. **PRAY MEDITATIVELY**

The Profession of Faith in your Missal or Missalette.

6. **THINGS TO DO**

Read: Genesis 24; 25; 27; 29; 32:22, etc.; 37—50.

If something is not clear in your Bible, be sure to look at the footnotes first. If they do not give an adequate explanation, ask your parish priest or someone who is familiar with the Bible.

When reading your Bible, do not pass over the important introduction before each book.

MOSES

4. God Protects Moses

"Abraham was the father of Isaac, Isaac the father of Jacob, Jacob the father of Judah and his brothers" (Matthew 1:2).

One of the eleven brothers of Judah was Joseph. Because the brothers were jealous of Joseph, they sold him to merchants who were on their way to Egypt. But God changed the bitter fate of Joseph and made him the co-ruler (vice-king) of all Egypt.

During a time of starvation in Canaan, Jacob and his whole family emigrated to Egypt. The Pharaoh (king) of Egypt gave Jacob and his family a fertile piece of land, called Goshen, along the river Nile. The clan of Jacob, also called Israel, stayed about four hundred years in Egypt. They were faithful to the God of their ancestors Abraham, Isaac and Jacob, and to the Covenant formerly established.

As the clan of Israel became increasingly larger, the kings of Egypt (Ramses II, 1292-1225 B.C., and Mernephtah I) began to persecute the chosen people of God. Finally, one Pharaoh, probably Mernephtah I, commanded that all male children of Israel be killed immediately after they were born. However, God did not forget His chosen people who had remained faithful among so many pagans. He bestowed a leader upon the people of Israel who led them out of slavery in Egypt. The name of this leader was

6. Moses.

In Chapters 4—8 we will read and discuss traditions in which Moses plays the principal role. These traditions should be understood in the same way as those of the Abraham cycle. (See Chapter 1, no. 2 and Chapter 2, no. 2.) God, the Covenant and
7. worship are the main themes.

1. Now a certain man of the house of Levi married a Levite woman, who conceived and bore a son. Seeing that he was a goodly child, she hid him for three months. When she could hide him no longer, she took a papyrus basket, daubed it with bitumen and pitch, and putting the child in it, placed it among the reeds on the river bank. His sister stationed herself at a distance to find out what would happen to him.

Pharaoh's daughter came down to the river to bathe, while her maids walked along the river bank. Noticing the basket among the reeds, she sent her handmaid to fetch it. On opening it, she looked, and lo, there was a baby boy, crying! She was moved with pity for him and said, "It is one of the Hebrews' children." Then his sister asked Pharaoh's daughter, "Shall I go and call one of the Hebrew women to nurse the child for you?" "Yes, do so," she answered. So the maiden went and called the child's own mother. Pharaoh's daughter said to her, "Take this child and nurse it for me, and I will repay you." The woman therefore took the child and nursed it. When the child grew, she brought him to Pharaoh's daughter, who adopted him as her son and called him Moses; for she said, "I drew him out of the water" (Exodus 2:1-10).

2. Prepared for his task. God loved the people of Israel, though He permitted them to endure pain and humiliation in Egypt. According to the Pharaoh's command, Moses, at infancy, was to have been killed, but that did not happen. Instead, Moses was brought into the palace of the Pharaoh. There he received a splendid education that prepared him for his task as leader of his people. Since the Egyptians were already writing on stone some 2,000 years before Moses, we can easily understand how Moses with his Egyptian education could later write on stone tablets in the desert (see Exodus 32:15).

3. Suffering a mystery. God is a good and loving Father. Pain may be a punishment for your sins. Possibly it is a trial. Often it is a mystery. But from eternity it is God's plan to make man happy. Also, pain and sorrow permitted by God are implied in this plan. Sorrow will always be changed into joy by God, if not in this world, then surely in the future life. You must remember this truth, especially when you are troubled by sorrow and grief.

Joseph had been persecuted by his brothers but elevated by God; hence he pointed out to his brothers in Egypt: "Even though you meant harm to me, God meant it for good, to achieve his present end, the survival of many people" (Genesis 50:20).

The Church sees a parallel between what happened to the chosen people of God in Egypt and what happens to the elected people of the New Covenant: Sinners are in the slavery of evil, just as the people of Israel were in the slavery of Egypt. As God bestowed a leader upon Israel, so He gave a Savior to mankind, enslaved to sin and evil. The name of our Redeemer is Jesus Christ, the Son of God, Who became Man.

4. THINKING IT OVER

How can God be called "good" when there is so much trouble and pain in the world? Explain the parallel between: Moses and the chosen people in slavery in Egypt and their liberation, and what happens to the elected people of the New Covenant.

5. PRAY MEDITATIVELY

Our Father (see Treasury of Prayers, p. 290) and Psalm 103 "Bless the Lord . . ." (see your Bible).

6. THINGS TO DO

Read: Exodus 1—2:1-22.

To make efficient use of this book: (1) Read the chapter attentively once or twice. (2) Then try to answer the questions under "Thinking It Over."

5. God Reveals Himself in the Burning Bush

1. A long time passed, during which the king of Egypt died. Still the Israelites groaned and cried out because of their slavery. As their cry for release went up to God, he heard their groaning and was mindful of his covenant with Abraham, Isaac and Jacob. He saw the Israelites and knew . . . (Exodus 2:23-25).

Meanwhile Moses was tending the flock of his father-in-law Jethro, the priest of Midian. Leading the flock across the desert, he came to Horeb, the mountain of God. There an angel of the Lord appeared to him in fire flaming out of a bush. As he looked on, he was surprised to see that the bush, though on fire, was not consumed. So Moses decided, "I must go over to look at this remarkable sight, and see why the bush is not burned."

When the Lord saw him coming over to look at it more closely, God called out to him from the bush, "Moses! Moses!" He answered, "Here I am." God said, "Come no nearer! Remove the sandals from your feet, for the place

Ch. 5 God Reveals Himself in the Burning Bush

where you stand is holy ground. I am the God of your father," he continued, "the God of Abraham, the God of Isaac, the God of Jacob." Moses hid his face, for he was afraid to look at God. But the Lord said, "I have witnessed the affliction of my people in Egypt and have heard their cry of complaint against their slave drivers, so I know well what they are suffering. Therefore I have come down to rescue them from the hands of the Egyptians and lead them out of that land into a good and spacious land, a land flowing with milk and honey, the country of the Canaanites, Hittites, Amorites, Perizzites, Hivites and Jebusites" (Exodus 3:1-8).

"But," said Moses to God, "when I go to the Israelites and say to them, 'The God of your fathers has sent me to you,' if they ask me, 'What is his name?' what am I to tell them?" God replied, "I am who am." Then he added, "This is what you shall tell the Israelites: I AM sent me to you."

God spoke further to Moses, "Thus shall you say to the Israelites: The Lord, the God of your fathers, the God of Abraham, the God of Isaac, the God of Jacob, has sent me to you.

This is my name forever;
    this is my title for all generations" (Exodus 3: 13-15).

2a. A God of salvation. "Abraham planted a tamarisk at Beer-sheba, and there he invoked by name the Lord, God the Eternal" (Genesis 21:33). This eternal God appeared five centuries later as the still merciful Protector of His chosen people. God said to Moses: "I am who am," meaning: "I am not a far-away God, but your present God-Protector." It is a saving God Who called Moses for his lifetime task of leading the chosen people out of bondage.

Who is God? The God of the Bible is the God of a people's historical experience. Faith in the Biblical God is first and foremost Faith in *a God of Salvation:* it was as a saving God that Israel first experienced Yahweh and that Paul experienced Christ and the God revealed in Christ. God saves man from the meaninglessness of existence—an existence which the Bible recognizes as "life" only when it has taken on a meaning and purpose.

2b. Who is God? As already mentioned the Hebrews did not care too much who God is in Himself. They were mainly concerned with God insofar as He is related to man. And though modern man knows that he cannot express adequately who God is in Himself, he goes on trying.

Who is God and where can I meet Him? A strong trend in contemporary theology points to the positive experiences "in the midst of life": love, creative fidelity, dedication, concern, commitment, encounter in dialogue, trust in the basic goodness of life, sense amidst so much nonsense. These offer modern man privileged moments of "disclosure," of sensitivity, for the deeper and transcending element that is experienced as underlying all, as co-present

Can we call this "deeper and transcending element that is experienced as underlying all" God? Modern theologians do. And if we dare to call this ultimate depth, which offers itself to our experience in the midst of our life, "Person" and "Father," we rely for this on Jesus and the living tradition of people who have kept alive Jesus' word of revelation to this very day.

In other words, in our most sensitive moments we experience the ultimate depth of our being not just as immanent (present in creation, the self and fellowmen) but as deeper, as transcending all. The Ultimate Reality is both immanent and transcendent.

The question is, can I address myself to "the ground of my being," the Ultimate Reality, as to a "You"? The answer is that man's experience as such seems not to force him to see the Ultimate Reality as a "You." But it can be done in Faith. Recognizing the transcendent reality as "You," we follow the example of Jesus and even address this "You" as Father, as "God our Father."

8.

God is immanent in all of creation. Paul states: "In him we live and move and have our being" (Acts 17:28). Consequently, I meet God as immanent in my fellowmen, in creation. But God transcends creation as an absolute "You." Hence, it is valuable to address Him as such in both private prayer and community worship. And God, immanent and transcendent, is the same God!

3. Meeting God. If God reveals Himself in history, it is there that, challenged by the experience of the Hebrews, I must find Him. If God is immanent in creation, I must meet Him in the eyes of my mother, husband or wife, children, any good person. I must love and serve Him in all my fellowmen. If God transcends creation as an absolute "You," I must address Him as such in prayer and worship.

God Reveals Himself in the Burning Bush

If God did in fact speak through the Prophets, we cannot absolve ourselves from the task of discovering what was said and what is meant. If God did in fact speak to us through the Life, Death, and Resurrection of Jesus, it is vitally important for us to know as fully and as accurately as possible what sort of life and death and resurrection became the medium of the Divine Revelation. In other words, you should read your Bible and study it prayerfully every day.

4. THINKING IT OVER

Describe God as the Hebrews experienced Him! Why can we not express adequately Who God is in Himself? Describe how modern theologians approach the mystery of God! What about your own experience in life—a sensitivity or openness to that deeper element experienced as underlying all? Why do Christians dare to call the deepest ground of their being "Person" and "Father"? What has Chapter 1, no. 3 to say about this? What do we mean by God's immanence and God's transcendence? Where do you meet God as immanent and where as transcendent?

5. PRAY MEDITATIVELY

Glory to God in the highest,
    and peace to his people on earth.
Lord God, heavenly King,
almighty God and Father,
    we worship you, we give you thanks,
    we praise you for your glory *(From the liturgy of the Mass).*

6. THINGS TO DO

Read one of the Prefaces to the Eucharistic Prayer in your Missal. Read also Exodus 2:23-25; 3:12-36.

Inquire as to where you will be able to see a series of slides about the Biblical countries and research work (excavations) of the last half century.

A book with splendid pictures and maps is: *Atlas of the Bible* by Rev. L. H. Grollenberg, O.P., published by Thomas Nelson and Sons, New York, N. Y.

6. The Departure of Israel from Egypt

Moses repeatedly conveyed to the Pharaoh the command of God to give Israel its liberty. Only after severe punishment had been inflicted upon him did the Pharaoh let the Israelites go.

On the night before Israel's departure, the Passover lamb was eaten and the houses were marked with its blood. God had promised: "Seeing the blood, I will pass over you," that is, not kill your first-born.

1. "This is how you are to eat it: with your loins girt, sandals on your feet and your staff in hand, you shall eat like those who are in flight. It is the Passover of the Lord. For on this same night I will go through Egypt, striking down every first-born of the land, both man and beast, and executing judgment on all the gods of Egypt—I, the Lord! But the blood will mark the houses where you are. Seeing the blood, I will pass over you; thus, when I strike the land of Egypt, no destructive blow will come upon you.

"This day shall be a memorial feast for you, which all your generations shall celebrate with pilgrimage to the Lord, as a perpetual institution" (Exodus 12:11-14).

When it was reported to the king of Egypt that the people had fled, Pharaoh and his servants changed their minds about them. "What have we done!" they exclaimed. "Why, we have released Israel from our service!" So Pharaoh made his chariots ready and mustered his soldiers (Exodus 14:5-6).

Then Moses stretched out his hand over the sea, and the Lord swept the sea with a strong east wind throughout the night and so turned it into dry land. When the water was thus divided, the Israelites marched into the midst of the sea on dry land, with the water like a wall to their right and to their left.

The Egyptians followed in pursuit; all Pharaoh's horses and chariots and charioteers went after them right into the midst of the sea (Exodus 14:21-23).

Then the Lord told Moses, "Stretch out your hand over the sea, that the water may flow back upon the Egyptians, upon their chariots and their charioteers." So Moses stretched out his hand over the sea, and at dawn the sea flowed back to its normal depth. The Egyptians were fleeing head on toward the sea, when the Lord hurled them into its midst. As the water flowed back, it covered the chariots and the charioteers of Pharaoh's whole army which had followed the Israelites into the sea. Not a single one of them escaped (Exodus 14:26-28).

Ch. 6   The Departure of Israel from Egypt   27

Then Moses led Israel forward from the Red Sea, and they marched out to the desert of Shur. After traveling for three days through the desert without finding water, they arrived at Marah, where they could not drink the water, because it was too bitter. Hence this place was called Marah. As the people grumbled against Moses, saying, "What are we to drink?" he appealed to the Lord, who pointed out to him a certain piece of wood. When he threw this into the water, the water became fresh (Exodus 15:22-25).

Then the Lord said to Moses, "I will now rain down bread from heaven for you. Each day the people are to go out and gather their daily portion; thus will I test them, to see whether they follow my instructions or not" (Exodus 16:4).

"Show me, O Lord, Your way" (Ps. 27:11).

2a. The story of the exodus. Israel is another name for Jacob. The people of Jacob are also called "the house of Jacob," or "Israel," or "Israelites."

We see in the above story:

(1) Israel was protected by the blood of the Passover lamb (also: Paschal lamb).

(2) The chosen people of the Old Covenant went through the Red Sea and got their freedom from Pharaoh's slavery.

(3) Under the leadership of Moses they wandered in the desert for forty years and hoped to enter the Promised Land of their ancestors.

(4) Whatever they needed in the desert: water, meat and bread, they received through the intercession of Moses.

2b. The point of the story. The traditions concerning the exodus from Egypt, as related in Chapters 4—8, were written down about 300 B.C. As was true of the traditions concerning

Abraham (see Chapter 1, no. 2, and Chapter 2, no. 2), the sacred writer did not intend to write history as such. He did not spend much time to find out what had really happened during the time of the exodus and what had been introduced by way of colorful addition during the oral transmission of these traditions over the centuries.

For example, consider the account of the plagues in Exodus 7—11. The sacred writer used these traditions, as he knew them, to teach religious values to God's people of his time. His point was that they should be grateful for what God had done for His people in ancient times and faithful to the custom of the Passover Sacrifice.

2c. The Passover. We know that Jesus, as a faithful Jew, followed this custom. He celebrated the Passover Sacrifice with His disciples. After the lamb was offered in the temple the meat was taken home for the Passover meal. Pilgrims who came from outside Jerusalem would rent a room for the meal. This is what Jesus did; then in the upper room He gave a new meaning to the Passover Sacrifice and Sacrificial repast, stating that He Himself was that Passover Lamb from that moment on. Read Matthew 26:17-19 and 26-28. This will be discussed more extensively later.

3a. Parallel. The people of God of the New Covenant are called the Church of Jesus Christ. The Church is also called the Catholic (universal) Church or the Roman Catholic Church because the bishop of Rome, as head of all the bishops, rules the Church in the name of Jesus Christ. (This will be more thoroughly explained in the second part of this book, Chapters 31-39.)

As already briefly indicated in Chapter 4, the Apostle Paul and the Church Fathers saw a parallel between the happenings above and what happens to the new holy people of God, the Church.

3b. The Easter Lamb. The holy people of the New Covenant are protected by the Blood of the Easter Lamb Who takes away the sins of the world. The Easter Lamb on the altar during Mass is prefigured by the Passover lamb of the Old Covenant.

3c. The waters of Baptism. The Church gets her freedom from the bondage of evil through the waters of Baptism. When you are baptized, the priest says an exorcism over you, in order to drive away evil influence. This rite indicates how each individual member of the Church secures "freedom from the bondage of evil" through Baptism.

3d. Promised Land of Heaven. Under the leadership of Christ, the Church travels through the desert of life, hoping to enter the Promised Land—Heaven.

3e. Through Christ. All that the people of God in this world need in order to realize God's Kingdom now and hereafter is given through Christ, our Lord.

4. THINKING IT OVER

What is meant by "Paschal lamb"? Read attentively the above-mentioned parallel between the people of the Old and the New Covenant, and compare it with the Paschal Proclamation of Holy Saturday night (the part after "Let us give thanks to the Lord . . ."), the Preface of the Easter Mass and the Communion Antiphon (see your Missal).

5. PRAY MEDITATIVELY

Psalms 114 and 115, "When Israel came forth from Egypt . . ." (see Bible). (This liberation epic of Israel is also our epic of freedom from the slavery of sin and evil.)

6. THINGS TO DO

Read: Exodus 12:37—18.

Spend a quarter to half an hour each day meditating upon these chapters and the spiritual reading indicated.

7. The Covenant

1. Moses himself was told, "Come up to the Lord, you and Aaron, with Nadab, Abihu, and seventy of the elders of Israel. You shall all worship at some distance, but Moses alone is to come close to the Lord; the others shall not come too near, and the people shall not come up at all with Moses."

When Moses came to the people and related all the words and ordinances of the Lord, they all answered with one voice, "We will do everything that the Lord has told us." Moses then wrote down all the words of the Lord and, rising early the next day, he erected at the foot of the mountain an altar and twelve pillars for the twelve tribes of Israel. Then, having sent certain young men of the Israelites to offer holocausts and sacrifice young bulls as peace offerings to the Lord, Moses took half of the blood and put it in large bowls; the other half he splashed on the altar. Taking the book of the covenant, he read it aloud to the people, who answered, "All that the Lord has said, we will heed and do." Then he took the blood and sprinkled it on the people, saying, "This is the blood of the covenant which the Lord has made with you in accordance with all these words of his" (Exodus 24:1-8).

> Fear not, you shall not be put to shame;
> > you need not blush, for you shall not be disgraced.
> The shame of your youth you shall forget,
> > the reproach of your widowhood no longer remember.
> For he who has become your husband is your Maker;
> > his name is the Lord of hosts;
> Your redeemer is the Holy One of Israel,
> > called God of all the earth.
> The Lord calls you back,
> > like a wife forsaken and grieved in spirit,
> A wife married in youth and then cast off,
> > says your God.
> For a brief moment I abandoned you,
> > but with great tenderness I will take you back.
> In an outburst of wrath, for a moment
> > I hid my face from you;
> But with enduring love I take pity on you,
> > says the Lord, your redeemer.
> This is for me like the days of Noah,
> > when I swore that the waters of Noah
> > should never again deluge the earth;
> So I have sworn not to be angry with you,
> > or to rebuke you.
> Though the mountains leave their place
> > and the hills be shaken,
> My love shall never leave you
> > nor my covenant of peace be shaken,
> > says the Lord, who has mercy on you (Isaiah 54:4-10).

And if anyone, whether of the house of Israel or of the aliens residing among them, partakes of any blood, I will set myself against that one who partakes of blood and will cut him off from among his people. Since the life of a living body is in its blood, I have made you put it on the altar, so that atonement may thereby be made for your own lives, because it is the blood, as the seat of life, that makes atonement. That is why I have told the Israelites: No one among you, not even a resident alien, may partake of blood (Leviticus 17:10-12).

2a. How is man related to God or to his gods? This question has kept the human mind searching all through its existence. Various concepts have been used to describe that relationship. The one most used in Hebrew literature is the theme of "covenant" or "partnership." Since this search of the Hebrews, as reflected in the Bible, was inspired by God, we pay special attention to it. The fruit of their ages-long thinking may guide us.

2b. The covenant theme. This theme, used to describe man's relationship to the divinity and vice-versa, is not specifically Hebrew. We have numerous examples of it outside the Bible. Moreover, we should keep in mind that this concept of covenant or partnership is conditioned by time and Old Testament culture, where it is based on the so-called suzerainty treaty: a relationship between unequal partners in which the stronger (a mighty king) grants a covenant to the weaker (a petty king), who, in turn, is obligated within definite boundaries.

9.

2c. Covenant based on love. The Biblical writers used this political concept of their time to describe Israel's relationship to Yahweh, their God. We find it already in the traditions that record the primitive history of the Hebrews. See the traditions of the Abraham cycle in Genesis 12—17 (Chapter 1 and no. 1a, above).

But since the Biblical writers saw Yahweh as a father and Israel as His child, later this Covenant was seen more as a partnership based on love—more or less like a father taking his son into his business as a partner in our society. His son has plenty of opportunity for new, personal and creative initiatives in the business, but with his father!

Other Biblical writers (Hosea, Isaiah: see no. 1b above) saw the Yahweh-Israel relationship as a marital one. God loves Israel as a husband loves his wife. In their writings, the Covenant assumes marital characteristics, but necessarily as in the patriarchal marriage pattern of that time: Israel should love God with the submissive love of a wife for her husband, as was the custom in Hebrew culture.

2d. Mediator and blood involved. Observe that, according to the tradition, Moses was the mediator between God and the people when the Sinai Covenant was solemnly ratified. Observe also that blood, "the substance of life" for the Hebrews, plays a role. The Covenant is effected by the shedding of blood, i.e., in the power of the blood, the substance of life. See nos. 1c and 1a, above. Sometimes animals were cut into two parts and one passed between the parts cursing the party that would infringe the Covenant. (See Jeremiah 34:18.)

These are symbols, conditioned by the Biblical situation. We should make the effort to understand this symbolism, since the early theologians of the Church used it to explain the Christian's new relationship with God. They speak of Jesus as the Mediator of a New Covenant (partnership), effected in the power of His blood (substance of life!), which was shed on the Cross. New Testament symbolism cannot be understood without a knowledge of the symbolism of the Hebrew Bible (Old Testament) in which it is rooted.

3a. Fidelity and infidelity. The Bible passages of this chapter mention fidelity and infidelity to the Covenant. If you are faithful, you are dearer to God than all other people (no. 1a). If you have been unfaithful, God will take you back (no. 1b). But there must be repentance and a serious will to do better.

3b. Creative participation. Man is God's partner with plenty of room for his own creative initiatives in his Father's "business" to make this world a better place to live in. Apply this to your own situation! Being a Christian is no excuse to take it easy. Man is God's partner, His co-worker! Politicians, sociologists, medical doctors, teachers, housewives, you—all of us are responsible for the future of this planet. Ecology is a Christian concern!

The Covenant theme, elaborated by the Hebrew genius under God's guidance, has inspiring aspects for man of all ages and cultures!

4. THINKING IT OVER

In the Bible, which theme is most used to describe man's relationship to God? Describe the concept "covenant" both in its early Hebrew setting and later development! The ideas of "mediator" and "blood" are related to the Covenant-theme. Describe and explain! Why is it useful to study this Covenant-theme and its symbolism? What does all of this mean to Christians of our time and culture? What does ecology mean in your situation, and what has it to do with the Covenant idea?

5. PRAY MEDITATIVELY
Psalm 111.

6. THINGS TO DO

Read: Exodus 19; 20; 24. Thunder, lightning, clouds, smoke, fire, calamities, earthquakes, persecutions, etc. are the usual Biblical imagery to describe a theophany (manifestation of God). They are to be understood not literally but as a literary form or figure of speech. See also Psalm 97 and Matthew 24:26-32.

8. The Public Worship of the Old Covenant

The Sacred Liturgy

1. But Moses passed into the midst of the cloud as he went up on the mountain; and there he stayed for forty days and forty nights (Exodus 24:18).

This is what the Lord then said to Moses: "Tell the Israelites to take up a collection for me. From every man you shall accept the contribution that his heart prompts him to give me" (Exodus 25:1-2).

"They shall make a sanctuary for me, that I may dwell in their midst. This Dwelling and all its furnishings you shall make exactly according to the pattern that I will now show you.

"You shall make an ark of acacia wood, two and a half cubits long, one and a half cubits wide, and one and a half cubits high. Plate it inside and outside with pure gold, and put a molding of gold around the top of it" (Exodus 25:8-11).

"You shall make a lampstand of pure beaten gold—its shaft and branches —with its cups and knobs and petals springing directly from it" (Exodus 25:31).

"You shall order the Israelites to bring you clear oil of crushed olives, to be used for the light, so that you may keep lamps burning regularly" (Exodus 27:20).

"The Dwelling itself you shall make out of sheets woven of fine linen twined and of violet, purple and scarlet yarn, with cherubim embroidered on them" (Exodus 26:1).

"You shall make an altar of acacia wood, on a square, five cubits long and five cubits wide; it shall be three cubits high. At the four corners there are to be horns, so made that they spring directly from the altar. You shall then plate it with bronze" (Exodus 27:1-2).

"From among the Israelites have your brother Aaron, together with his sons Nadab, Abihu, Eleazar and Ithamar, brought to you, that they may be my priests" (Exodus 28:1).

"Now, this is what you shall offer on the altar: two yearling lambs as the sacrifice established for each day; one lamb in the morning and the other lamb at the evening twilight. With the first lamb there shall be a tenth of an ephah of fine flour mixed with a fourth of a hin of oil of crushed olives and, as its libation, a fourth of a hin of wine. The other lamb you shall offer at the evening twilight, with the same cereal offering and libation as in the morning. You shall offer this as a sweet-smelling oblation to the Lord. Throughout your generations this established holocaust shall be offered before the Lord at the entrance of the Meeting Tent, where I will meet you and speak to you" (Exodus 29:38-42).

2. Old Testament worship. The editors of the Bible have put the whole Torah or Law under the name of Moses. We accept the fact that Moses wrote laws on stone tablets (Chapter 4), but the above Bible passages actually reflect the final result of a long evolution in Hebrew worship (liturgy). In other words, they describe how the Hebrews worshiped throughout the centuries of the Old Testament.

There were sacrifices as a symbolical self-surrender of the people to the Creator. There were priests who were anointed with holy ointments. They were to pray and to offer the sacrifices in the name of the people.

3a. General lines—details. Liturgy is the public worship of the Church. Private prayers are not considered part of the liturgy.

Christ Himself sketched, in general lines, the liturgy of His chosen people. In the name of Christ, the Church indicates the details.

There is a sacrifice. But the sacrifice that symbolizes the self-surrender of the Church to God is not a lamb. It is the Sacred Body and Blood of Jesus Christ. This sacrifice is called the Sacrifice of the Cross. In the symbols of bread and wine, it is offered daily all over the world, and as such it is called the Sacrifice of the Mass.

There are priests. First of all, there is the High Priest of the holy people, Jesus Christ Himself. He surpasses in excellence the high priest of the Old Covenant. The word "Christ" means "The Anointed." God the Father Himself anointed His Son as the High Priest of mankind.

3b. All must join in. The Second Vatican Council *(Constitution on the Sacred Liturgy)* has stressed again that all of us share in Christ's royal priesthood through Faith and Baptism. This means that all of us are responsible for the public worship of the Church. All must join in and consider it a duty of honor to pay their tribute to God through the splendor of the liturgy. The primary purpose of public worship is not to satisfy personal religious feeling, but to honor and worship God. Bishops and priests share in Christ's priesthood in a special way and lead the congregation in worship. These ideas will be discussed more extensively in Chapters 22 and 23.

4. THINKING IT OVER

What does "liturgy" mean? Who established the liturgy of the Church? Study attentively the parallel between the sacrifices and the priests of the Old and the New Covenant. What do sacrifices symbolize? What is your relation to the public worship of the Church?

5. READ ATTENTIVELY

What does the author of the Letter to the Hebrews say about the task of the priest?

Hebrews says: "Every high priest is taken from among men and made their representative before God, to offer gifts and sacrifices for sins" (Hebrews 5:1).

6. PRAY MEDITATIVELY

Psalm 84, "How lovely is your dwelling place. . . ."
Psalm 122, "I rejoiced because they said to me. . . ."

7. THINGS TO DO

Discuss with your parish priest any difficulties that may arise about the use of your Missal.

For outlines to the History of Salvation, read: Leviticus 23; 27; Numbers 1:1-3; 10:11-26; 11:1-15; 12; 13; 16:1-11; 17:16-27; 21:1-9; 27:12-23; Deuteronomy 1:19-25; 4:32-40; 31:14-29; 34.

DAVID

9. David King of Israel

The Kingdom of God

It was Joshua who led the chosen people into the Promised Land. The settling of Israel in the Promised Land involved long years of fighting with the peoples living in that country.

About 1000 B.C., King David succeeded finally in ending the constant war with the pagan Canaanites. He united the tribes of Israel into a strong and great nation.

Israel's history from the time of the patriarchs to the great kings David and Solomon portrays the gradual development of a nomadic tribe to a "writing" civilization. The mainly oral traditions of Israel were written down about 1000-900 B.C. and in succeeding years. This national literature of the chosen people is the Bible, namely, the Old Testament. The final edition of the Hebrew text is to be dated around 300 B.C.

1a. All the tribes of Israel came to David in Hebron and said: "Here we are, your bone and your flesh. In days past, when Saul was our king, it was you who led the Israelites out and brought them back. And the Lord said to you, 'You shall shepherd my people Israel and shall be commander of Israel.'" When all the elders of Israel came to David in Hebron, King David made an agreement with them there before the Lord, and they anointed him king of Israel. David was thirty years old when he became king, and he reigned for forty years (2 Samuel 5:1-4).

Ch. 9   **David King of Israel**   **37**

1b. Pilate went back into the praetorium and summoned Jesus. "Are you the King of the Jews?" he asked him. Jesus answered, "Are you saying this on your own, or have others been telling you about me?" "I am no Jew!" Pilate retorted. "It is your own people and the chief priests who have handed you over to me. What have you done?" Jesus answered:

> *"My kingdom does not belong to this world.*
> *If my kingdom were of this world,*
> *my subjects would be fighting*
> *to save me from being handed over to the Jews.*
> *As it is, my kingdom is not here."*

At this Pilate said to him, "So, then, you are a king?" Jesus replied:

> *"It is you who say I am a king.*
> *The reason I was born,*
> *the reason why I came into the world,*
> *is to testify to the truth.*
> *Anyone committed to the truth hears my voice"* (John 18:33-37).

    2a. Interpreting history. In order to understand the traditions concerning the illustrious king David, you should keep in mind the typically Hebrew way of interpreting its national history, namely under the aspect of God's presence to His people. God had promised to Abraham: "I will give you and your descendants after you this land. I will make nations of you and kings shall stem from you" (see Genesis 17:8. 6). The Hebrews saw a first fulfillment of God's promise to Abraham in the Kingdom of God with His servant David as king in His name.

    This kingdom of David—the golden age of Israel!—was ever more idealized in Hebrew literature during the centuries. In their political insignificance of later ages, nostalgically the Hebrews dreamed and wrote about the restoration of that colorful kingdom of David.

    2b. A new interpretation. Finally Jesus and the early theologians of the Church used this literary theme to explain the Reign of God, as initiated by our Lord. It was seen as a restored Kingdom of God with His servant Jesus as king (Messiah) in His name. Hence, figuratively, Luke could put into the mouth of the angel Gabriel these words: "The Lord God will give him [Jesus Christ] the throne of David his father. He will rule over the house of Jacob forever and his reign will be without end" (Luke 1:32-33).

11.

New Testament literature calls Jesus of Nazareth "Christ" (Greek) or "Messiah" (Hebrew), which means "The Anointed (king)." And Jesus confirms that He sees Himself as a king, though in His own way, when He addresses Pontius Pilate (see John 18:33-37 in no. 1b, above).

2c. Finding the Kingdom. We find the Kingdom (Reign) of God with Jesus Christ as king *in* the Catholic Church, which does not mean that we do not find it in the churches which are separated from us. Together with all brethren who seek Christ sincerely, be it in separation or error, we establish the Church in her full sense. And in this sinful and divided Church we find the Kingdom or elements of it.

God's Kingdom as established in this world is a fulfillment of God's promise to Abraham; this fulfillment also contains a further promise, namely: The Kingdom of God to come in all its splendor when Christ will deliver it to His Father (1 Corinthians 15: 26-28).

3. How to join the Kingdom. You join the Kingdom of God by Faith and Baptism. It is worthwhile to be obedient to Christ Whose yoke is sweet and Whose burden is light. It is worthwhile to realize that Reign (Dominion-Kingdom) of God evermore in yourself!

4. THINKING IT OVER

What is characteristic of the Hebrew way of interpreting its national history? How did Jesus of Nazareth and the early theologians of the Church see the Kingdom (Reign) of God as initiated by our Lord? How does Luke bring out this idea? How did our Lord Himself qualify the Kingdom He established? Where do you find the Kingdom of God? What does this mean to you? (See no. 3, above.)

5. PRAY MEDITATIVELY

The Preface for the feast of Christ the King in your Missal. Also Psalm 110, and study the explanation in the *New American Bible!*

6. THINGS TO DO

Read about the History of Salvation: Joshua 1; 2; 3; 1 Samuel 8; 10; 16; 17; 18; 19; 24; 26; 31; 2 Samuel 2:1-7; 5; 6; 7; 11; 12; 15; 22; 1 Kings 1; 2: 1-12; 8:1-21; 10.

If, in reading the Bible, you have any questions, please always ask your parish priest. Read also "How to Read Your Bible," no. 4, p. 298.

THE PROPHETS OF THE OLD TESTAMENT

10. God Created Heaven and Earth

As a very precious heritage, God bestowed Faith upon His chosen people. He made a Covenant with them, first with Abraham, the patriarch of the nation (Chapter 1), consolidating it with Moses, the elected leader (Chapter 7).

In order to prevent His chosen people from losing the grace of Faith, and to help them to be faithful to the Covenant, God sent the Prophets who were to teach and to advise the people. By "Prophets" we mean not only the writers of the Prophetical Books in the Bible, but also, in the broad sense, the other sacred writers and preachers of the Old Testament.

The greatest among the Prophets were Moses, David, Isaiah, Jeremiah, and John the Baptizer.

Inspired by God's Spirit, these wise men taught the people of Israel, frequently using stories and examples adapted to their intellectual comprehension. Often it is not easy to find out whether certain stories in the Bible are history in our sense or tales with a historical core used to teach religious values. When reading the Bible, a Catholic follows the guidance of the Church whose authority is backed by Christ Himself. She teaches us how to understand the Bible.

1. The inspired writer teaches that God created all things in the following poem on creation:

1a. In the beginning, when God created the heavens and the earth, the earth was a formless wasteland, and darkness covered the abyss, while a mighty wind swept over the waters. Then God said, "Let there be light," and there was light. God saw how good the light was. God then separated the light from the darkness. God called the light "day," and the darkness he called "night." Thus evening came, and morning followed—the first day (Genesis 1:1-5).

1b. Then God said, "Let there be a dome in the middle of the waters, to separate one body of water from the other." And so it happened: God made the dome, and it separated the water above the dome from the water below it. God called the dome "the sky." Evening came, and morning followed—the second day (Genesis 1:6-8).

1c. Then God said, "Let the water under the sky be gathered into a single basin, so that the dry land may appear." And so it happened: the water under the sky was gathered into its basin, and the dry land appeared. God called the dry land "the earth," and the basin of the water he called "the sea." God saw how good it was. Then God said, "Let the earth bring forth vegetation: every kind of plant that bears seed and every kind of fruit tree on earth that bears fruit with its seed in it." And so it happened: the earth brought forth every kind of plant that bears seed and every kind of fruit tree on earth that bears fruit with its seed in it. God saw how good it was. Evening came, and morning followed—the third day (Genesis 1:9-13).

1d. Then God said: "Let there be lights in the dome of the sky, to separate day from night. Let them mark the fixed times, the days and the years, and serve as luminaries in the dome of the sky, to shed light upon the earth." And so it happened: God made the two great lights, the greater one to govern the day, and the lesser one to govern the night; and he made the stars. God set them in the dome of the sky, to shed light upon the earth, to govern the day and the night, and to separate the light from the darkness. God saw how good it was. Evening came, and morning followed—the fourth day (Genesis 1:14-19).

1e. Then God said, "Let the water teem with an abundance of living creatures, and on the earth let birds fly beneath the dome of the sky." And so it happened: God created the great sea monsters and all kinds of swimming creatures with which the water teems, and all kinds of winged birds. God saw how good it was, and God blessed them, saying, "Be fertile, multiply, and fill the water of the seas; and let the birds multiply on the earth." Evening came, and morning followed—the fifth day (Genesis 1:20-23).

1f. Then God said, "Let the earth bring forth all kinds of living creatures: cattle, creeping things, and wild animals of all kinds." And so it happened:

Ch. 10 God Created Heaven and Earth

God made all kinds of wild animals, all kinds of cattle, and all kinds of creeping things of the earth. God saw how good it was. Then God said: "Let us make man in our image, after our likeness. Let them have dominion over the fish of the sea, the birds of the air, and the cattle, and over all the wild animals and all the creatures that crawl on the ground" (Genesis 1:24-26).

1g. Thus the heavens and the earth and all their array were completed. Since on the seventh day God was finished with the work he had been doing, he rested on the seventh day from all the work he had undertaken. So God blessed the seventh day and made it holy, because on it he rested from all the work he had done in creation (Genesis 2:1-3).

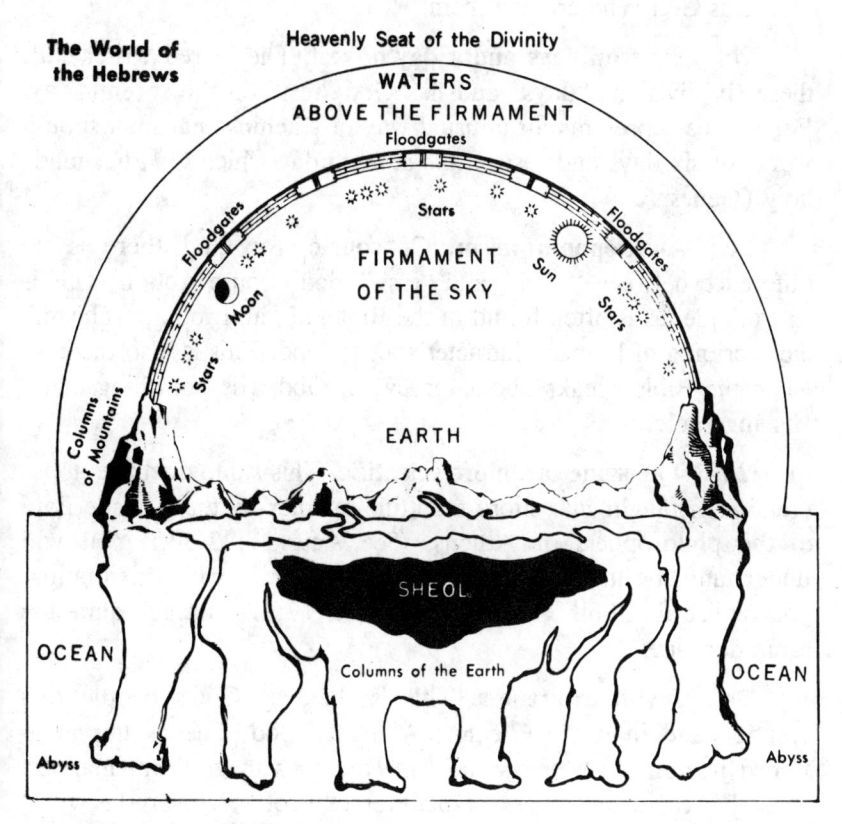

The World of the Hebrews

Heavenly Seat of the Divinity
WATERS ABOVE THE FIRMAMENT
Floodgates
Stars
Floodgates
Floodgates
FIRMAMENT OF THE SKY
Moon
Sun
Stars
Stars
Columns of Mountains
EARTH
SHEOL
OCEAN
Columns of the Earth
OCEAN
Abyss
Abyss

2a. All things created by God. The vision of the sacred writer on nature is the Jewish vision of that time: The earth is a large plate. At its edge is the abyss. Above the plate is a huge vault, or inverted bowl, in which there are windows, or floodgates. Water is all around this bowl. If God opens the gates, it starts raining. Against this background (the Bible does not discuss whether it is true or not), the sacred writer explains extensively the mystery of Creation. His conclusion is: "All things were created by God." "All things" were divided in this manner:

(a) Light and darkness (see no. 1a).
(b) Heaven and earth (see no. 1b).
(c) Sea, dry land and vegetation (see no. 1c).
(d) Sun, moon and stars (see no. 1d).
(e) Fishes and birds (see no. 1e).
(f) Animals and mankind (see no. 1f).

12. It is God Who created them!

2b. Six workdays and a day of rest. The sacred writer calls these six divisions "days" and has God "rest" on the seventh day. For us this represents an unusual way of teaching that man should work for six days and rest on the seventh day which God has made holy (Genesis 2:3).

2c. Anthropomorphism. Of course, for God there is no difference between "work" and "rest." God is pure Action. This is an example, as is often found in the Bible, of "anthropomorphism," the ascribing of human characteristics to God. This is also the case when the Bible speaks about the eye of God, His punishing hand, His anger, etc.

2d. The same but more scientific. This same doctrine about creation is taught in a more scientific manner by the Apostle Paul to the philosophers of Athens. (See Acts 17:22-34.) You will understand the first chapter of Genesis better if, while meditating, you realize that both Genesis 1 and Acts 17:22-34 teach quite the same doctrine.

3a. Joyful awareness. This is the way God's people sees creation and in it the Creator, Almighty God. The psalms mentioned in number 5 below illustrate this in a magnificent manner. It is the joyful awareness of believers: "Brothers, over the world of the stars, a loving Father must reside." ("Ode to Joy" in the 9th symphony of Beethoven.) Cultivate this awareness!

3b. God in the process of evolution. God creates all things by His almighty will. More and more scientists are questioning a certain evolution (unfolding) of things, but in this evolutionary process we see the constantly creative activity of God.

With His will God also keeps all things in "being." God is everywhere present to continue His task as Creator. We are never alone. God is everywhere present to protect His children. The Apostle Paul says God "is not far from any one of us. 'In Him we live and move and have our being'" (Acts 17:27-28). The loving God is in you, and you are in Him. Never forget this, especially in times of sorrow.

3c. Man, God's co-worker. Note also that the sacred writer of Genesis discusses extensively how God orders the chaos (unorganized matter) into a habitable world and how He chose man as His co-worker. Read again Genesis 1 and especially Genesis 2:18-23: "Whatever the man called each of them would be its name." And in the beautiful allegory that teaches the oneness of husband and wife, it is the man who gives a name (meaning) to sex. Together God and man devise the emblems and meanings by which anarchic confusion becomes a world.

Whether man is inventing the wheel in ancient times or building today's chemical plants, computers and spacecrafts, he is God's co-worker. When you are repairing a car, giving birth to a child, cooking a meal for the family or studying in school, you are creatively busy fashioning the chaos (unordered or less ordered matter) into a better world! Artists are especially conscious and proud of their creativity; but all can have these same sentiments, particularly when creatively occupied in education, molding and fashioning children into better men and women.

4. THINKING IT OVER

What is anthropomorphism? Compare Genesis 1 with Acts 17:22-34. What does St. Paul say about the omnipresence of God? God made the world incomplete. What is there still to be done? What can *you* do as God's co-worker in the great process of evolution?

5. PRAY MEDITATIVELY

Psalm 104, "Bless the Lord, O my soul..."
Psalm 148, "Praise the Lord from the heavens..."

6. THINGS TO DO

Israel considered itself as God's chosen people, living with Him in a sacred partnership (Covenant). We see in Israel a growing awareness of God's loving presence. This process of growing wisdom was guided (inspired) by God. Read about it in: Proverbs 3; 8:22-36; Wisdom 15:1-5.

Listen, if possible, to *Die Schoepfungg* (Creation) of Haydn on a record player.

11. The Bible on Angels

God's Concern for Man

1a. The Lord has established his throne in heaven,
*   and his kingdom rules over all.*
Bless the Lord, all you his angels,
*   you mighty in strength, who do his bidding,*
*   obeying his spoken word.*
Bless the Lord, all you his hosts,
*   his ministers, who do his will (Psalm 103:19-21).*

Now the serpent was the most cunning of all the animals that the Lord God had made. The serpent asked the woman, "Did God really tell you not to eat from any of the trees in the garden?" The woman answered the serpent: "We may eat of the fruit of the trees in the garden; it is only about the fruit of the tree in the middle of the garden that God said, 'You shall not eat it or even touch it, lest you die'" (Genesis 3:1-3).

No evil shall befall you,
*   nor shall affliction come near your tent,*
For to his angels he has given command about you,
*   that they guard you in all your ways.*
Upon their hands they shall bear you up,
*   lest you dash your foot against a stone (Psalm 91:10-12).*

2a. Familiar imagery. When reading about angels in the Bible, you should remember that the sacred writers describe God, His greatness, His loving care and His justice, with the aid of a terminology taken from their time and cultural background. They knew about the splendor of their kings and their courts, such as the Egyptian pharaohs, their own king Solomon and the kings of Babylon.

Using this familiar imagery, the sacred writers describe God as an Oriental king with many servants and messengers or angels. (The Latin word for messenger is "angelus"; hence we speak of angels.) Oriental kings did not have newspapers, telephones or radio, nor could they go on television. They had to communicate with their people by means of messengers.

A king who did not have a multitude of servants and messengers (angels) would indeed be a sorry little king! Hence, describing God as the almighty King and Ruler of heaven and earth, the sacred writers surrounded Him with a multitude of servants and angels, who conveyed His messages, His blessings and His judgment down to His people on earth. (Remember that the ancient Hebrews saw the earth as a plate with a huge vault over it and God's palace "up" somewhere!)

2b. God communicates with man. You should not be "shocked" at this human wording used to describe God's greatness. We must use human imagery when we speak of God. We cannot do otherwise. Another question is: Do these angels of the Bible really exist or are they just literary characters used to describe God's communication with man? In other words, did God create an invisible world of angels next to the visible world of man, as discussed in Chapter 10?

Some say that the teaching authority of the Church does not give a definitive answer. Others say that it does. Bible scholars are not unanimous. When you read about angels in your Bible and Missal, always remember that you are reading about God Who communicates with His people. He is present to our being by His message, His blessings and His judgment, whether via angels or not. Bible passages on angels tell us about God's concern for man and as such you should appreciate them.

13.

2c. Devils in the Bible. The Bible has no consistent doctrine on the devil. Satan and his angels appear in the Old Testament not as fallen angels but as God's assistants, who call men to account for their failings. In the New Testament the devil is the evil ruler of the world who must give way to the Messiah. His fall "like lightning" (Luke 10:18) and his defeat at the hands of

Michael (Revelation 12:9) refer to his Messianic and eschatological (final) overthrow.

The Church regards the devils as fallen angels in a permanent state of revolt against God, attempting to lead man to evil. This concept is not clearly stated in the Bible, *but is rather the fruit* of theological reflection, generally accepted since the time of St. Augustine (4th Century).

3a. God is concerned. One of the most inspiring truths of our religion is that God is concerned about us. Thank God as often as you read a Bible passage, which describes that Divine concern which brought angels into the picture!

As for prayers in which angels are mentioned—for example, the Preface to the Eucharistic Prayer—think of all the creatures ever created by God! Actually, what do we know of other creatures who perhaps live and have lived in other galaxies and/or are now "in heaven"? And it may be even that the traditional angels really exist. Anyway, all of them are "His angels," "His hosts" and "His ministers." (See first Bible passage above!)

3b. Your adversary. We know that primitive man was and still is inclined to personify evil. Is this perhaps the reason why the Bible describes evil as a person? (See 2c.) However, evil exists in and around us and that is why we should heed the Apostle's warning: "Your opponent the devil is prowling like a roaring lion looking for someone to devour. Resist him, solid in your faith" (1 Peter 5: 8-9).

4. THINKING IT OVER

From the above Bible passages it is clear that God is concerned about you. Find two Bible passages that describe God as a King surrounded by servants and angels. Explain how these passages imply God's concern for man! What about the real existence of angels and devils? What do Bible passages on angels teach us? What advice does Peter give us concerning the danger of evil?

5. PRAY MEDITATIVELY

Almighty and eternal God, your bounteous kindness exceeds

the merits and fondest hopes of our prayers. Shower your mercy upon us, forgive us the sins that strike fear in our consciences, and grant us the blessings we dare not presume to ask for *(Eleventh Sunday after Pentecost).*

6. THiNGS TO DO

Examine the Mass of Sts. Michael, Gabriel and Raphael on September 29 and find passages indicating that God communicates a message, that He punishes, and that He bestows favors on man!

Read about God's wisdom: Job 1; 2; 19; 42. Notice how God conveys His wisdom in the striking tale about Job! It is a lesson about man's attitude toward evil, temptation and sorrow.

12. God Created Man

God's Blueprint

1. Then God said: "Let us make man in our image, after our likeness. Let them have dominion over the fish of the sea, the birds of the air, and the cattle, and over all the wild animals and all the creatures that crawl on the ground."

God created man in his image;
in the divine image he created him;
male and female he created them.

God blessed them, saying: "Be fertile and multiply; fill the earth and subdue it. Have dominion over the fish of the sea, the birds of the air, and all the living things that move on the earth" (Genesis 1:26-28).

Then the Lord God planted a garden in Eden, in the east, and he placed there the man whom he had formed. Out of the ground the Lord God made various trees grow that were delightful to look at and good for food, with the tree of life in the middle of the garden and the tree of the knowledge of good and bad (Genesis 2:8-9).

The Lord God gave man this order: "You are free to eat from any of the trees of the garden except the tree of knowledge of good and bad. From that tree you shall not eat; the moment you eat from it you are surely doomed to die" (Genesis 2:16-17).

2a. Finding the message. Catholic Bible scholars, who submit their opinions to the final decision of Christ's Church, teach that Chapters 2 and 3 of Genesis should be regarded as an allegory (a symbolical narrative) rather than history in the modern sense. Chapter 2 teaches God's original plan concerning man. "Paradise" existed only in the mind of God. The allegory tells us about God's blueprint for man. The story of Eve's creation is a dramatic expression of the truth concerning woman's essential similarity to man.

Chapter 3 teaches that sin, which is everyman's "situation" at his origin, is the reason why God did not realize the plan He had in mind. Man ate from the tree of knowledge of good and evil, which means, he experienced what evil is by committing serious sin.

2b. Conditioned by thought patterns. You may ask, how did the writer know this? Theologians approach this problem as follows: The Biblical writer—like all of us—was conditioned by the thought patterns of his time and culture.

(1) One man at the beginning. A close look at the Book of Genesis reveals to us that world history, as related there, is actually the history of families and clans that were somehow related to one another. Primitive tribes paid great attention to genealogy (the history of descent from certain ancestors). According to their way of thinking, the clan or tribe began with a famous ancestor who mysteriously came from "somewhere," took a wife and often proved his greatness by acts of great heroism, courage and strength.

The clan itself was frequently named after its ancestor. Judah was the ancestor of the tribe of Judah, and Jacob, the ancestor of Israel, received the name "Israel" from God. Even when primitive people today relate the history of their tribe, this thought pattern is followed constantly. Thus it is small wonder that the Biblical history of mankind followed the same pattern, the clan beginning with an ancestor called Adam, which means "The Man."

(2) All disasters caused by sin. As for what happened at the beginning of man's history, the Biblical author believed that since God is a good Father, His original plan for man *must* have been good (see Genesis 2). Why then did God not make man according to that original plan? The answer given is: At the very beginning "The Man" sinned (see Genesis 3).

In school we have learned that "man" is at least one million years old, and that he evolved from lower kinds of life. How then did the sacred writer know about sin at the very beginning of that history? Guided by God, he inferred this as a logical conclusion that was conditioned by another thought pattern, namely: "All disasters in life are punishment for sin." This thought pattern recurs throughout Hebrew literature. Whenever the Bible relates a story of a war, famine, disease, or defeat it is interpreted as punishment for sin. In writing the history of the human clan, the Biblical writer followed this thought pattern.

As a perceptive observer he saw all the misery experienced by the human race throughout history, and to his way of thinking sin at the very beginning *must* have caused such misery. This is the Faith experience of Israel, as expressed in Genesis 2—3: Human misery is caused by sin and infidelity to God, in which all somehow participate. Christians believe that Christ has redeemed man from this situation.

2c. Friction? The teachings of modern science indicate evolution from lower kinds of life to gradually higher ones. There are different opinions about the details of this process of unfolding (evolution), but its basic principles are a hypothesis, which is accepted by many.

Is there any reason for friction between contemporary science and the Christian Faith in the message of the Bible, especially Genesis 2—3?

(1) Scientists admit that there are "leaps" (gaps) in the process of evolution (unfolding) as far as we know it now. They explain these leaps as part of a natural process, and state or hope that they will some day find the "missing links." For them the process of humanization (from lower forms of life becoming man) is a natural thing.

15.

(2) **Many theologians** require a specially creative interference of God to explain the leap from a lower form of life to a human being. "God created man" means to them that God infused an intelligent "soul" into a lower form of life.

(3) **Other theologians** leave it up to science to find the missing link and to explain the leaps in evolution. Scientific details are not their concern as theologians. They see in and behind that great process of evolution the *constant* creative activity of Almighty God. Hence, instead of saying "God *created*" (as the Bible does, speaking from a *static* world vision which is no longer ours), it is better to say "God *creates.*" At this very moment God creates the universe. St. Paul states: "In him we live and move and have our being" (Acts 17:28).

3. Your parents did not want "you." This creative will of God made "you" come into being. Your parents did not want "you" and could not even want "you." They wanted a child, a boy, a girl. God wanted "you" at the very moment that you originated in the womb of your mother.

"You," as being in God's mind from all eternity and realized in time, should be a wholehearted party of God's great plan of evolution and growth. Indeed, God is your Father, Who wants you to be happy and to grow to even more perfect happiness and intimacy with Him.

4. THINKING IT OVER

What is the message of Genesis 2 and 3? Mention two Hebrew thought patterns that conditioned the way the writer of Genesis 2 and 3 conveys the message. Is there reason for friction between modern science and the Christian Faith in the message of Genesis 2 and 3? Explain the opinions of scientists and theologians!

5. PRAY MEDITATIVELY
Psalms 23; 121.

6. THINGS TO DO
Read Genesis 1; 2; 3.

13. Adam and Eve Disobeyed God

Temptation and Sin. God Is All-knowing and All-just

1. Now the serpent was the most cunning of all the animals that the Lord God had made. The serpent asked the woman, "Did God really tell you not to eat from any of the trees in the garden?" The woman answered the serpent: "We may eat of the fruit of the trees in the garden; it is only about the fruit of the tree in the middle of the garden that God said, 'You shall not eat it or even touch it, lest you die.' " But the serpent said to the woman: "You certainly will not die! No, God knows well that the moment you eat of it you will be like gods who know what is good and what is bad." The woman saw that the tree was good for food, pleasing to the eyes, and desirable for gaining wisdom. So she took some of its fruit and ate it; and she also gave some to her husband, who was with her, and he ate it (Genesis 3:1-6).

When they heard the sound of the Lord God moving about in the garden at the breezy time of the day, the man and his wife hid themselves from the Lord God among the trees of the garden. The Lord God then called to the man and asked him, "Where are you?" (Genesis 3:8-9).

The Lord God therefore banished him from the garden of Eden, to till the ground from which he had been taken. When he expelled the man, he settled him east of the garden of Eden; and he stationed the cherubim and the fiery revolving sword, to guard the way to the tree of life (Genesis 3:23-24).

2a. Every man's sin. Describing the sin of Adam, the Biblical "first man" and figure of Him Who was to come (the Redeemer), the Bible describes everybody's sin. Adam (the Man) is Everyman of the medieval morality play.

As already mentioned in Chapter 12, Bible scholars, after detailed research, tell us how to understand Chapters 1—3 of Genesis: as an allegory which teaches us about the mystery of evil in this world. From it we learn how it happens over and over again that man is tempted, plays with temptation and finally gives in. Man may try to hide himself from God, but it is impossible. God is all-knowing and all-just when He punishes.

17.

2b. Eating from the tree. As it is, we are incomplete beings. And though man has come a long way from caveman to astronaut, we are only at the very beginning of an evolution. As co-workers of God we are supposed to take part in that great process of evolution. We are to order the chaos into a better world. We are to grow to maturity, as the Bible states, "into maturity in Christ," which means to become ever more Christ-like.

To sin, however, means to refuse to be part of all of this. Man who does not want to project himself to that great process of growth and evolution and refuses to be God's co-worker for a better world (himself included) is termed a sinner.

The first beings, who became self-conscious and therefore "men," were innocent. Only through a growing self-consciousness did man become capable of saying "no" to God's plan, i.e., to commit serious sin. Sometime, somehow, man has been so foolish as to "eat from the tree of the knowledge of good and evil," that is, to commit serious evil.

The sin of the world is a fact. All of us are born into this sinful situation, which is the root of all misery in this world.

"Death thus has come to all men inasmuch as all sinned" (Romans 5:12).

Documents of the Church call this situation, or state, "original sin." St. John speaks about "the sin of the world" as the cause of all trouble. St. Paul simply calls it "sin."

3a. "The ego not master in his own house." Whether we call the tempter satan, environment, structure, public opinion, indoctrination, your own inclination or "the ego not master in his own house" (Freud), temptation is there. In itself, temptation is no sin, so long as you do not give in of your free will. To lessen temptations, you (especially the young) must be careful in your choice of reading, movies, etc. See in your Catholic newspaper the list of movies classified by the National Catholic Office on Motion Pictures! When assailed by temptation, resist by praying, and try to distract yourself by working, by conversation, by reading, by being creatively busy.

3b. Your most secret thoughts. Never forget that God is all-knowing. As your Creator, He knows even your most secret thoughts, words and actions. Do not, however, regard God as some secret policeman who is constantly after you. God is a loving Father who desires what is best for you.

4. THINKING IT OVER

What is your present attitude regarding temptation and sin? How would you discuss these topics: "sin and God" and "sin and yourself"?

5. READ ATTENTIVELY

What does the Apostle Paul say about temptations?

The Apostle Paul says: "Let everyone who thinks he is standing upright watch out lest he fall! No test has been sent you that does not come to all men. Besides, God keeps his promise. He will not let you be tested beyond your strength. Along with the test he will give you a way out of it so that you may be able to endure it" (1 Corinthians 10:12-13).

6. PRAY MEDITATIVELY

Psalm 130, "Out of the depths . . ."

7. THINGS TO DO

Read: "The Vineyard Song" in Isaiah 5:1-7.

Notice the disappointment of God when His people (the Church) are unfaithful!

14. The Consequences of Sin for the Human Race

Patience and Penance

1. To the woman he said:
   "I will intensify the pangs of your childbearing;
      in pain shall you bring forth children.
   Yet your urge shall be for your husband,
      and he shall be your master."

To the man he said: "Because you listened to your wife and ate from the tree of which I had forbidden you to eat,

   "Cursed be the ground because of you!
      In toil shall you eat its yield
      all the days of your life.
   Thorns and thistles shall it bring forth to you,
      as you eat of the plants of the field.

> *By the sweat of your face*
>   *shall you get bread to eat,*
> *Until you return to the ground,*
>   *from which you were taken;*
> *For you are dirt,*
>   *and to dirt you shall return"* (Genesis 3:16-19).

2. Collectivity in evil. The approach to this Genesis passage is the same as that described in Chapters 12 and 13.

A child born and reared in an irreligious family of evildoers and thieves is seriously handicapped in becoming and remaining a good person. Similar to this is the human condition into which we are born. Only the Blessed Virgin Mary was preserved from that sinful state called "original sin." Hence we speak of the Immaculate Conception of the Virgin Mary.

We have already mentioned that the Bible speaks of the "sin of the world" or simply "sin." Documents of the Church use the term "original sin." Note that "original sin" is not sin in the usual sense of the word. No man will be condemned solely because of "original sin," but because of personal decisions by which he gives shape to "original sin."

Original sin may be described as that **collective refusal of the** first sinner and all his fellow sinners to live up to what we should be in the mind of God. Jesus also mentions this evil. See Matthew 23:35; John 1:29). This mysterious collectivity in evil is something which we cannot understand completely. Evil will always be obscure.

3a. Do not blame God. Let us be grateful that Jesus became the Lamb Who took away the sin of the world and made it possible to overcome evil! Through Jesus' meritorious death we are now dead to sin and able to grow into what God wants us to be for all eternity.

As for our human condition, the message of Genesis 2—3 is: Do not blame God for evil in this world! His original plan was good. Blame yourself, the sin of the world which took shape in your own sins!

3b. A mysterious process. As long as you are in this world, you must carry your cross. That is to say: you must be patient in sorrow and sickness, until death finally comes to you from the hands of God.

God permits pain and death to cleanse you and to release you from your strong inclination to evil. He wants your heart directed to Him.

The aim of Christian penance is quite the same: direction of your heart to God. By the acceptance of pain and its climax: death, and by mortification, you free yourself from the bondage of evil, so that you are able to surrender yourself totally to God.

Accepting wholeheartedly pain and death and, moreover, mortifying yourself is called by St. Paul "crucifying the flesh." The Wise Man of the Bible compares mankind with gold, that must be cleansed in the furnace (Wisdom 3:6). Jesus speaks of the grain of wheat that falls into the ground and dies in order to bring forth fruit (John 12:24). Penance, pain, frustration, death—it is a mysterious process that all of us must go through.

Christ set the example. You must carry your cross as He did, and try to become free from all attachment to evil in order to become perfect in love of God.

4. THINKING IT OVER

Explain the difference between the terms "original sin" and "actual sin." What is the aim of pain, death and Christian penance? Supplement the explanation given here with what is said in Chapter 4 about this subject. What does St. Paul mean by "crucifying the flesh"? How do Wisdom 3:1-6 and John 12:33-35 approach this mystery?

5. READ ATTENTIVELY

What does St. Paul say about unregulated desires?

St. Paul says: "Those who belong to Christ Jesus have crucified their flesh with its passions and desires" (Galatians 5:24).

6. PRAY MEDITATIVELY

Psalm 51, "Have mercy on me, O God . . ."

7. THINGS TO DO

Read: Genesis 1-11.

Using folklore. Bible scholars tell us that these Chapters of Genesis do not teach history in our sense of the word; rather they are allegories. The sacred writer used these stories, often the folklore of his time, to instruct the people concerning the great problems of Creation, God's original plan for man, evil and penance. As long as the Church does not condemn a particular Bible scholar's explanation of the Bible, you remain a Catholic in good standing if you follow these contemporary visions on the Biblical message.

Nothing wrong with the Bible. From time to time Christians have to reconsider their understanding of the Bible. When Copernicus and Galileo set forth their views that the world is not a plate (see Chapter 10) but a bowl, the first reaction of the Church was that science was wrong, since these new views were supposedly incompatible with God's word in the Bible. When it became evident that Galileo was right, the Church became conscious that there was nothing wrong with the Bible (God's message cannot be wrong!) but that there was something wrong with our understanding of the Bible.

The same happened in the early days of the theory of evolution. Again the first reaction of the Church was that evolution is incompatible with the Bible; yet today the basic outlines of this theory can scarcely be denied. This has resulted in a reconsideration not of the Bible as God's infallible message but of our understanding of it.

Not a science book. As it is, scholars are constantly exploring the Bible and its literary forms. Archeologists make excavations in the Near East and investigate ancient cultures and languages from the environment in which the Bible came into being. These scholars tell us how we are to understand the Bible against the back-

Archeologists make excavations. Stepped and battered terracewall of Temple 1 at Eridu c. 3500 B.C.

ground of modern science on nature and the past. They tell us that the Bible is not a science textbook for high school or college; that the sacred writers described nature as they saw it, without pronouncing a scientific opinion (see Chapter 10); and that they, in describing nature as they saw it, teach us religious truths with Divine authority.

19.

Scholars tell us that not only the intellect, but the "whole" man has to approach the Bible not as a problem but as a mystery, as an expression of a faithful view of life inspiring your own Faith.

It may happen, therefore, that as a result of scientific investigation certain Bible stories (such as Jonah and Job) more or less lose their character of being history, but gain more worth as to doctrine, understanding of Faith, theology, pastoral tendencies, etc.

In communion with the Church. Christians in the Catholic tradition firmly believe that the Spirit is guiding God's people and that this Divine guidance somehow culminates in the teaching authority of the Church, the collective bishops and their head, the Bishop of Rome. That is why Catholic Bible scholars explain the Bible in communion with the Church and make their opinions ultimately subject to its teaching authority. By doing so, they will not fall into extremes, as happens outside the Church when scholars sometimes go so far as to declare the Bible a collection of fairy tales. Chapter 35 and the section on "How to Read Your Bible," p. 298 give further explanation on Bible reading.

15. God Promised a Redeemer

God Is Merciful

From the time of Moses there were always Prophets in Israel (see Chapter 10). They were men sent by God to keep Israel's Faith in the Covenant alive. (See the section on "How to Read Your Bible," no. 10, p. 302.)

We may cite here the Prophet Elijah who lived in the northern kingdom of Palestine around 800-700 B.C., and Amos who preached at the gate of the sanctuary in Bethel.

Toward the end of the eighth Century B.C., Samaria was defeated and a large part of the population exiled to Assyria. The king of Assyria transferred other people to Samaria, and they mixed with the Israelites who had remained. You can understand, then, why the Samaritans in the time of Christ were not regarded as real Israelites. (See the parable of the Good Samaritan, Luke 10:25-37, and Jesus' meeting with the Samaritan woman, John 4:1-42.)

There were also Prophets in the southern kingdom of Judah. We now mention: Joel, the "Pentecost prophet" (Peter quoted him in his first sermon on Pentecost; see Acts 2: 14-24); Isaiah (the acclamation "Holy . . ." of the Mass is taken from his writings; see Isaiah 6:1-3); Micah, and Jeremiah. Jeremiah predicted the destruction of the kingdom of Judah because of its infidelity to God.

In 605 B.C., Judah was defeated by the king of Babylon. In 589 B.C., the destruction of Jerusalem and the Temple followed. Thousands of Israelites were carried off into exile in Babylon.

A Prophet who lived with the exiles in Babylon was Ezekiel. After about seventy years of exile many Israelites came back to their holy city with the sacred vessels that had been robbed by the king of Babylon. They established a new temple. Prophets of the post-exile era (500 B.C.) were Haggai and Malachi.

We possess in the books of Judith and Esther great treasures stemming from those Israelites who, instead of returning from exile, remained in Persia.

After the exile Israel no longer had any political significance. It was subject successively to Persia, Greece (Alexander the Great), and Rome. (See diagram on page 309.)

But this national calamity and occupation gave birth to Judaism as a religion. Anguish and disaster had caused the best part of Israel to reflect on the real values of life. Synagogues were established everywhere and the new Temple in Jerusalem became the religious center for the Jews both in Israel and abroad.

"But holy men of God spoke as they were moved by the Holy Spirit" (2 Peter 1:21).

A Prophet. French School.

God Promised a Redeemer

1a. *Then the Lord God said to the serpent:*

> "Because you have done this, you shall be banned
> > from all the animals
> > and from all the wild creatures;
>
> On your belly shall you crawl,
> > and dirt shall you eat
> > all the days of your life.
>
> I will put enmity between you and the woman,
> > and between your offspring and hers;
>
> He will strike at your head,
> > while you strike at his heel" *(Genesis 3:14-15).*

1b. Again the Lord spoke to Ahaz: Ask for a sign from the Lord, your God; let it be deep as the nether world, or high as the sky! But Ahaz answered, "I will not ask! I will not tempt the Lord!" Then he said: Listen, O house of David! Is it not enough for you to weary men, must you also weary my God? Therefore the Lord himself will give you this sign: the virgin shall be with child, and bear a son, and shall name him Immanuel *(Isaiah 7:10-14).*

> *1c.* If he gives his life as an offering for sin,
> > he shall see his descendants in a long life,
> > and the will of the Lord shall be accomplished through him.
>
> Because of his affliction
> > he shall see the light in fullness of days;
>
> Through his suffering, my servant shall justify many,
> > and their guilt he shall bear.
>
> Therefore I will give him his portion among the great
> > and he shall divide the spoils with the mighty,
>
> Because he surrendered himself to death
> > and was counted among the wicked;
>
> And he shall take away the sins of many,
> > and win pardon for their offenses *(Isaiah 53:10-12).*

> *1d.* The people who walked in darkness
> > have seen a great light;
>
> Upon those who dwelt in the land of gloom
> > a light has shone.
>
> You have brought them abundant joy
> > and great rejoicing,
>
> As they rejoice before you as at the harvest,
> > as men make merry when dividing spoils.
>
> For the yoke that burdened them,
> > the pole on their shoulder,

> And the rod of their taskmaster
>> you have smashed, as on the day of Midian.
> For every boot that tramped in battle,
>> every cloak rolled in blood,
>> will be burned as fuel for flames.
> For a child is born to us, a son is given us;
>> upon his shoulder dominion rests.
> They name him Wonder-Counselor, God-Hero,
>> Father-Forever, Prince of Peace.
> His dominion is vast
>> and forever peaceful,
> From David's throne, and over his kingdom,
>> which he confirms and sustains
> By Judgment and justice,
>> both now and forever.
> The zeal of the Lord of hosts will do this (Isaiah 9:1-6)!

1e. The days are coming, says the Lord, when I will make a new covenant with the house of Israel and the house of Judah. It will not be like the covenant I made with their fathers the day I took them by the hand to lead them forth from the land of Egypt; for they broke my covenant and I had to show myself their master, says the Lord. But this is the covenant which I will make with the house of Israel after those days, says the Lord. I will place my law within them, and write it upon their hearts; I will be their God, and they shall be my people (Jeremiah 31, 33-33).

> 1f. The spirit of the Lord God is upon me,
>> because the Lord has anointed me;
> He has sent me to bring glad tidings to the lowly,
>> to heal the brokenhearted,
> To proclaim liberty to the captives
>> and release to the prisoners,
> To announce a year of favor from the Lord
>> and a day of vindication by our God,
>> to comfort all who mourn (Isaiah 61:1-2).

> 1g. As the visions during the night continued, I saw
>> One like a son of man coming,
>> on the clouds of heaven;
> When he reached the Ancient One
>> and was presented before him,
> He received dominion, glory, and kingship;
>> nations and peoples of every language serve him.
> His dominion is an everlasting dominion
>> that shall not be taken away,
>> his kingship shall not be destroyed (Daniel 7:13-14).

2a. The Messiah-Redeemer theme. The Hebrews dreamed about the formerly great kingdom of David. Steadily oppressed by mighty neighbors, they desired to see a restoration of that kingdom. Their prophets, men inspired by God, promised a redeemer to deliver them from all bondage, a great king:

"Behold, the days are coming, says the Lord,
   when I will raise up a righteous shoot to David;
As king he shall reign and govern wisely,
   he shall do what is right and just in the land"
                                    (Jeremiah 23:5).

"The kings of Tarshish and the Isles shall offer gifts;
   the kings of Arabia and Seba shall bring tribute.
All kings shall pay him homage,
   all nations shall serve him" (Psalm 72:10-11).

See also Chapter 9, no. 2b.

The above very brief Bible excerpts illustrate that there was a Messiah-expectation in ancient Israel. Jesus has evaluated it, demonstrating that He was the long-expected one. Read Luke 4:14-32 and note how Jesus demonstrated His mission with the aid of the quotation in no. 1f, above.

2b. Turning to the quotations themselves, we see that no. 1a is a promise known from the Paradise story. We must understand this passage in the light of the Hebrew belief that all disaster was caused by sin. There will be enmity between the offspring of the serpent (evil) and the offspring of the woman (man). We experience this daily in and around us. But man will overcome! The Christian interpretation is: Man will overcome evil in Christ, Who defeated evil on the Cross of Calvary.

The passage in no. 1b is the oracle of Isaiah 7:10-16. The young maiden who will be with child and bear a son is probably Abi, the young wife of King Ahaz. "Immanuel" (means: "with us is God") is his son, later called Hezekiah. Matthew quotes this oracle of Isaiah when he proclaims the virgin birth of Jesus in the first of his five "fulfillment-episodes" (see Matthew 1:18-25; 2:1-6. 13-15. 16-18. 19-23).

In no. 1c, we see a new element in the Messiah idea. Isaiah describes the savior (redeemer) as a servant of Yahweh, who will make up for the sins of many. But finally as a great king he will defeat his enemies and the Covenant will be renewed (see nos. 1d, e, f, g).

Encouraged by its sacred writers, Israel could pray:

"Let justice [the Savior] descend, O heavens [God], like dew from above,
like gentle rain let the skies drop it down" (Isaiah 45:8).

It is the author of the Gospel according to Matthew, writing among Jews for Jews, who makes a special point to demonstrate that the Scriptures are fulfilled in the person and work of Jesus. In every significant passage of his work he makes use of the Old Testament to prove that Law and Prophets are "fulfilled." For examples, look in the Gospel version of Matthew!

3. **Faith pointing toward a future.** The Church calls forth, each year, the time of waiting and longing for a Redeemer during Advent, the four weeks preceding Christmas. "Advent" means "coming." During this time Christians prepare themselves for the coming of Christ through grace, and His final coming on "Judgment Day." Never forget that Hope, an aspect of which contemporary theologians speak of as "Faith pointing toward a future," is a typically Christian attitude toward life and its problems. (See Chapter 43, no. 2b.)

4. THINKING IT OVER

Describe and explain the Messiah expectation in Hebrew literature! How did our Lord evaluate this expectation, demonstrating that He was the long-expected one? (See Luke 4:14-32.) Give some examples and explain how Matthew shows that "the Law and the Prophets" are fulfilled in our Lord. How would you describe "hope"?

5. PRAY MEDITATIVELY

The Masses of the first and second Sundays of Advent.

6. THINGS TO DO

Read the following passages of the Bible, which form a brief anthology on the above mentioned sacred authors: 1 Kings 19:9-21; 2 Kings 2:1-14; Joel 2:27-32; Isaiah 9:1-7; Micah 4:1-4; Jeremiah 2:1-9; Lamentations 1:1-14; Ezekiel 34:11-16; Daniel 6:14-28; Malachi 1:11; Isaiah 60:1-3.

JOHN THE BAPTIZER

16. Saint John Introduces Christ

The Redeemer Is Priest and Victim

1a. In the fifteenth year of the rule of Tiberius Caesar, when Pontius Pilate was procurator of Judea, Herod tetrarch of Galilee, Philip his brother tetrarch of the region of Ituraea and Trachonitis, and Lysanias tetrarch of Abilene, during the high-priesthood of Annas and Caiaphas, the word of God was spoken to John son of Zechariah in the desert. He went about the entire region of the Jordan proclaiming a baptism of repentance which led to the forgiveness of sins, as is written in the book of the words of Isaiah the prophet:

> *"A herald's voice in the desert, crying,*
> *'Make ready the way of the Lord,*
> *Clear him a straight path.*
> *Every valley shall be filled*
> *And every mountain and hill shall be leveled.*
> *The windings shall be made straight*
> *And the rough ways smooth,*
> *And all mankind shall see the salvation of God'"* (Lk 3:1-6).

1b. John answered them: "I baptize with water. There is one among you whom you do not recognize—the one who is to come after me—the strap of whose sandal I am not worthy to unfasten."

This happened in Bethany, across the Jordan, where John was baptizing.

The next day, when John caught sight of Jesus coming toward him, he exclaimed:

> *"Look! There is the Lamb of God*
> *who takes away the sin of the world!*

64 Saint John Introduces Christ　　　　　　　　　　Ch. 16

It is he of whom I said:
> *'After me is to come a man*
> *who ranks ahead of me,*
> *because he was before me.'*

I confess I did not recognize him, though the very reason I came baptizing with water was that he might be revealed to Israel."

> *John gave this testimony also:*
> *"I saw the Spirit descend*
> *like a dove from the sky,*
> *and it came to rest on him.*

But I did not recognize him. The one who sent me to baptize with water told me, 'When you see the Spirit descend and rest on someone, it is he who is to baptize with the Holy Spirit.' Now I have seen for myself and have testified, 'This is God's chosen One'" (Jn 1:26-34).

"Make ready the way of the Lord" *(Luke 3:4)*

2a. John a Qumran monk? Archeologists have discovered the ruins of a Jewish monastery at Qumran close to the Dead Sea in the desert. In nearby caves they have uncovered valuable scrolls and manuscripts from the time of Jesus. The monks of Qumran lived together, prayed and studied the Scriptures. There is some conjecture that John the Baptizer, who baptized in the Jordan only a few miles away, may have been one of them.

It was the task of John the Baptizer to introduce the Messiah to the people of Israel.

As John baptized Christ in the Jordan, the Holy Spirit descended in the shape of a dove. This event revealed to John that the Person Whom he baptized was the promised Messiah and the Son of God.

Because the Son of God is eternal, even though He comes *after* John, He is, nevertheless, *before* him (see the above passage from St. John).

2b. The very core of Christ's task. John the Baptizer announced the very core of Christ's task, namely, to become a Lamb without spot, patient and meek of heart, sent by God to carry all the sins of mankind on His shoulders (or on His head) and to take them away from the world. This happened when Jesus hung on the Cross, as a Lamb that was slaughtered.

Christ is anointed a High Priest (see Chapter 8) and at the same time He is also a Victim of atonement for your sins.

3. In the signs of bread and wine. Our High Priest offered Himself as a Lamb without spot on the altar of the Cross. As often as the Sacrifice of the Mass is offered, the supreme Sacrifice of the Cross is offered. The High Priest offers Himself through the mouth and hands of the priest at the altar. In the signs of bread and wine, Christ becomes the Lamb of God Who takes away the sin of the world.

You must be thankful for God's love; He bestowed His Son to become our High Priest and Victim.

4. THINKING IT OVER

What was the task of John the Baptizer? How did he recognize Jesus as the promised Messiah? How could John say that Christ comes *after* him and is nevertheless *before* him? What did St. Paul say about the task of a priest? (See Chapter 8.) Why did John the Baptizer call Christ "the Lamb of God, Who takes away the sin of the world"? When is the Sacrifice of the Cross present for us?

5. PRAY IN YOUR MISSAL

"Lamb of God . . ." (*Ordinary of the Mass.*)

6. THINGS TO DO

Read the Masses for the third and fourth Sundays of Advent. Notice how, in these Masses, the desire for Christ's coming in grace is expressed.

Read: Luke 1:1-25; 3; 7:18-30; John 1:6-8; Mark 6:14-29.

"Last of all in these days He [God] has spoken to us by His Son" (Heb. 1:2).

JESUS CHRIST

17. Jesus Christ Proclaims the Kingdom of God

Reform your lives!

1a. *In times past, God spoke in fragmentary and varied ways to our fathers through the prophets; in this, the final age, he has spoken to us through his Son, whom he has made heir of all things and through whom he first created the universe (Hebrews 1:1-2).*

> 1b. *The Word became flesh
> and made his dwelling among us,
> and we have seen his glory:
> The glory of an only Son coming from the Father,
> filled with enduring love.
> The light shines on in darkness,
> a darkness that did not overcome it (John 1:14, 5).*

1c. *During that time, Jesus came from Nazareth in Galilee and was baptized in the Jordan by John. Immediately on coming up out of the water he saw the sky rent in two and the Spirit descending on him like a dove. Then a voice came from the heavens: "You are my beloved Son. On you my favor rests."*

At that point the Spirit sent him out toward the desert. He stayed in the wasteland forty days, put to the test there by Satan. He was with the wild beasts, and angels waited on him.

After John's arrest, Jesus appeared in Galilee proclaiming the good news of God: "This is the time of fulfillment. The reign of God is at hand! Reform your lives and believe in the gospel!" (Mark 1:9-15).

1d. *Now John in prison heard about the works Christ was performing, and sent a message by his disciples to ask him, "Are you 'He who is to come' or do we look for another?" In reply, Jesus said to them: "Go back and report to John what you hear and see: the blind recover their sight, cripples walk, lepers are cured, the deaf hear, dead men are raised to life, and the poor have the good news preached to them" (Matthew 11:2-5).*

2a. On communication. Communication is a complicated thing. It is more than just uttering sounds either in English or

Chinese. Often barriers must first be taken away. Emotions, hard feelings, prejudice, ignorance, closed-mindedness must be patiently done away with and only then communication becomes possible. Which means should God use to communicate with man? He is so entirely different and so much greater than we are. He is so incomprehensible that we cannot possibly develop an adequate concept of Him.

"In this, the final age, God has spoken to us through his Son." (See no. 1a.) God speaks to us through Jesus of Nazareth: a child in a crib, a person, His kindness, goodness, justice, honesty, miracles, parables, Death and Resurrection.

It is this very core of New Testament literature which John tries to explain in the introduction of his Gospel version. He uses figures of speech. He calls Jesus God's *word* to those who are ignorant. He calls Him *light* to people who walk in darkness. Jesus of Nazareth, His charming personality, is God's word to man. Prejudice, lack of interest, closed-mindedness prevent understanding. But could God speak a clearer language than He has done through the appealing personality of Jesus of Nazareth? (See no. 1b.)

2b. The time fulfilled. The celestial proclamation, as related by Mark, is an invitation to see Jesus as the Messiah foretold by the Prophets. The Spirit urges Jesus to begin His mission as such. Hence, Jesus started preaching and proclaiming the Kingdom of God, saying: "The reign of God is at hand! Reform your lives and believe in the gospel."

The Prophets had foretold that Kingdom. Pious men had prayed: "Let justice descend, O heavens, like dew from above, like gentle rain let the skies drop it down." Now the time is fulfilled: "Justice" from above, the Messiah, has come and proclaims His kingdom.

The one condition necessary to enter the Kingdom of God is: reform your life and believe in the Gospel, namely, the good tidings of Jesus Christ.

2c. Faithful in love. Faith is very closely related to "Love," as it still resounds in the Anglo-Saxon word be-*lieve* (*love*). The language does not lie! The "faithful" are in love with God. Reasons can be adduced for the fact that two persons are in love. But the ultimate reason escapes the logic of an outsider. Only those in love with one another experience this fact! In similar fashion do we approach the mystery of Faith. You are "in Faith"! Reasons can be adduced for the fact that you have Faith in God, but the ultimate reason escapes the logic of the outsider (unbe-*liever*).

Faith is a gift of God. No one is able to believe if God does not call him. However, there are very possibly people who, when offered the gift of Faith, resist it. They hear the good tidings of Jesus Christ with their ears, and their hearts are touched by the grace of God, but they continue to doubt and refuse God's great gift.

To help those "of little faith," our Lord accompanied the proclamation of His Kingdom by showing the fulfillment of the prophecies in Him (see Chapter 15, no. 2a, and no. 1d above), and by working many miracles, even raising Himself from the dead.

2d. Miracles are symbols through which God reveals Himself. Telling of Jesus' first miracle in Cana, St. John writes: "Thus [by working this sign] did he reveal his glory" (John 2:11). You might read, in Matthew 9:1-8, how Jesus healed a sick man and forgave him his sins: "At the sight, a feeling of awe came over the crowd, and they praised God." On reading the Gospels, a similar kind of awe may come over you and may reach the conclusion that led Nicodemus to Jesus: "Rabbi [teacher], we know you are a teacher come from God, for no man can perform signs and wonders such as you perform unless God is with him" (John 3:2).

2e. Signs which summon. When reading the Gospels, one should distinguish historical facts from midrashic elaboration. (Midrash is a figure of speech, namely, "a theological interpretation of events in the past.") Catholic Bible scholars usually accept the fact that Jesus worked miracles. However, the miracle stories of the Gospels are not simply a record of what actually happened, but above all theological reflections about what happened in order to bring out its meaning for the Christian Faith. Moreover, some of these stories may simply be adaptations of similar Old Testament miracle stories in order to bring out the Christian belief in the importance of Jesus' person and mission. From this observation we learn that miracles are not signs which compel assent. Rather they are signs which summon those with an open mind. They do not give Faith but rather strengthen it.

3. First the Kingdom. Jesus says: "Seek first his kingship over you, his way of holiness, and all these things will be given you besides" (Matthew, 6:33). But do not forget the condition for joining the Kingdom: Reform your life, and believe! This is of first importance because once you have done it, all other things shall be given you besides.

4. THINGS TO DO

Describe the process of communication! What language does a mother choose to communicate with her little child? What means did God use to communicate with man? Which figures of speech does John use to indicate to all of us Who Jesus is? Describe Faith as related to love! What is midrash? What has it to do with the miracle stories of the Gospels? What is the function of miracles in regard to Faith?

5. PRAY MEDITATIVELY

Almighty and eternal God, you have renewed all creation through your beloved Son, the King of the whole universe. May all peoples of the earth, now torn apart by the wound of sin, become subject to the gentle rule of your only-begotten Son. Amen *(Prayer for the feast of Christ the King).*

6. THINGS TO DO

Read: John 12:37-50; John 11:1-44 (esp. 42).

18. Jesus of Nazareth

Mary Conceives of the Holy Spirit

1. In the sixth month, the angel Gabriel was sent from God to a town of Galilee named Nazareth, to a virgin betrothed to a man named Joseph, of the house of David. The virgin's name was Mary. Upon arriving, the angel said to her: "Rejoice, O highly favored daughter! The Lord is with you. Blessed are you among women." She was deeply troubled by his words, and wondered what his greeting meant. The angel went on to say to her: "Do not fear, Mary. You have found favor with God. You shall conceive and bear a son and give him the name Jesus. Great will be his dignity and he will be called Son of the Most High. The Lord God will give him the throne of David his father. He will rule over the house of Jacob forever and his reign will be without end."

Mary said to the angel, "How can this be since I do not know man?" The angel answered her: "The Holy Spirit will come upon you and the power of the Most High will overshadow you; hence, the holy offspring to be born will be called Son of God. Know that Elizabeth your kinswoman has conceived a son in her old age; she who was thought to be sterile is now in her sixth month, for nothing is impossible with God."

Mary said: "I am the servant of the Lord. Let it be done to me as you say." With that the angel left her (Luke 1:26-38).

2a. Without mediation of man. The angel said to Mary: "The Holy Spirit will come upon you and the power of the Most High will overshadow you." Directly through the almighty will of God the Holy Spirit, without the mediation of man, the human life of Jesus had its origin in the womb of His Mother. This is the meaning of the words in the Angelus: "And she [Mary] conceived of the Holy Spirit."

The Feast of the Anunciation of the Blessed Virgin Mary is March 25.

2b. Composed of flesh and blood. The Bible, comparing Jesus with the Jewish high priest, states: "For we do not have a high priest who is unable to sympathize with our weakness, but one who was tempted in every way that we are, yet never sinned" (Hebrews 4:15). Jesus of Nazareth is first of all a man composed of flesh and blood, born of a woman as all of us are. He suffered hunger and thirst; He was grieved, and joyful, and afraid to die.

As He grew up Jesus became more and more conscious that He had a very particular mission, that He was the Messiah promised by the Prophets and about Whom He heard the Rabbi read and preach in the synagogue on the Sabbath. Moreover, especially during His public life, Jesus became ever more conscious of His intimate relationship with God, which was such as to make Him the Son of God. This will be discussed more extensively in the next Chapter.

2c. Mother of God. Christ is called "God and Man"; because He is not only Man but also God, His Mother is indeed the Mother of God.

Mary was highly honored by God. She was, from the first moment of her conception, free from original sin. She is called "Holy Virgin of Virgins" because she remainded a virgin before and after the birth of her Child. St. Joseph was only the foster father of Jesus. Mary never committed a sin. She shares in God's life in a very special way—much more than other Christians do through Faith and Baptism. Mary is full of grace.

These special gifts were given to Mary not because of her own merits, but because of the merits of Jesus Christ on the Cross.

You may ask: "Did Mary fully understand whom she was bringing into the world?" She had an initial intimation of it. Her faith grew in clearness and depth. The resurrection of Jesus must also have thrown new light for Mary on the mystery of the Son of God.

2d. A poetical expression? In Chapter 14, number 7, we mentioned that the Church had to reconsider her understanding of the Bible because of new findings of science and Biblical scholarship (Galileo—Evolution). There cannot possibly be anything wrong with the Bible (God's word), but man can misunderstand some part of the Bible even for generations.

Something similar could sometime possibly occur concerning the *bodily* virginity of Mary. There are theologians who refer to the literary forms in Matthew 1 (one of the five "fulfillment-episodes" that introduce this Gospel version) and Luke 1-3 and reason as follows: Both Matthew and Luke announce Jesus' roots in our humanity as solemnly as possible by a genealogy. But at the same time they also announce Jesus' origin from God.

Jesus is a child of promise. The Prophets had promised a Redeemer to come. For centuries God's people had prayed: "Come . . ." (Chapter 15). Jesus was born entirely out of grace, entirely out of promise: "received from the Holy Spirit." This is what the Gospel wishes to announce by stating that Jesus had His origin not from the will of a man.

Hence the *virgin* birth would be a poetical expression of Jesus' uniqueness as the Son of God. These contemporary theologians also state that the dogma of Mary's Immaculate Conception would in no way be affected if she would have had a sexual relationship with Joseph.

May we accept this new interpretation of the Biblical message? Though several contemporary theologians state that the *bodily* virginity of Mary is not a dogma of the Church, and offer some Biblical reasons for their opinion (the virginity of Mary being a poetical expression of Jesus' uniqueness), we may not easily do away with at least ordinary statements of the Teaching Authority and the generally accepted interpretation of the centuries, as explained in 2a, b, c.

2e. **And St. Joseph.** Next to Mary, Christians also give St. Joseph a special veneration. He is the foster father of Jesus, the chaste spouse of Mary and the protector of Holy Mother Church. St. Joseph protected the holy family for many years. That is why Christians ask him to protect also the great holy family of God's children in this world with his prayers before God.

St. Joseph is the special protector of workmen because he had to make a living for his family with the work of his hands.

The Feast of Saint Joseph, Spouse of the Blessed Virgin Mary, Confessor and Patron of the Universal Church, is March 19.

The Feast of Saint Joseph the Workman is May 1.

Joseph and Mary were a lawfully married couple, who gave each other the marriage right, though they never made use of that right.

3. A Christian custom. It is a Christian custom to commemorate three times a day the tremendous mystery of God's Incarnation. The prayer Christians say is the Angelus and, during Easter time, the Regina Coeli (see Treasury of Prayers, p. 291). In many churches, the chimes are rung at 6 a.m., 12 noon, and 6 p.m. to remind Christians of this mystery.

4. THINKING IT OVER

Was Jesus always explicitly conscious of the fact that He was the promised Messiah and the Son of God? Why is Mary indeed the Mother of God? Who alone remained free from original sin? (See Chapter 14). Why can Mary be called "Holy Virgin of Virgins"? Because of Whose merits did Mary receive her fullness of grace? Who is St. Joseph? Why is St. Joseph the protector of the workman?

5. PRAY MEDITATIVELY

The Angelus (see Treasury of Prayers, p. 291).

6. THINGS TO DO

Read: The Masses of March 25 and May 1; also Luke 1:39-56; Matthew 1:18-25; 2:13-23.

For the human qualities of Jesus, see Mark 10:13-16; Luke 7:36-50; Matthew 23:27-39; Matthew 26:36-46.

Listen, if possible, to a recording of the first part of *The Messiah* of Handel.

Compare the story of Jesus' conception and birth in Luke 1:26-38; 1:46-55; 2:1-20 with 1 Samuel 1 and 2 (birth of the

Prophet Samuel), Judges 13:1-24 (birth of Samson, a savior of his people by defeating the Philistines time and again) and Luke 1:5-25; 1:57-80 (birth of John the Baptizer). Note the same pattern: a barren woman (young maiden)—an unusual conception—an angel of the Lord—a miracle of God—a song, figuratively put into the mouth of the happy mother or father. What did the writers have in mind? Is it perhaps a classical figure of speech to introduce a great man (prophet, savior) to the readers?

19. Jesus Christ Is the Son of God

1. When Jesus came to the neighborhood of Caesarea Philippi, he asked his disciples this question: "Who do people say that the Son of Man is?" They replied, "Some say John the Baptizer, others Elijah, still others Jeremiah or one of the prophets." "And you," he said to them, "who do you say that I am?" "You are the Messiah," Simon Peter answered, "the Son of the living God!" Jesus replied, "Blest are you, Simon son of John! No mere man has revealed this to you, but my heavenly Father" (Matthew 16:13-17).

It was winter, and the time came for the feast of the Dedication in Jerusalem. Jesus was walking in the temple area, in Solomon's Portico, when the Jews gathered around him and said, "How long are you going to keep us in suspense? If you really are the Messiah, tell us so in plain words." Jesus answered:

> "I did tell you, but you do not believe.
> The works I do in my Father's name
> give witness in my favor.
> The Father and I are one."

When some of the Jews again reached for rocks to stone him, Jesus protested to them, "Many good deeds have I shown you from the Father. For which of these do you stone me?" "It is not for any 'good deed' that we are stoning you," the Jews retorted, "but for blaspheming. You who are only a man are making yourself God." Jesus answered:

> "Is it not written in your law,
> 'I have said, You are gods'?
> If it calls those men gods
> to whom God's word was addressed—
> and Scripture cannot lose its force—
> do you claim that I blasphemed

> when, as he whom the Father consecrated
> and sent into the world,
> I said, 'I am God's Son'?
> If I do not perform my Father's works,
> put no faith in me.
> But if I do perform them,
> even though you put no faith in me,
> put faith in these works,
> so as to realize what it means
> that the Father is in me
> and I in him."

At these words they again tried to arrest him, but he eluded their grasp (John 10:22-25, 30-39).

2a. Growing consciousness. From the above Bible passages we learn that Jesus was conscious of a very particular fact, namely that He was not just an ordinary man, but a man so intimately related to God that He could truly be called the Son of God. "The Father and I are one" (John 10:30).

As we have mentioned in the previous Chapter, Jesus was probably not so explicitly conscious of this fact from the beginning of his life. The Bible states: "Jesus progressed steadily in wisdom . . . before God and men" (Luke 2:52). Theologians speak of a growing human consciousness of Jesus that He had a particular mission, that He was the Messiah promised by the Prophets and spoken about by the Rabbi in the synagogue.

2b. Turning points in the life of Jesus concern His relations with John the Baptizer. Jesus came to John ready to undergo his Baptism of repentance and to be one among many sinners. However, a remarkable experience took place: the Spirit descended on Him and a voice spoke to Him from the heavens: "You are my beloved Son. On you my favor rests." (See Mark 1:1-11 and John 1:24-34.)

Then Jesus was confronted with the idea of being a material and political Messiah (Anointed King) with its accompanying human privileges of wealth, glory, and power. He chose instead utter dependence on God, humility, and obedience to God's will. (See Luke 4:1-13.)

Later, John the Baptizer was thrown into prison. Is it possible that Jesus felt called upon to take John's place to proclaim the good news of the Kingdom at hand? In any case, the message with which Jesus began His teaching was the same as John's: "Reform your lives! The kingdom of heaven [God] is at hand." (See Matthew 4:11-17.)

Ultimately, John the Baptizer was put to death. "When Jesus heard this, he withdrew by boat from there to a desert place by himself" (Matthew 14:13). Did Jesus perhaps see His own impending death in the beheading of John the Baptizer? To continue his mission of preaching the Kingdom was to risk death. He dreaded this prospect: "My Father, if it is possible, let this cup pass me by. Still, let it be as you would have it, not as I" (Matthew 26:39).

Jesus was clearly aware that He could forgive sins, that He was the Lord of the Sabbath, and that He was one with the Father. But He had to go through darkness. Listen to Jesus' cry on the Cross: "My God, my God, why have you forsaken me? (Matthew 27:46). It is the cry of a human being in real distress, but not a sign of despair. As He breathed His last, Jesus prayed: "Father, into your hands I commend my spirit" (Luke 23:46). Jesus' consciousness of being God's Son was clouded, but never denied.

Jesus Christ is not merely an ordinary Man. He is the Son of God. Jesus Christ is both God and Man:

> "We believe in one Lord, Jesus Christ,
>   the only Son of God,
>   eternally begotten of the Father,
>   God from God, Light from Light,
>   true God from true God,
>   begotten, not made, one in Being with the Father."
> *(Profession of Faith of the Mass)*

2c. No mere man. We learn from the first Bible passage that Peter and the other Apostles believed. But Jesus made it plain to them that they must be thankful because they believed in God: "No mere man has revealed this to you, but my heavenly Father" (Matthew 16:17). Faith is a gift from God! (See Chapter 17, no. 2c.)

3. Dark periods. You believe and confess with Peter: "You are the Messiah . . . the Son of the living God!" You are able to do so because God has called you to the Faith.

Jesus' human consciousness of being the Son of God was clouded by the sad circumstances of life. By Faith and Baptism you are an adopted child of God. But you also will go through dark periods in your life of Faith. This seems to be part of our human condition. Faith, like love, is not a value that can be enjoyed without shadows of doubt interfering. Pray as Jesus did!

4. THINKING IT OVER

Describe Jesus' growing awareness of Himself and His mission! Can man come to Faith only by his own efforts? How should you handle doubts in your life of Faith?

5. PRAY MEDITATIVELY

"We worship you, we give you thanks,
  we praise you for your glory.
Lord Jesus Christ, only Son of the Father,
Lord God, Lamb of God,
you take away the sin of the world:
  have mercy on us;
you are seated at the right hand of the Father:
  receive our prayer.
For you alone are the Holy One,
you alone are the Lord,
you alone are the Most High,
  Jesus Christ,
  with the Holy Spirit,
  in the glory of God the Father. Amen."

(Glory to God of the Mass)

6. THINGS TO DO

Read: John 1:1-18 (with the aid of the footnote in your Bible explain why John calls the Son "Word").

When reading your Bible in the family, do you always read also the short introductions to the Books? They are very important for a better understanding of the Bible.

20. Christ a Light of Revelation to the Gentiles

The Apostolate

1a. *There were shepherds in that locality, living in the fields and keeping night watch by turns over their flocks. The angel of the Lord appeared to them as the glory of the Lord shone around them, and they were very much afraid. The angel said to them: "You have nothing to fear! I come to proclaim good news to you—tidings of great joy to be shared by the whole people. This day in David's city a savior has been born to you, the Messiah and Lord. Let this be a sign to you: in a manger you will find an infant wrapped in swaddling clothes." Suddenly, there was with the angel a multitude of the heavenly host, praising God and saying,*

> *"Glory to God in high heaven,*
> *peace on earth to those on whom his favor rests."*

When the angels had returned to heaven, the shepherds said to one another: "Let us go over to Bethlehem and see this event which the Lord has made known to us." They went in haste and found Mary and Joseph, and the baby lying in the manger; once they saw, they understood what had been told them concerning this child (Luke 2: 8-17).

Grotto of the Nativity in Bethlehem

1b. When the eighth day arrived for his circumcision, the name Jesus was given the child, the name the angel had given him before he was conceived (Luke 2:21).

Christmas is on December 25. On this day, after the winter solstice, the pagan Romans celebrated the feast of the Undefeated Sun. This pagan feast was Christianized in honor of the Sun of Justice, i.e., our Lord Jesus Christ.

1c. When the day came to purify them according to the law of Moses, the couple brought him up to Jerusalem so that he could be presented to the Lord (Luke 2:22).

1d. There lived in Jerusalem at the time a certain man named Simeon. He was just and pious, and awaited the consolation of Israel, and the Holy Spirit was upon him. It was revealed to him by the Holy Spirit that he would not experience death until he had seen the Anointed of the Lord. He came to the temple now, inspired by the Spirit, and when the parents brought in the child Jesus to perform for him the customary ritual of the law, he took him in his arms and blessed God in these words:

> *"Now, Master, you can dismiss your servant in peace;*
>   *you have fulfilled your word.*
> *For my eyes have witnessed your saving deed*
>   *displayed for all the peoples to see:*
> *A revealing light to the Gentiles,*
>   *the glory of your people Israel" (Luke 2:25-32).*

The Feast of the Purification of the Blessed Virgin Mary is February 2.

1e. After Jesus' birth in Bethlehem of Judea during the reign of King Herod, astrologers from the east arrived one day in Jerusalem inquiring, "Where is the newborn king of the Jews? We observed his star at its rising and have come to pay him homage." At this news King Herod became greatly disturbed, and with him all Jerusalem. Summoning all of the chief priests and scribes of the people, he inquired of them where the Messiah was to be born. "In Bethlehem of Judea," they informed him. "Here is what the prophet has written:

> *'And you, Bethlehem, land of Judah,*
>   *are by no means least among the princes of Judah,*
>   *since from you shall come a ruler*
>   *who is to shepherd my people Israel.' "*

Herod called the astrologers aside and found out from them the exact time of the star's appearance. Then he sent them to Bethlehem, after having instructed them: "Go and get detailed information about the child. When you have found him, report it to me so that I may go and offer him homage too."

After their audience with the king, they set out. The star which they had observed at its rising went ahead of them until it came to a standstill over the place where the child was. They were overjoyed at seeing the star, and on entering the house, found the child with Mary his mother. They prostrated themselves and did him homage. Then they opened their coffers and presented him with gifts of gold, frankincense, and myrrh.

They received a message in a dream not to return to Herod, so they went back to their own country by another route (Matthew 2:1-12).

The Feast of the Epiphany is January 6.

1f. After they had left, the angel of the Lord suddenly appeared in a dream to Joseph with the command: "Get up, take the child and his mother, and flee to Egypt. Stay there until I tell you otherwise. Herod is searching for the child to destroy him." Joseph got up and took the child and his mother and left that night for Egypt. He stayed there until the death of Herod, to fulfill what the Lord had said through the prophet:

"Out of Egypt I have called my son."

Once Herod realized that he had been deceived by the astrologers, he became furious. He ordered the massacre of all the boys two years old and under in Bethlehem and its environs, making his calculations on the basis of the date he had learned from the astrologers. What was said through Jeremiah the prophet was then fulfilled:
"A cry was heard at Ramah,
  sobbing and loud lamentation:
Rachel bewailing her children;
  no comfort for her, since they are no more" (Matthew 2:13-18).

The Feast of the Holy Innocents is December 28.

2. Catechisms. Bible scholars tell us that the Gospels are not biographies of Jesus, but catechisms or digests of Christian teaching concerning the risen Lord Jesus. (See "How to Read Your Bible" no. 13a, b, c, p. 302). Keeping this in mind, we should read the Infancy Narratives given above.

Both Luke and Matthew made use of traditions as they found them in the early Christian congregations. How did they handle them? They took these narratives and frequently even remolded and refashioned them to bring out the lesson they wanted to teach.

For example, take nos. 1c and d of this Chapter. Experts on the Bible tell us that a horoscope of the expected King-Messiah circulated during the time of Jesus' birth. Astrologers (wise men from the East) were watching the sky for the appearance of the Messiah's star. King Herod, superstitious and upset by these people, killing children of two and under, is extremely probable. Kings could make and break people! People leaving Bethlehem to escape the massacre is equally acceptable. This could be the historical background of this tradition.

The rest is interpretation, elaborated by early Jewish-Christian communities and by the author of Matthew. Its purpose is to show Jesus as the true Israel (God's chosen one!), in whose history the history of the old Israel is recapitulated. Note: Israel was in Egypt! God's dealings with Israel in the past are being reproduced in His dealings with Jesus (the new Israel—the new chosen one)! This is a strange literary device, but the ancient writers loved to work with this kind of figurative speech.

3a. Others may share. Every Christian must exert himself to radiate the light of Christ. Our fellowmen, who walk in the semi-darkness of their religions, will not be barred from salvation if they honestly follow their conscience. God is a loving Father, Who guides every man in His own unsearchable way. But we, who walk in the brightness of God's light, should do whatever we can, that others may share in that light. Faith, with all its benefits for this life and the life hereafter, is a special gift of God. But how can our fellowmen believe, if there is no one to preach? (See Romans 10:14-17.) A good Christian must necessarily also be an apostle.

3b. God calling. Young persons ought to consider the possibility that God may be calling them to become a Priest, a Brother, or a Sister. Do not close your heart to the invitation of the Lord! Pray often: "Come, Holy Spirit, fill the hearts of your faithful and kindle in them the fire of your love."

3c. Unbelievers. All of us must remember the commandment of our Lord: "In the same way, your light must shine before men so that they may see goodness in your acts and give praise to your heavenly Father" (Matthew 5:16). The modern existentialist philosopher, Gabriel Marcel, a convert, writes (in a way, about himself): "An unbeliever can begin by believing in the faith of others, until this openness to belief leads to his own call and his own response."

You became "a child of light" by Faith and Baptism. You must radiate your light by your apostolate. You may do it through your prayers for the heathen, by giving good example to non-Catholics, and even by giving tactful advice; further, by making sacrifices and supporting the papal works of the foreign missions.

3d. The Church a sign. The Church must necessarily be Missionary. However this does not mean that other great Religions such as Hinduism, Buddhism, and Islamism will certainly disappear. Must Christianity then be labeled a failure? Must we despair at the shrinking proportion of Christians on the earth today? We need not, if we simply avoid thinking of ourselves as the exclusive Community of the Saved. The Church, with an authentic Asiatic, African, European, and American membership, will represent a sign of unity and brotherhood. Aside from converting individuals (there will always be people in every culture who demand the ultimate intimacy of knowing Christ), the Church, as a Sign or a Light (1d), may leaven entire societies, formally Hindu, Buddhist or whatever.

4. THINKING IT OVER

What did the Gospel writers want to present to us? How did they handle existing traditions on Jesus? Apply this to nos. 1e and 1f of this chapter and find the lesson! Mention some ways in which you can radiate your light to your fellowmen! What about Christianity and the other great Religions of the world—is there reason to despair? Explain this! What does Luke 13:20-21 teach in this connection?

5. PRAY MEDITATIVELY

O God, you desire that all men should be saved and come to the knowledge of your truth. Send laborers into your harvest, and grant that they may spread the Word with complete confidence, so that your gospel may everywhere be heard and glorified, and all nations know you, the one true God, and him whom you have sent, Jesus Christ, your Son, our Lord. Amen. (*Prayer of the Mass for the Propagation of the Faith.*)

6. THINGS TO DO

Listen, if possible, to the Christmas Concert of Corelli.

21. His Own Did Not Accept Him

1. The chief priests, with the whole Sanhedrin, were busy trying to obtain false testimony against Jesus so that they might put him to death. They discovered none, despite the many false witnesses who took the stand. Finally two came forward who stated: "This man has declared, 'I can destroy God's sanctuary and rebuild it in three days.'" The high priest rose to his feet and addressed him: "Have you no answer to the testimony leveled against you?" But Jesus remained silent. The high priest then said to him: "I order you to tell us under oath before the living God whether you are the Messiah, the Son of God." Jesus answered: "It is you who say it. But I tell you this: Soon you will see the Son of Man seated at the right hand of the Power and coming on the clouds of heaven." At this the high priest tore his robes: "He has blasphemed! What further need have we of witnesses? Remember, you heard the blasphemy. What is your verdict?" They answered, "He deserves death!" Then they began to spit in his face and hit him. Others slapped him (Matthew 26:59-67).

2a.   A political Messiah. St. John writes about the Savior:

"To his own he came, yet his own
did not accept him" (John 1:11).

Christ Himself said: "O Jerusalem, Jerusalem [people of Israel], murderess of prophets and stoner of those who were sent to you! How often have I yearned to gather your children, as a mother bird gathers her young under her wings, but you refused me" (Matthew 23:37).

The people of Israel were offered the gift of Faith. They saw the signs that Jesus worked to help their lack of Faith. Nevertheless, many rejected the invitation of God. They would accept only a "political" Messiah, one who would expel the Romans from their country and establish the former kingdom of David. They so emphasized temporal values that they could not appreciate the spiritual values brought by Christ. A Messiah Who was going to establish an everlasting universal kingdom (God's reign on earth) was not acceptable.

Painting by Gerard van Honthorst (1590-1656). Netherlands.
"His own did not accept him" *(John 1:11)*

2b. More enormous in us. Yet considering the fact that "his own did not accept him" does not entitle anybody to condemn the Jewish people, especially the Jews living today, for the crucifixion of Jesus. Read attentively Romans 9:1-5 and 11:29-32.

"The Church, therefore, cannot forget that she received the revelation of the Old Testament through the people with whom God in His inexpressible mercy deigned to establish the Ancient Covenant. . . . True, authorities of the Jews and those who followed their lead pressed for the death of Christ (cf. Jn 19:6); still, what happened in His Passion cannot be blamed upon all the Jews then living, without distinction, nor upon the Jews of today" (Vatican II: *Declaration on the Relationship of the Church to Non-Christian Religions,* no. 4).

Moreover, "the guilt for Christ's death seems more enormous in us than in the Jews, since according to the testimony of the Apostle: 'If they had known it, they would never have crucified the Lord of glory' (1 Corinthians 2:8); while we, on the contrary, professing to know Him, yet denying Him by our actions, seem in some sort to lay violent hands on Him" (*Catechism of the Council of Trent, 1556*).

3. A precious pearl. You receive the full gift of Faith on the day of your Baptism. But just as love can be lost (see Chapter 17 for the relationship of Faith and love), so also can you lose your Faith in God.

You might endanger your Faith by lack of attention during religious instruction (the Sunday sermon), by disregarding prayer, by failure to do spiritual reading, such as reading your Bible, by only seldom receiving the Sacraments of Penance and Holy Communion, and by overemphasis on temporal prosperity (having an extra job, even on Sunday, leaving no time for the worship of God).

You must be careful to protect your Faith as a precious pearl. Just as love must be fostered by the means indicated by nature, so must you foster your Faith in God. Read books about your religion. Suscribe to at least one Catholic newspaper or magazine.

4. THINKING IT OVER

What reasons brought the authorities of the Jews to their final rejection of Christ? Why in a way are we Christians more to be blamed for Jesus' death than are the Jews? What may endanger your Faith?

5. PRAY MEDITATIVELY

We have come to a new life by your gift of redemption, O Lord. May the true faith always advance through this aid to our eternal salvation. Amen (*Prayer after Communion of the Votive Mass for the Propagation of the Faith*).

6. THINGS TO DO

Read: John 7:1-14. For the reaction of the Jews on the raising of Lazarus, read: John 11:45-56; 12; 18.

22. The Suffering Servant of the Lord

1a. He was spurned and avoided by men,
   a man of suffering, accustomed to infirmity,
One of those from whom men hide their faces,
   spurned, and we held him in no esteem.
Yet it was our infirmities that he bore,
   our sufferings that he endured,
While we thought of him as stricken,
   as one smitten by God and afflicted.
But he was pierced for our offenses,
   crushed for our sins,
Upon him was the chastisement that makes us whole,
   by his stripes we were healed.
We had all gone astray like sheep,
   each following his own way;
But the Lord laid upon him
   the guilt of us all.
Though he was harshly treated, he submitted
   and opened not his mouth;
Like a lamb led to the slaughter
   or a sheep before the shearers,
   he was silent and opened not his mouth.
Oppressed and condemned, he was taken away,
   and who would have thought any more of his destiny?
When he was cut off from the land of the living,
   and smitten for the sin of his people,
A grave was assigned him among the wicked
   and a burial place with evildoers,
Though he had done no wrong
   nor spoken any falsehood (Isaiah 53:3-9).

1b Judas took the cohort as well as guards supplied by the chief priests and the Pharisees, and came there with lanterns, torches and weapons. Jesus, aware of all that would happen to him, stepped forward and said to them, "Who is it you want?" "Jesus the Nazorean," they replied, "I am he," he answered. (Now Judas, the one who was to hand him over, was there with them.) As Jesus said to them, "I am he," they retreated slightly and fell to the ground. Jesus put the question to them again, "Who is it you want?" "Jesus the Nazorean," they repeated. "I have told you, I am he," Jesus said. "If I am the one you want, let these men go" (John 18:3-8).

Then the soldiers of the cohort, their tribune, and the Jewish guards arrested Jesus and bound him (John 18:12).

> When they brought Jesus to the site of Golgotha (which means "Skull Place"), they tried to give him wine drugged with myrrh, but he would not take it. Then they crucified him and divided up his garments by rolling dice for them to see what each should take. It was about nine in the morning when they crucified him. The inscription proclaiming his offense read, "The King of the Jews."
>
> With him they crucified two insurgents, one at his right and one at his left (Mark 15:22-27).
>
> One of the criminals hanging in crucifixion blasphemed him: "Aren't you the Messiah? Then save yourself and us." But the other one rebuked him: "Have you no fear of God, seeing you are under the same sentence? We deserve it, after all. We are only paying the price for what we've done, but this man has done nothing wrong." He then said, "Jesus, remember me when you enter upon your reign." And Jesus replied, "I assure you: this day you will be with me in paradise" (Luke 23:39-43).

2a. Meaningful tragedy. The cruel Death of Jesus of Nazareth was a tragedy, but actually not that exceptional. Confucius died an apparent failure. Socrates, the prophets of the Old Testament, many great men of our own time: Gandhi, John F. Kennedy, Martin Luther King—all finished the same way. What is exceptional in Jesus' cruel Death is its meaning.

In order to understand the tragedy of Calvary, the way Jesus Himself and the early theologians of the Church interpreted it, we must go back to the Hebrew Bible. Both Jesus and the authors of the New Testament were Jews, who lived and thought in the framework of Jewish tradition. Jesus' life and assignment was understood as the fulfillment of the Old Testament aspirations. Hence, it was from that background that this mysterious life and tragic Death was interpreted.

2b. The Servant of the Lord. Consider the first Bible passage of this chapter, which is part of the fourth oracle of the Servant of the Lord in the Book of Isaiah. Who is this Servant of the Lord? Often Isaiah speaks of Israel as a servant of the Lord, chosen to be God's witness before the nations. But in this fourth oracle, Isaiah seems to distinguish him from Israel. This mysterious Servant suffers vicariously for the sins of his fellowmen.

2c. Vicarious suffering. The concept of vicarious suffering, possible because of God's positive ordinance, was well-known in

Jewish tradition. Jesus has explained the meaning of his cruel Death in terms of this type of expiation: "This is my body to be given for you" (Luke 22:19). Luke has done the same by relating Jesus' Suffering and Death to the expiatory suffering of Isaiah's Servant of the Lord. Read Acts 8:26-35, especially verses 32 to 35, and the Bible passages in no. 1b, above.

3. Meditating on the suffering. Christians usually meditate on the Suffering and Death of our Lord by making the Stations of the Cross. If you follow each scene (picture at each Station) on the Way of the Cross you do not necessarily have to use a prayerbook. Look at the picture and meditate on Jesus' pain and Death. This prayer is an acceptable thanksgiving after Confession, because it is through Jesus' vicarious Suffering and Death that you obtain forgiveness of sin.

Palm Sunday procession toward Jerusalem.

You may also keep in mind the Passion of our Lord by praying the Rosary, meditating on the five sorrowful mysteries. Quite a few Catholics have given up the family Rosary and replaced it with a family Bible reading. Many others still love to say the Rosary. Let us all follow our own conscience and enjoy our freedom!

The cross on the church, as well as a crucifix on the wall of your living room or bedroom, or a crucifix worn on your person—all remind you of Jesus' cruel Death, which took away the sin of the world.

Holy Thursday and Good Friday are the special remembrance days of the Passion of Jesus Christ.

4. THINKING IT OVER

What is conventional and what is exceptional in Jesus' Death? Who is the Servant of the Lord in the oracle of Isaiah? What is vicarious suffering? How did Jesus use this theme to explain His Death and how did Luke do the same? How do Christians meditate on the Suffering of the Lord?

5. READ ATTENTIVELY

"He [God] rescued us from the power of darkness and brought us into the kingdom of his beloved Son. Through him we have redemption, the forgiveness of our sins" (Colossians 1:13-14.)

6. THINGS TO DO

Listen, if possible, to highlights of *Matthew's Passion* by Bach or, if it is your taste, *Jesus Christ Superstar*. Read the Servant-of-the-Lord oracles in Isaiah: 42:1-4; 49:1-7; 50:4-11; 52:13—53:12; and one of the Passion accounts in the Gospels. Relate your understanding to your existence or life-situation! (See "How to Read the Bible," no. 17 on p. 307.)

23. A Sin Offering

1a. "Then he shall slaughter the people's sin-offering goat, and bringing its blood inside the veil, he shall do with it as he did with the bullock's blood, sprinkling it on the propitiatory and before it. Thus he shall make atonement for the sanctuary because of all the sinful defilements and faults of the Israelites. He shall do the same for the meeting tent, which is set up among them in the midst of their uncleanness" (Leviticus 16:15-16).

"When he has completed the atonement rite for the sanctuary, the meeting tent and the altar, Aaron shall bring forward the live goat. Laying both hands on its head, he shall confess over it all the sinful faults and transgressions of the Israelites, and so put them on the goat's head. He shall then have it led into the desert by an attendant. Since the goat is to carry off their iniquities to an isolated region, it must be sent away into the desert" (Leviticus 16:20-22).

1b. It is impossible for the blood of bulls and goats to take sins away. Wherefore, on coming into the world, Jesus said:
  "Sacrifice and offering you did not desire,
   but a body you have prepared for me;

Ch. 23   A Sin Offering

> *Holocausts and sin offerings you took no delight in.*
> *Then I said, 'As is written of me in the book,*
>   *I have come to do your will, O God.'*"

First he says,

> *"Sacrifices and offerings, holocausts and sin offerings,*
>   *you neither desired nor delighted in."*

(These are offered according to the prescriptions of the law.) Then he says,

> *"I have come to do your will."*

In other words, he takes away the first covenant to establish the second.

By this "will," we have been sanctified through the offering of the body of Jesus Christ once for all (Hebrews 10:4-10).

After that, Jesus realizing that everything was now finished, said to fulfill the Scripture, "I am thirsty." There was a jar there, full of common wine. They stuck a sponge soaked in this wine on some hyssop and raised it to his lips. When Jesus took the wine, he said, "Now it is finished." Then he bowed his head, and delivered over his spirit (John 19:28-30).

2a. Reconciled through Christ. We have mentioned that seemingly Jesus' cruel Death was very similar to that of a civil rights' worker. Because of God's ordinance however, expiation for the sins of the world was granted through Christ's "obedience to death." "All this has been done by God, who has reconciled us to himself through Christ" (2 Corinthians 5:18). Jesus Himself and also Luke have explained the tragedy of Calvary as a vicarious expiation (see Chapter 22).

The entrance of the Holy Sepulchre.

"Sanctified through the offering of the body of Jesus Christ once for all" (Hebrews 10:10).

2b. Sin offering. With reference to Isaiah's Servant-of-the Lord oracle, we have mentioned that according to Jewish thought one person could pray, suffer, and make up for others. Symbolically, this could be done by sin offerings (sacrifices for sin) and the scape-goat ritual (see no. 1a).

Inspired by God, the early theologians of the Church used this theme to interpret Jesus' Death as a sin offering. The author of the Letter to the Hebrews describes details of Jewish sacrificial worship and uses them to explain the meaning of Jesus' cruel Death. Figuratively, he puts words into the mouth of Jesus (see no. 1b) which were very clear to Christians from a Jewish background, since they were familiar with those ritual sacrifices and sin offerings.

Christians of our time can also appreciate this approach if they take the time to read about Jewish sacrificial worship in the Hebrew Bible (Old Testament). (See no. 6 of this chapter!)

Both Jesus Himself and Luke (Chapter 22) and the author of the Letter to the Hebrews explain the tragic Death of Calvary as a vicarious expiation. Jesus and Luke did so by referring to the Suffering Servant of the Lord in Isaiah. The author of Hebrews does the same by portraying Jesus' Death as an antitype of the ritual sacrifices of the Old Law: Jesus both High Priest and "Lamb of God who takes away the sin of the world."

2c. Symbolic self-surrender. The custom of offering sacrifices to God is very old. Mankind knows that it has been created by a Supreme Being. A sacrifice is a symbolic self-surrender to that Supreme Being in order to acknowledge dependence on Him. Man gives some of his possessions (his cattle, his crops) to symbolize himself. So the chosen people of the Old Covenant offered sacrifices to God according to the regulations given by Moses. Pagans still offer chickens, pigs, cows, rice, and corn to their gods.

2d. Traditional sacrifices superfluous. When the Church became ever more conscious of Jesus' Death as a sacrifice of which our Lord was both the offering priest and the offered victim, in other words, as an offering definitely "taking away" or "making up for" the sins of the world, traditional sacrifices (lambs, bulls, etc.) were considered superfluous.

However, we Catholics speak of the Sacrifice of the Mass. Later, we will discuss the point that the Mass is a sacrifice related to the Sacrifice of the Cross. It is a symbolical representation (calling forth) of Jesus' sacrifice of Calvary in the signs of bread and wine. (See Chapters 47-49.)

3. Your self surrender. Christ's sacred Body and Blood are a symbol also of your self-surrender to God. That is why you must partake in the ceremonies of the Mass and unite yourself with the sacrifice. Thus you see that the sacrifice on the altar of your parish church is a real symbol of your self-surrender to your Creator!

4. THINKING IT OVER

How did Jesus Himself and also Luke explain the expiatory character of Jesus' Death on the Cross? What theme did the author of Hebrews use to explain the Death of Jesus as a vicarious expiation of the sins of the world? (See nos. 1a and 1b.) What are sacrifices supposed to be symbols of? After Jesus' Death, why did the Church consider the traditional sacrifices superfluous? How is the Sacrifice of the Mass related to the Sacrifice of the Cross? What does this mean whenever you attend Mass?

5. PRAY MEDITATIVELY

O God, you ordained your only-begotten Son the eternal High Priest for the glory of your divine majesty and the salvation of man. Grant that those whom he has chosen as ministers and dispensers of his mysteries may be faithful in fulfilling their appointed duties.

6. THINGS TO DO

Read leviticus 16 and see how the author of Hebrews 5: 1-10; 7; 8; 9; 10:1-18 uses similar concepts to explain what Jesus' Death on the Cross means to all of us. Read also 1 Peter 2:4-8; 3:18-22 and Philippians 2:6-11.

24. The New Covenant in His Blood

1a. *This is why he is mediator of a new covenant: since his death has taken place for deliverance from transgressions committed under the first covenant, those who are called may receive the promised eternal inheritance. Where there is a testament, it is necessary that the death of the testator be confirmed. For a testament comes into force only in the case of death; it has no force while the testator is alive. Hence, not even the first covenant was inaugurated without blood. When Moses had read all the commandments of the law of the people, he took the blood of goats and calves, together with water and crimson wool and hyssop, and sprinkled the book and all the people, saying, "This is the blood of the covenant which God has enjoined upon you." He also sprinkled the tabernacle and all the vessels of worship with blood. According to the law almost everything is purified by blood, and without the shedding of blood there is no forgiveness.*

It was necessary that the copies of the heavenly models be purified in this way, but the heavenly realities themselves called for better sacrifices. For Christ did not enter into a sanctuary made by hands, a mere copy of the true one; he entered heaven itself that he might appear before God now on our behalf. Not that he might offer himself there again and again, as the high priest enters year after year into the sanctuary with blood that is not his own; if that were so, he would have had to suffer death over and over from the creation of the world. But now he has appeared at the end of the ages to take away sins once for all by his sacrifice. Just as it is appointed that men die once, and after death be judged, so Christ was offered up once to take away the sins of many; he will appear a second time not to take away sin but to bring salvation to those who eagerly await him (Hebrews 9:15-28).

1b. *You who want to be subject to the law, tell me: do you know what the law has to say? There it is written that Abraham had two sons, one by the slave girl, the other by his freeborn wife. The son of the slave girl had been begotten in the course of nature, but the son of the free woman was the fruit of the promise. All this is an allegory: the two women stand for the two covenants. One is from Mount Sinai, and brought forth children to slavery: this is Hagar. The mountain Sinai [Hagar] is in Arabia and corresponds to the Jerusalem of our time, which is likewise in slavery with her children. But the Jerusalem on high is freeborn, and it is she who is our mother. That is why Scripture says:*

> *"Rejoice, you barren one who bear no children;*
> *break into song, you stranger to the pains of childbirth!*
> *For many are the children of the wife deserted—*
> *far more than of her who has a husband!"*

Ch. 24   **The New Covenant in His Blood**   **95**

You, my brothers, are children of the promise, as Isaac was. But just as in those days the son born in nature's course persecuted the one whose birth was in the realm of spirit, so do we find it now. What does Scripture say on the point? "Cast out slave girl and son together; for the slave girl's son shall never be an heir on equal terms with the son" of the one born free.

Therefore, my brothers, we are not children of a slave girl but of a mother who is free (Galatians 4:21-31).

2a. We were hoping. Only weakly can we imagine the tremendous impact of our Lord's Death on those who had faith in Him. Think of those who had faith in Dr. Martin Luther King or had campaigned for Senator Robert Kennedy! "We were hoping that he was the one to be next president of the USA." And then the utter dismay in the hotel lobby in Los Angeles when he was assassinated.

This same disappointment resounds in the statement of the disciples of Emmaus on their way back home: "We were hoping that he was the one to set Israel free" (Luke 24:21). And then the fact that Jesus was seen by witnesses! He is alive!

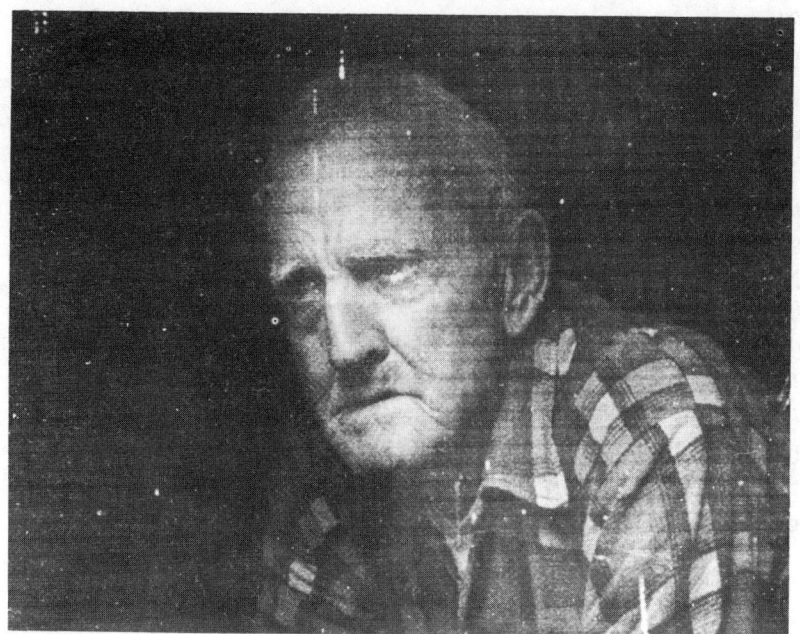

"We were hoping . . ." (cf. Luke 24:21).

2b. Positive results. Small wonder, that early theologians of the Church searched the Scriptures to find themes to clarify the meaning of Jesus' seemingly senseless Death. We have mentioned the theme of the suffering Servant of the Lord (Chapter 22) and the theme of ritual sin offerings in Jewish worship (Chapter 23). Both themes were used to clarify that our Lord's Death was an expiation for the sins of the world.

But atonement and reconciliation are mainly negative concepts: Sins have been forgiven. Inspired by God, the early theologians of the Church also saw a beautiful positive result in Jesus' Death. To describe this result they once again used themes of the Hebrew Bible, the Old Testament. We will discuss here the theme of the Covenant, which became "a new covenant" in the early Church.

2c. His legacy. In Chapter 7, we studied the very fecund theme of Covenant. Read this chapter again! During the last centuries before Christ, the concept "Covenant" was very much seen as a gift and a unilateral action on the part of God, though it still required a personal response of man who lives under this God-given partnership. Perhaps this was the reason that the word "diateke" (will-testament or testamentary disposition) was chosen to translate "berit" (covenant) from Hebrew into Greek.

In New Testament literature, the Covenant became Jesus' testamentary disposition, His legacy. Just as Moses was the mediator of the Old Covenant, so Jesus became the mediator of the New Covenant (Hebrews 9:15). This new Covenant (partnership) is effected by the shedding of Jesus' blood on the Cross (blood, the substance of life; see Chapter 7 and Mark 14:24). Paul states that the new Covenant was effected in Jesus' blood (i.e., in the power of His blood!). (See 1 Corinthians 11:25.) This blood-symbolism is again a way of explaining the meaning of Jesus' cruel Death, namely, as meritorious, well deserving of God's gracious mercy, which has chosen us as His partners.

2d. Understanding the symbolism. The Bible passage in 1a is not easy. But after you have read Chapter 7, you should be able to understand its symbolism, taken from Jewish worship.

Notice in verse 15: The Moses-Jesus relation.

In verse 17: A testament (will): The covenant as testamentary disposition or legacy.

In verses 23 and 24: The sacrifices of Jewish worship superseded by Jesus' Death, which the author sees as a sacrifice, in which Jesus is both the offering priest and the offered lamb.

The second Bible reading (1b) also requires some effort to be understood.

Verses 21 and 22: Read this tradition of the Abraham cycle: Genesis 16:15 and 21:1-21. Abraham's behavior was not very Christian. But he was not a Christian. Paul takes this tradition as an allegory to explain what he has to say about the two Covenants. Pay attention to the point made in verse 31.

3. Son and partner. We could print here no. 3 of Chapter 7. Read it again! Only, you should relate all of it to the Death of our Lord, seen as a sacrifice, that was meritorious and well deserving of God's mercy, giving you the status of "son" and "partner." These are reasons to be grateful!

4. THINKING IT OVER

How would you clarify the impact Jesus' Death had on His friends, followers, and campaigners for his Messiahship? Mention themes chosen by Biblical writers to explain the seemingly senseless Death of our Lord. Describe the development of the concept "Covenant" in the Bible as found in Chapter 7. What meaning did the concept "Covenant" have around Jesus' time? Explain the notions "mediator" and "blood" as related to "Covenant." Which allegory does Paul use to explain the Old and New Covenants? What does all of this mean to you as a Christian?

5. PRAY MEDITATIVELY

Father, all-powerful and ever-living God, we do well always and everywhere to give you thanks. You decreed that man should be saved through the wood of the cross. The tree of man's defeat became his tree of victory; where life was lost, there life has been restored through Christ our Lord *(Preface of the Holy Cross).*

25. The Resurrection of Our Lord

We Shall Arise with Him

To be a Christian does not consist primarily in admiring Jesus as a great genius, nor even in following Him in His capacity as a leader. Basically, it means to adhere to the belief in His Resurrection and to what it implies: Jesus is indeed the Messiah Who has been promised by the Prophets of the Old Testament and Who by His exaltation in glory is established as supreme Lord. His present Reign (Kingdom) tends toward a complete accomplishment, which will be strikingly manifested at His Second Coming.

A dramatic way of expression. The Apostles' Creed says Jesus died, was buried and descended into hell. (The meaning of "hell" here is limbo, or waiting-place. There Jesus announced the Redemption to the just who were waiting.) This is a dramatic way of expressing our Faith that Jesus' redemption was for all men, past, present, and future! In the "hereafter" there is neither time nor space; hence, we cannot speak of "when" and "where"!

> **1a.** *I handed on to you first of all what I myself received, that Christ died for our sins in accordance with the Scriptures; that he was buried and, in accordance with the Scriptures, rose on the third day; that he was seen by Cephas, then by the Twelve. . . . This is what we preach and this is what you believed (1 Corinthians 15:3-5.11).*

Paul writes this about 56 or 57 A.D. He makes a reference to the Gospel (Good News) he preached at Corinth in 51. Moreover, Paul declares that he himself "received" this Gospel, as witnessed by the Apostles and Palestinian disciples. This summary of Paul's preaching, which was drafted previous to the Gospel versions, testifies to the central place which the proclamation of the Death, Resurrection and Ascension of our Lord occupied in the preaching of the early Church.

1b. With respect to the Gospel traditions on the Resurrection of our Lord, Bible scholars distinguish three groups:

(1) Primary accounts. The accounts of Christ's apparitions to the Apostolic group: apparitions of an "official" character, such as the impressive summary found in Matthew's Gospel.

> The eleven disciples made their way to Galilee, to the mountain to which Jesus had summoned them. At the sight of him, those who had entertained doubts fell down in homage. Jesus came forward and addressed them in these words:
> > "Full authority has been given to me
> > both in heaven and on earth;
> > go, therefore, and make disciples of all the nations.
> > Baptize them in the name
> > 'of the Father,
> > and of the Son,
> > and of the Holy Spirit.'
> > Teach them to carry out everything I have commanded you.
> > And know that I am with you always, until the end of the world!"
> > (Matthew 20:16-20).

Similar to this is the account found in John 20:19-23.

> On the evening of that first day of the week, even though the disciples had locked the doors of the place where they were for fear of the Jews, Jesus came and stood before them. "Peace be with you," he said. When he had said this, he showed them his hands and his side. At the sight of the Lord the disciples rejoiced. "Peace be with you," he said again.
> > "As the Father has sent me,
> > so I send you."
>
> Then he breathed on them and said:
> > "Receive the Holy Spirit.
> > If you forgive men's sins,
> > they are forgiven them;
> > if you hold them bound,
> > they are held bound" (John 20:19-23).

You might also read Mark 16:14-18 and Luke 24:36-49 in your Bible.

These "official" accounts can be called "primary," because of their close correspondence with the fundamental proclamation of the early Church's preaching.

(2) Apparition to individuals. A second group of accounts are the apparitions to individuals. See Luke 24:13-35: the disciples of Emmaus; John 20:14-18: the apparition to Mary Magdalene; Matthew 28:8-10: the apparition to the Holy Women.

(3) The Empty Tomb. Accounts about the Empty Tomb and the Legend of the Removal of Jesus' Body (Matthew 28:1-8 and 11-15).

2. Teaching Death and Resurrection. The traditions found in numbers (2) and (3) are more elaborated than the very sober traditions found in number (1). The Gospel versions comprise a whole body of accounts which affirm the Resurrection of Christ and report its manifestations. These reports are dependent on traditions which, before being collected by the Evangelists, were alive in the early Christian communities.

The Evangelists merely exercised a choice. They were not concerned to discover every historical detail. They related these traditions as they were living in the local congregations and refashioned them for their purpose: teaching the Death and Resurrection of our Lord to which the Apostles bore witness.

3a. You too will arise. St. Paul says: "If we believe that Jesus died and rose [as we do], God will bring forth with him from the dead those also who have fallen asleep believing in him" (1 Thessalonians 4:14). You too will arise and live glorified with Christ. We know and believe Jesus' own words to Martha in Bethany:

> "I am the resurrection and the life:
> whoever believes in me,
> though he should die, will come to life;
> and whoever is alive and believes in me
> will never die" (John 11:25).

3b. Two mysteries. On Easter, Christians celebrate two mysteries: Christ's Resurrection from the tomb and our resurrection with Him from the tomb of sin and entry into God's light.

These two mysteries are celebrated at the Easter Vigil on Holy Saturday as follows: The church is dark. The priest blesses the Easter (Paschal) candle. The lighted candle is a symbol of the risen Christ.

The priest enters the dark church and intones: "The Light of Christ." The faithful answer: "Thanks be to God." The people in the church light their candles from the Easter candle, symbolizing that they share in the light of Christ. The previously dark church is then flooded with the light of candles and the church lights. With Christ we arise from the darkness of sin and become "children of light."

With this symbolism Christians yearly celebrate the mystery of their Baptism, i.e., their mysterious resurrection with Christ. That is why baptismal water is blessed during the Easter Vigil, why catechumens (those preparing to become Christians) are baptized, and the faithful renew their baptismal vows.

The Easter candle at the side of the main altar will be lighted every Sunday Mass until after the reading of the Gospel on Ascension Day.

(Discuss here and read at home the Easter Vigil ceremonies in your Missal for Holy Saturday. The blessing of baptismal water may be discussed in Chapter 40).

3c. Old and new Passover. The chosen people of the Old Covenant yearly celebrated the Passover as a remembrance of their liberation from bondage in Egypt. They prayed, read the Bible, and ate the Passover lamb with unleavened bread.

The chosen people of the New Covenant celebrate Easter as a remembrance of their liberation from the bondage of evil. **Our Passover (Paschal, Easter) Lamb is Christ, Who died and arose from the tomb. We eat the Passover Lamb when we receive Holy Communion.**

(Read Easter Mass, especially the Preface to the Eucharistic Prayer, and the Communion Antiphon.)

3d. The greatest sign. Finally, the Resurrection of our Lord is the greatest sign of Jesus to strengthen our "littleness of faith." (For the meaning of "miracles," see Chapter 17.) "To them [the Apostles] also He showed Himself alive after His passion by many proofs, during forty days appearing to them and speaking of the kingdom of God" (Acts 1:3).

4. THINKING IT OVER

What does St. Paul say about the risen Christ? What two mysteries do Christians celebrate at Easter? Explain the symbolism of the Easter Vigil and apply it to yourself. Compare the above explanation about the Christian Easter Lamb with that given in Chapter 6 of this book.

5. PRAY MEDITATIVELY

The *Regina Coeli* (see Treasury of Prayers, p. 291).

6. THINGS TO DO

Read: Peter's discourse on Pentecost: Acts 2:14-41, and St. Paul: 1 Corinthians 15.

Listen, if possible, to a recording of the last part of *The Messiah* of Handel.

26. The Ascension of Jesus Christ

1. In my first account, Theophilus, I dealt with all that Jesus did and taught until the day he was taken up to heaven, having first instructed the apostles he had chosen through the Holy Spirit. In the time after his suffering he showed them in many convincing ways that he was alive, appearing to them over the course of forty days and speaking to them about the reign of God (Acts 1:1-3).

On one occasion when he met with them, he told them not to leave Jerusalem: "Wait, rather, for the fulfillment of my Father's promise, of which you have heard me speak. John baptized with water, but within a few days you will be baptized with the Holy Spirit" (Acts 1:4-5).

No sooner had he said this than he was lifted up before their eyes in a cloud which took him from their sight.

They were still gazing up into the heavens when two men dressed in white stood beside them. "Men of Galilee," they said, "why do you stand here looking up at the skies? This Jesus who has been taken from you will return, just as you saw him go up into the heavens" (Acts 1:9-11).

2a. Actually one event. To obtain proper understanding of the traditions concerning the Resurrection and Ascension of our Lord, we should remember that the Resurrection of Jesus, His glorious Ascension, and the Communication of His Spirit is actually *one* event. Immediately after His Resurrection, Jesus is at the right hand of the Father (i.e., shares power with Him) and starts communicating the Spirit. St. Luke (author of the Acts) explains this mystery by discussing several aspects of it separately (Resurrection-Ascension-Communication of the Spirit), using a literary form and the sacred numbers of 3, 40, and 9. And that is the way we celebrate this mystery very meaningfully at Easter, Ascension Day, and Pentecost: three aspects of one Mystery! [37]

2b. No "when" and "where." The Bible passages of this lesson describe the last of Jesus' apparitions to His disciples as a group. "Ascending" into heaven is also symbolical and adapted to the ancient outlook on the universe, as mentioned in Chapter 10. As we stated in Chapter 25, in the "hereafter" there is neither time nor space; hence we cannot speak of "when" and "where."

2c. Hope for all. Jesus said these words to the Apostles: "I am indeed going to prepare a place for you, and then I shall come back to take you with me, that where I am you also may be" (John 14:3). This is a truth filled with hope for all of us.

The author of the First Letter of John states:
> "I am writting this to keep you from sin.
> But if anyone should sin,
> we have, in the presence of the Father,
> Jesus Christ, an intercessor who is just.
> He is an offering for our sins,
> and not for our sins only,
> but for those of the whole world."
> (1 John 2:1-2)

After Jesus "ascended into heaven," His task as Redeemer was not yet finished. Jesus Christ is constantly Head of His people as their Supreme Teacher, King and eternal High Priest, constantly interceding for us.

3a. Teaching authority. Jesus rules and teaches God's people (the Church) through the successors of the Apostles: the bishops with their head, the Holy Father (the Pope), and further on through the priests and all who are authorized to teach. For a more extensive discussion on the teaching authority of the Church, see Chapters 27, 34, 35. Christians honor Christ the King in the procession of Palm Sunday and on the Feast of Christ the King, on the last Sunday of the liturgical year.

3b. He prays for us. Christ is our High Priest "in heaven." He defends us sinners. He prays for us and offers His sacred Body and Blood to His Father through the hands of His priests throughout the world. That is why Christians often end their official prayers to God by saying: "Through Jesus Christ, your Son, our Lord, who lives and reigns with you in the unity of the Holy Spirit, God, forever and ever. Amen."

4. THINKING IT OVER

What literary form do the Gospels use to describe the risen Lord? What is Jesus doing for you "in heaven"? On which days do Christians especially honor Christ the King? What does the author of the Letter to the Hebrews say about a priest's task? (See Chapter 8.) Why do Christians often end their prayers with "through Jesus Christ . . ."?

5. THINGS TO DO

Read: the ceremonies that precede the Mass of Palm Sunday and the Mass of Ascension Day, and Hebrews 4:14-16.

THE HOLY SPIRIT

27. Descent of God's Spirit

1. On one occasion when he met with them, he told them not to leave Jerusalem: "Wait, rather, for the fulfillment of my Father's promise, of which you have heard me speak. John baptized with water, but within a few days you will be baptized with the Holy Spirit" (Acts 1:4-5).

When the day of Pentecost came it found them gathered in one place. Suddenly from up in the sky there came a noise like a strong, driving wind which was heard all through the house where they were seated. Tongues as of fire appeared, which parted and came to rest on each of them. All were filled with the Holy Spirit. They began to express themselves in foreign tongues and make bold proclamation as the Spirit prompted them.

Staying in Jerusalem at the time were devout Jews of every nation under heaven. These heard the sound, and assembled in a large crowd. They were much confused because each one heard these men speaking his own language. The whole occurrence astonished them. They asked in utter amazement, "Are not all of these men who are speaking Galileans? How is it that each of us hears them in his native tongue? We are Parthians, Medes, and Elamites. We live in Mesopotamia, Judea and Cappadocia, Pontus, the province of Asia, Phrygia and Pamphylia, Egypt, and the regions of Libya around Cyrene. There are even visitors from Rome—all Jews, or those who have come over to Judaism; Cretans and Arabs too. Yet each of us hears them speaking in his own tongue about the marvels God has accomplished" (Acts 2:1-11).

2a. Symbolic meaning. In Chapter 26 we have discussed how Luke describes three aspects of one event. Many outpourings and communications of the Spirit are mentioned in the Bible. One is mentioned at Christ's first apparition to His disciples (John 20:21-22). The one in Acts 2:1-11 (printed above) has been described extensively and very dramatically.

The violent but invisible wind blowing symbolizes the strength of the Holy Spirit. The Apostles did indeed receive a special strength! Consider the fact that these simple fishermen extended the Church of Christ all over the Roman Empire, and far beyond its boundaries.

Also, "fire" and "tongues" have their symbolic meaning. Suddenly the Apostles dared to speak and to proclaim the good tidings of our Lord. The fire of the Holy Spirit enlightened their hearts and gave them courage and strength to preach Jesus Christ to all nations.

2b. Extraordinary phenomena. The Spirit has been given to God's people. When we read in the above Bible passage as well as elsewhere in the Bible (see 1 Corinthians 12:1-11 and 1 Corinthians 14) about extraordinary gifts, such as new languages, prophecies and ecstasies, accompanying the outpouring of the Spirit, we should not forget that every gift of God receives its shape from the environment in which it is poured out. Religious customs, character, and culture have something to do with the way in which the Spirit manifests Himself.

Extraordinary phenomena no longer occur too often in our day. This is because of the difference in our age, culture and way of living our religion. It may also be that something different was needed for establishing the Church than for building her up.

2c. Gifts of the Spirit to all. However, the Church does receive extraordinary or charismatic gifts of the Spirit even in our time. Recall, for example, the remarkable renewal movement in the Church animated and promoted by the charismatic Pope John XXIII and his Church Council!

The gifts of the Spirit are given to all. Think of St. Francis of Assisi, a deacon, and St. Catherine of Siena, a nun, who advised Popes concerning what should be done. Nowadays, too, ordinary lay people, priests and nuns sometimes offer progressive and outstanding suggestions and try to advise pastors and bishops as to what should be done in the Church. Pastors and bishops should listen attentively wherever the Spirit is breathing!

2d. Properly and in order. It is a notable fact that the first to receive the Spirit at Easter (John 20:21-22) and Pentecost (see no. 1) were the rulers of the Church. Paul noted this. After describing the gifts of the Spirit, he states: "If anyone thinks he is a prophet or a man of the Spirit, he should know that what I have written you is the Lord's commandment. Set your hearts on prophecy, my brothers, and do not forbid those who speak in tongues, but make sure that everything is done properly and in order" (1 Corinthians 14:37.39.40).

Not as in a democracy. Indeed, bishops receive their mission and authority in the name of God's people (when we speak of "God's people," we do not of course exclude bishops and priests), and as such your bishop stands before God as any other receiving faithful. On the other hand, authority is not given to the bishops as in a democracy. Christ gave authority to God's people by putting it into hands of His Apostles and their successors, the bishops: "I send you . . ." [39]

2f. Brotherly characteristics. Another question is how episcopal authority should be exercised. In countries like Africa and Southeast Asia, where civil authority is still exercised paternalistically, bishops should perhaps adapt to what people there are used to. In our democratic society, many would like episcopal authority to do away with paternalistic overtones and adopt more brotherly characteristics. Christians are adult brothers in Christ and able to accept co-responsibility with their bishops and pastors. Vatican II encourages the idea of collegiality (Pope and bishops together making decisions!). Moreover, it wants diocesan councils to be erected, so that all Christians can take part in the decision-making process.

3a. Quitting no solution. The Church is a congregation of human beings which is holy but always in need of being purified (Vatican II: *Dogmatic Constitution on the Church*). Reform will be necessary as long as the Church, both members and rulers, consists of human beings. If you have sorrows, do not become embittered or discouraged, but persevere patiently. Quitting the Church, as some do, is no solution. The Reformers of the 16th Century did this. The result was a painfully divided and torn-up Christianity, consisting of groups that in turn also need reforms because they too consist of human beings!

3b. "Creative fidelity." Our bishops are human beings. Some are conservative, some are progressive, others are just careful. Nevertheless, with their full share in Christ's office they have received the Spirit more intensively than any other members of the Church. Hence, thinking with our bishops, should never result in bitter and disrespectful criticism. "Creative fidelity," a cherished Christian value, contributes much more to the solution of the problems of our pilgrim Church.

4. THINKING IT OVER

What are charismatic gifts? What can we say about the extraordinary phenomena accompanying the outpouring of the Spirit in the early Church? Is the outpouring of the Spirit limited only to the rulers of the Church? Are there gifts of the Spirit in the Church today? What should be kept in mind if the Spirit prompts you to improve certain situations in the Church (your parish)?

5. PRAY MEDITATIVELY

Come, Holy Spirit, fill the hearts of Your faithful and enkindle in them the fire of Your Love.

> Send forth Your Spirit, and they shall be created.
> And You shall renew the face of the earth.
> *Let us pray.*

O God, Who did instruct the hearts of the faithful by the light of the Holy Spirit, grant us by the same Spirit to have a right judgment in all things and ever to rejoice in His consolation. Through Christ our Lord. Amen.

6. THINGS TO DO

Read: The Prophet Joel: 2:27-32; Peter's Discourse: Acts 2:14-22; the Mass of Pentecost and the Votive Mass of All Holy Apostles.

28. The Gift of the Spirit

*1a. Then he breathed on them and said:
"Receive the Holy Spirit.
If you forgive men's sins,
they are forgiven them;
if you hold them bound,
they are held bound" (John 20:23).*

When they heard this, they were deeply shaken. They asked Peter and the other apostles, "What are we to do, brothers?" Peter answered: "You must reform and be baptized, each one of you, in the name of Jesus Christ, that your sins may be forgiven; then you will receive the gift of the Holy Spirit. It was to you and your children that the promise was made, and to all those still far off whom the Lord our God calls" (Acts 2:27-39).

While Apollos was in Corinth, Paul passed through the interior of the country and came to Ephesus. There he found some disciples to whom he put the question, "Did you receive the Holy Spirit when you became believers?" They answered, "We have not so much as heard that there is a Holy Spirit." "Well, how were you baptized?" he persisted. They replied, "With the baptism of John." Paul then explained, "John's baptism was a baptism of repentance. He used to tell the people about the one who would come after him in whom they were to believe—that is, Jesus." When they heard this, they were baptized in the name of the Lord Jesus. As Paul laid his hands on them, the Holy Spirit came down on them and they began to speak in tongues and to utter prophecies. There were in the company about twelve men in all (Acts 19:1-7).

1b. When the designated time had come, God sent forth his Son born of a woman, born under the law, to deliver from the law those who were subjected to it, so that we might receive our status as adopted sons. The proof that you are sons is the fact that God has sent forth into our hearts the spirit of his Son which cries out "Abba!" ("Father!") You are no longer a slave but a son! And the fact that you are a son makes you an heir, by God's design (Galatians 4:4-7).

2a. A deep experience. The gift of God, the favor of God, the gift of the Holy Spirit, in other words, God's self-communication to men, is called "Grace" in Biblical language. A renowned

Bible scholar was asked by a student: "Could you give me a definition of 'Grace'?" His answer was: "Grace cannot be given a definition. It is like Jesus seeing the tax-collector Zacchaeus up in the tree and saying to him: 'Come on down, I am going to have dinner in your house today.'" (Read Luke 19:1-10.) This example describes Grace as a deep experience that cannot be accurately defined in words. It conveys something of the joyful surprise that comes to a person as he suddenly feels the totally unexpected, unmerited, loving initiative of God.

2b. Person to person relationship. Contemporary theologians try to approach this "deep experience" with the concept "relationship." Often great men, who accomplished marvelous things in their lives, have admitted that they owed a great deal to the inspiring presence of their wives. The relationship to their wives was a dynamic force that transformed them, making them to a certain degree different persons. Analyzing such a relationship, we observe that "dynamic force" and "inspiring presence" cannot be separated from the woman involved. It is the woman, her dynamic inspiration, her presence, love, concern, and interest, related to this man, which establishes this person to person relationship—a grace to this man.

2c. God's self-communication. While relating this example to the relationship of God to man and calling it "Grace," we should remember that no example can adequately explain religious values. This example indicates in what direction theologians are groping for some more understanding of that mysterious concept "Grace" which is mentioned in the Bible so often.

Reading the Bible passages in no. 2 with this example in mind can help to give some more insight into the Biblical concept of "Grace" and an understanding of the following definition: "Grace is God's absolute self-communication to men, it is the personal sharing of life with God" (Schillebeeckx).

2d. Relationships transform. As the Bible passages indicate, "Grace" (gift, favor) cannot be separated from God. God communicates Himself. He is present in a very special way to those who share His life through Faith and Baptism. This special relationship of loving and dynamic presence transforms the Christian. The Bible calls it a rebirth from water and Spirit (John 3:1-4).

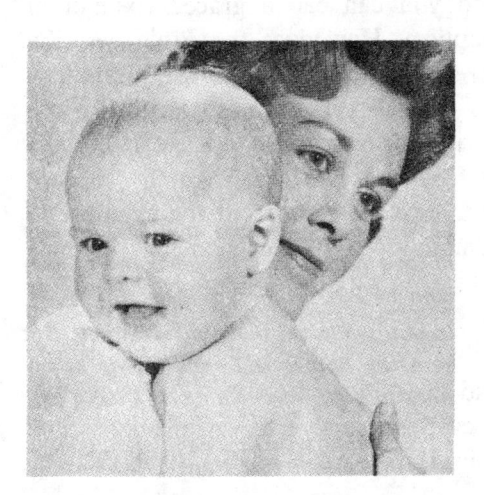

A mother is happy when people say about her baby: "He looks like his mother!" A father feels proud when his teen-age son is said to have some of his good qualities. A husband may owe a lot to his wife. Relationships transform us and make us different persons. By relating to one another we become more human.

Born and reborn to the image of God.

If this is true on the human level, it is even more true when man is drawn into that very intimate relationship with Almighty God which the Bible calls "Grace" (favor). By relating to God, man becomes more divine, more in His image!

3. Dialogue of love. You are locally present to people surrounding you in an overcrowded bus or subway. But this is not a personal presence. A person is personally present to you only if you disclose yourself to him. This is the presence of friends and lovers. The more there is a mutual openness of mind and heart, the more two persons are present to one another.

This should be the presence of the Spirit in you. The more you are open to the Spirit and establish a dialogue of love in prayer, the more He is present to you. Be open to the guidance of "God-with-you!" Read your Bible and meditate on it. God's Spirit speaks to you through the sacred text. For a better understanding of the presence of God (the Spirit, Jesus) see Chapter 47 and Chapter 45, no. 2a.

4. THINKING IT OVER

Can you recall a relationship in your life (with a teacher, spouse, priest, friend), which you can call a grace? Explain in this context the grace of Baptism. How does the Bible describe that change (transformation) worked by "Grace"? (See Galatians 4:4-7 above and John 3:1-4.) Describe how Zacchaeus was changed by his relationship with our Lord! (Read Luke 19:1-10.) In the Letters of Paul, look for texts which mention the concept "Grace" or "Favor" and try to explain them from the example in no. 2a. How should you remain open to God's loving presence in you?

5. PRAY MEDITATIVELY

Father, all-powerful and ever-living God,
we do well always and everywhere to give you thanks
through Jesus Christ our Lord.

He returned to you in glory
to take his place at your right hand.
. . . true to his promise,
he sent the Holy Spirit to dwell in us
and make us children of the Father.

So now in boundless joy the whole wide world
joins with the angels in their unending hymn of praise:

Holy, holy, holy Lord, God of power and might,
heaven and earth are full of your glory.
    Hosanna in the highest.
Blessed is he who comes in the name of the Lord.
    Hosanna in the highest. *(Preface of the Holy Spirit)*

6. THINGS TO DO

Read attentively Chapter 8 of Romans (including the footnotes) which describes "our being in grace" in a way found nowhere else in the Bible.

29. The Spirit Too Helps Us

1. Once, on the sabbath, we went ouside the city gate to the bank of the river, where we thought there would be a place of prayer. We sat down and spoke to the women who were gathered there. One who listened was a woman named Lydia, a dealer in purple goods from the town of Thyatira. She already reverenced God, and the Lord opened her heart to accept what Paul was saying. After she and her household had been baptized, she extended us an invitation: "If you are convinced that I believe in the Lord, come and stay at my house." She managed to prevail on us (Acts 16:13-15).

The Spirit too helps us in our weakness, for we do not know how to pray as we ought; but the Spirit himself makes intercession for us with groanings that cannot be expressed in speech (Romans 8:26).

2a. Suddenly courageous. The Lord touched the heart of the woman named Lydia. This woman was unable to join the holy people of God without the help of God's Spirit. Christ says: "Apart from me you can do nothing" (John 15:5).

The Apostles, who were commissioned by Jesus Christ to preach His Gospel (good tidings) all over the world, were afraid (see Chapter 27). But after the Holy Spirit had poured out His help, they suddenly became very courageous and were willing to take all risks to carry out Christ's command.

2b. A balanced judgment. In the life of a Christian there is a constant tension between total dependence on God and the knowledge that we are God's partners, fully responsible for the world-process. Marxists (see Chapter 43, no. 2d, e) often blame Christians for accepting situations like poverty, social injustice, and war too easily with the promise of a better life hereafter. Indeed, often Christians have overstressed the role of Grace! It requires a well-balanced judgment to accept the inevitable in Faith and to do whatever possible to improve a situation.

2c. One Grace. Traditionally, theologians distinguish between "sanctifying grace" (the situation—the special relationship between God and man) and "actual grace" (its dynamic aspect). Discussing them separately, we should not forget that we are really speaking of one grace, which is the presence of the Spirit. The Spirit Who comes to us is living. It is not correct to speak of grace as something impersonal or a "quantity of something," as if God's gifts were a sort of supernatural invisible liquid or a kind of badge of membership in the Church. Grace means being known and permeated by the Spirit of Jesus and the Father.

Furthermore, we should not forget that the Spirit can come to us also in others. Actually, the Spirit has been given to us together. Together we have One Spirit Who makes us the "Church," Who makes us brothers and sisters "in Christ."

3. Enkindle the fire. The Spirit helps our weakness. And this help of the Spirit is our guarantee that we are ultimately going to remain faithful to God. But we must cooperate with God's grace in us and pray often: "Come, Holy Spirit, fill my heart and enkindle in it the fire of Your love."

4. THINKING IT OVER

What does Jesus say about the necessity of actual grace? Illustrate this with the Bible quotation in this chapter and also with what happened at Pentecost. (See Chapter 27.) What do Marxists blame Christians for and what should we do about it? What does Grace mean and what misunderstanding of Grace is sometimes found among Christians?

5. READ ATTENTIVELY

a) What does St. Paul say about sufficient grace for all?
St. Paul says: "He [God] wants all men to be saved and come to know the truth" (1 Timothy 2:4).

b) What does St. Paul say about cooperation with God's help?

St. Paul says: "As your fellow workers we beg you not to receive the grace of God in vain" (2 Corinthians 6:1).

7. THINGS TO DO

In 1 Corinthians 15:9-11, study how Paul has handled the tension mentioned in No. 2b. Read also 2 Corinthians 12:7-9 and relate it to this chapter. Read some chapters from the Acts of the Apostles, which has been called the "Gospel of the Holy Spirit."

30. The Blessed Trinity

1a. How deep are the riches and the wisdom and the knowledge of God! How inscrutable his judgments, how unsearchable his ways! For "who has known the mind of the Lord? Or who has been his counselor? Who has given him anything so as to deserve return?" For from him and through him and for him all things are. To him be glory forever. Amen (Romans 11:33-36).

1b. Later Jesus, coming from Galilee, appeared before John at the Jordan to be baptized by him. John tried to refuse him with the protest, "I should be baptized by you, yet you come to me!" Jesus answered: "Give in for now. We must do this if we would fulfill all of God's demands." So John gave in. After Jesus was baptized, he came directly out of the water. Suddenly the sky opened and he saw the Spirit of God descend like a dove and hover over him. With that, a voice from the heavens said, "This is my beloved Son. My favor rests on him" (Matthew 3:13-17).

1c. The eleven disciples made their way to Galilee, to the mountain to which Jesus had summoned them. At the sight of him, those who had entertained doubts fell down in homage. Jesus came forward and addressed them in these words:

> *"Full authority has been given to me*
> *both in heaven and on earth;*
> *go, therefore, and make disciples of all the nations.*

> Baptize them in the name
> 'of the Father,
> and of the Son,
> and of the Holy Spirit.'
> Teach them to carry out everything I have commanded you.
> And know that I am with you always, until the end of the world!"
> (Matthew 28:16-20).

2a. Ineffable mystery. After we have discussed the Father, the Son, and the Holy Spirit, we must try to say something about the mystery of their Unity. Are we human beings able to do so? Can our human concepts and words express the ineffable mystery of God? Theologians tell us that all our speaking about God is analogous, corresponding only in some respects to a reality of God.

We have the concepts "Father" and "Son"; we have the concept of "Spirit" meaning "breath" or "breath of life." We apply these human concepts to God, always with the understanding that they are just an approach from far away, from the lowliness of our human condition. Is this perhaps the reason that the Church has us read the first Bible passage above (1a) during the Mass of Trinity Sunday? "How inscrutable his judgments, how unsearchable his ways!"

2b. Related to creation. Though we know that the mystery of God is ineffable, theologians try to penetrate it as far as humanly possible. Studying the data of the Bible, they understand God as Father, Son, and Holy Spirit first of all as God in relation to His creation and the work of salvation: *The Father* (as originator of all life, related to creation), sending *His Son or Word* (for our salvation) and communicating *the Spirit* (related to our rebirth from water and Spirit). The revelation of God as Father, Son, and Holy Spirit tells us first of all what God is for us men.

2c. The traditional way. Another question is, does the revelation of God as Father, Son, and Holy Spirit also indicate something about God Himself (as not related to man)? Theologians affirm this emphatically.

The traditional way of reasoning about this mystery of God in Himself is: In one God there are three persons: Father, Son, and Holy Spirit. As such, we speak about God as the Blessed Trinity. This traditional approach has its origin most of all in the doctrine taught by the Church Councils of Nicea (325) and Constantinople (381).

2d. Contemporary approach. Contemporary theologians try to approach this mystery of God in a different way. They want to give up the concept of "persons" in God. The reason to do so is that the meaning of the word "person" has changed over the centuries.

Initially, "persona" stood for the mask an actor wore to personify a certain character on the stage. Later, in the time of the Councils of Nicea and Constantinople, "persona" stood more for a man who played a role in society, hence a citizen: man in relation to society. That is why at that time "persona" was a very apt word to reason about God related to creation in a three-fold way: Father (related to creation), Son (related to man's salvation), and Holy Spirit (Related to man's sanctification).

But over the centuries, the meaning of "person" has changed. As it is now, person no longer stands for "man as related to . . ." It now stands for "a unique individual." And that is the reason why it seems confusing to go on speaking as if one were affirming that there are three individuals in God, since this would jeopardize the concept of "One God only."

Rather than speaking of three individuals in God, theologians are seeking a way to attempt to express the distinction and unity in God. As we have mentioned on p. 2, theology is not necessarily the Faith. All these theologians are trying to do is to shed some light on the Biblical data of Father, Son, and Holy Spirit. (See Bibliographical Notes, p. 325, no. 42.)

3. Knowing and knowing about. Man wants to know. But we must realize that more important than knowing about God, is knowing God! The most learned theologian, who knows a great deal about God, is not necessarily the best and the happiest Christian. To know God as "Love" (1 John 4:16) is much more important. This intimate person to person relationship gives a knowledge which cannot possibly be expressed in human terminology. You know your beloved and she/he knows you! It is that kind of knowledge of God, which ultimately satisfies a human being. (Read again No. 1a.)

Let your Sign of the Cross or your prayer "Glory be to the Father" be a thankful confession of Faith in this unsearchable mystery of God.

4. THINKING IT OVER

What do we mean when we say that our speaking of God is always analogous? What does the revelation of God as Father, Son, and Holy Spirit tell us first of all? Describe this! Studying the Biblical data of "Father, Son, and Holy Spirit," how do traditional theologians try to approach this mystery in God? Why do contemporary theologians try to approach the mystery of the Blessed Trinity in a different way?

5. PRAY MEDITATIVELY

Glory be to the Father, and to the Son, and to the Holy Spirit. As it was in the beginning, is now, and ever shall be, world without end. Amen.

6. THINGS TO DO

Read: First Mass of Christmas; Mass of Trinity Sunday; First and Second Letters of John.

PART II

PART II

The Church of Jesus Christ

The History of Salvation began with the calling of Abraham, reached its peak in the Death and Resurrection of Our Lord, and became complete with the descent of the Holy Spirit (Chapters 1—30). See Diagram on page 309.

But the history of (our) Salvation goes on. Christ did not abandon the Church He established. He leads the Church through the guidance of His Holy Spirit (Chapters 31—39). He continues to come to you and bless you through the Sacraments (Chapters 40—57). Your answer to God's call (a good life) is possible only with the help of Christ and His grace (Chapters 58—64). The History of Salvation will end with the second coming of Christ (Chapters 65—68).

Saint Peter's and the Vatican.

31. The Church of Jesus Christ

(Part 1)

The New People of God

1a. He left Nazareth and went down to live in Capernaum by the sea near the territory of Zebulun and Naphtali (Matthew 4:13).

As he was walking along the Sea of Galilee he watched two brothers, Simon now known as Peter, and his brother Andrew, casting a net into the sea. They were fishermen. He said to them, "Come after me and I will make you fishers of men." They immediately abandoned their nets and became his followers. He walked along farther and caught sight of two other brothers, James, Zebedee's son, and his brother John. They too were in their boat, getting their nets in order with their father, Zebedee. He called them, and immediately they abandoned boat and father to follow him (Matthew 4:18-22).

1b. Jesus toured all of Galilee. He taught in their synagogues, proclaimed the good news of the kingdom, and cured the people of every disease and illness. As a consequence of this, his reputation traveled the length of Syria. They carried to him all those afflicted with various diseases and racked with pain: the possessed, the lunatics, the paralyzed. He cured them all. The great crowds that followed him came from Galilee, the Ten Cities, Jerusalem and Judea, and from across the Jordan (Matthew 4:23-25).

1c. "I am the good shepherd;
the good shepherd lays down his life for the sheep.
The hired hand—who is no shepherd
nor owner of the sheep—
catches sight of the wolf coming
and runs away, leaving the sheep
to be snatched and scattered by the wolf.
That is because he works for pay;
he has no concern for the sheep.

"I am the good shepherd.
I know my sheep
and my sheep know me
in the same way that the Father knows me
and I know the Father;
for these sheep I will give my life" (John 10:11-15).

2a. The nucleus. Jesus gathered people around Him who believed and followed Him. He called His followers "disciples." From these disciples twelve were chosen to join Jesus in a special way. They were His "Apostles."

The disciples established the nucleus of the new people of God.

2b. Great crowds. Concerning the passage in no. 1b, we should keep in mind that the Hebrews of Jesus' time did not see a scientific connection between medication and disease. In their minds, sickness was caused by the evil power of demons. Hence, a sick person did not go first of all to the doctor but to the priest, who was asked to pray for him. That is why the preaching of the Gospel was accompanied by the "healing of every disease," signifying the defeat of evil.

Catholic Bible scholars usually accept the fact that Jesus worked miracles. But the miracle stories, as we have them in the Gospels, are mainly used by the inspired writers as literary forms, to signify (symbolize) the blessings of God's Kingdom (defeat of evil) on earth and hereafter. And great crowds followed Him!

"I am the good shepherd. I know my sheep and my sheep know me" (John 10:14).

2c. Together. The fact that both our Lord and his first co-workers repeatedly referred to the kingdom of David as an antitype to characterize the movement (the Kingdom!) they started, together with the comparison of the flock and the shepherd

(1c), clearly indicates that they intended Christianity to be lived not alone but in groups or congregations. How these groups should be organized is another question, which will be discussed later. However, two characteristics are involved in this set-up: (a) togetherness and (b) some kind of authority, since without them no group or congregation can exist.

2d. Germ from which. The new people of God, as established by our Lord, does not consist of one nation, as did Israel in former times, but of all men, chosen by God from all nations. "Those who believe are sons of Abraham" (Galatians 3:7).

The people of God, the Church, is not the same as the Kingdom of God. It is the germ from which the Kingdom (Reign) of God will develop into all its splendor at Christ's "Second Coming."

3. Birds of a feather. There are very few things man does alone. "Birds of a feather flock together." Both organized crime and organized religion follow the same human instinct. We do things together. Whether it is a ladies' garden club, the CYO, or the Shriners, there is no fun in doing it alone, and "alone" it does not last. Our Lord knew this.

Constantly living up to the beautiful ideals of Christianity (defeating evil in and around us; see no. 1b) must be done together. We need one another's inspiration. What do you contribute to a greater togetherness in your congregation? Criticizing others for lack of togetherness is easy. What do you do about it? A congregation (parish) cannnot be a sign of God's Reign to a community when members only attend Mass on Sunday and then hurry somewhere else.

4. THINKING IT OVER

Why do the Gospel-writers accompany the preaching of God's Kingdom (Reign) with miracle stories? (See no. 1b.) What does the Bible passage in no. 1c suggest as to how Christians should live their commitment in this world? What does the set-up of congregations as the life-environment of Christianity entail? Explain how the Church and the Kingdom (Reign) of God are related! What about a so necessary togetherness in your congregation and what can you do about it?

5. READ ATTENTIVELY

What does St. Paul say about the merits of Jesus Christ for the Church?

St. Paul says: "He [Jesus Christ] gave himself up for her [the Church] to make her holy, purifying her in the bath of water by the power of the word, to present to himself a glorious church, holy and immaculate, without stain or wrinkle or anything of that sort" (Ephesians 5:25-27).

6. PRAY MEDITATIVELY

Worthy is the Lamb [Jesus Christ] that was slain to receive power and riches, wisdom and strength, honor and glory and praise! With your blood you purchased for God men of every race and tongue, of every people and nation. You made of them a kingdom, and priests to serve our God, and they shall reign on the earth" (Revelation 5:12. 9. 10).

7. THINGS TO DO

Read some of the chapters in the Acts of the Apostles which tell about the establishment of the Church; also 1 Peter 2:9-10.

32. The Church of Jesus Christ

(Part 2)

The Unity of Life with Christ

1. *"I am the true vine
and my Father is the vinegrower.
He prunes away
every barren branch,
but the fruitful ones
he trims clean
to increase their yield"*
(John 15:1-2).

"He who lives in me and I in him, will produce abundantly" *(John 15:5).*

*"Live on in me, as I do in you.
No more than a branch can bear fruit of itself
apart from the vine,
can you bear fruit
apart from me.
I am the vine, you are the branches.
He who lives in me and I in him,
will produce abundantly,
for apart from me you can do nothing.
A man who does not live in me
is like a withered, rejected branch,
picked up to be thrown in the fire and burnt.
If you live in me,
and my words stay part of you
you may ask what you will—
it will be done for you"* (John 15:4-7).

Just as each of us has one body with many members, and not all the members have the same function, so too we, though many, are one body in Christ and individually members one of another (Romans 12:4-5).

Rather, let us profess the truth in love and grow to the full maturity of Christ the head. Through him the whole body grows, and with the proper functioning of the members joined firmly together by each supporting ligament, builds itself up in love (Ephesians 4:15-16).

2. More than a flock. The comparisons (similes) above explain that the Church of Jesus Christ (the people of God) establishes a unity of life with its Head, Jesus Christ.

The first comparison was made by Christ Himself; the second is St. Paul's comparison of the Mystical Body to the human body (related parts).

The Apostle teaches: The head is the center of life. All actions of man are directed by his head. So also is Christ the Center of Life for the holy people.

In Chapter 31, Christ compares the Church (the people of God) to a flock. He Himself is the Shepherd. But the Church of Jesus Christ is more than a flock. The Catholic (universal) Church is an impressive organization spread all over the world. Even unbelievers are impressed upon seeing all her churches and buildings, her societies, her effective administration, mission work, and spirit of sacrifice found among the clergy and religious. It is an impressive facade that becomes for many seekers of truth the very starting point of their thinking. But all this is only the facade! The essential beauty and the very core of the Church is the Divine Life of Christ within it, invisible but real! The Church of Jesus Christ is a spiritual family. All of us share the same Divine Life, as brothers and sisters share natural life in the family. This real splendor of the Church will be visible only at Christ's Second Coming.

God gives us the life of grace through Christ our Lord Who suffered death on the Cross. As a grain of wheat in the ground, He died in order to yield fruit a hundredfold. That is why Christ could say: "I came that they might have life, and have it to the full" (John 10:10).

3a. Your parish. When you are baptized, you receive the life of grace because of Jesus' merits on the Cross. Through the Sacrament of Penance, a spiritually dead man is restored to life because of Christ's Suffering and Death. And when you sustain life in you by eating the Bread of Life, do not forget that it is only because of Jesus' merits that you are able to live as a son of God.

As a member of the Mystical Body (the Church) you must constantly remain united with your Head, Jesus Christ, by hearing His Word, thinking it over in your heart and encountering Him in the Holy Signs which are called the Sacraments.

In Chapter 20 we have already discussed your duty of radiating your own light to your brothers in darkness. As a member of the Mystical Body of Christ, you must remember your responsibility toward the other members of the same Body, your fellow Christians. The welfare of your parish is not only your pastor's business!

3b. Making the Church present. Vatican II states: "The lay apostolate is a participation in the saving mission of the Church itself. Through Baptism and Confirmation all are commissioned to that apostolate by the Lord Himself. Now, the laity are called in a special way to make the Church present and operative in those places and circumstances where only through them can she become the salt of the earth" (*Constitution on the Church,* no. 33).

4. THINKING IT OVER

With what does Jesus compare the Church in Chapter 31? Is the Church only a "club" for people who perchance profess the same religion? What comparisons in the Bible teach you that the Church is more than a secular society? Through Whose mediation does God give you the life of grace? Explain "life of grace" from Chapter 29, no. 2c. What must you do to remain united with Christ? How can you radiate your light to others who still live in darkness? (See Chapter 20.) What is your responsibility to your fellow members of the Mystical Body? What can you do to make the Church present in your community?

5. READ ATTENTIVELY

To what is the Church compared in the Bible?

The Church is compared to:

(1) A People: Christ is the Leader (King) and we are His chosen people.

(2) A Flock: Christ is the Shepherd and the people of God are His sheep.

(3) A Vine: Christ is the Vine and the people of God are the branches.

(4) The Human Body: Christ is the Head and the people of God are the members.

6. PRAY MEDITATIVELY

Almighty and eternal God, you know that our divisions and problems are many. Help us overcome those obstacles so that those who are followers of Christ may be brought together in worship of Him Who lives and reigns with you in the unity of the Holy Spirit, God, forever and ever. Amen *(Octave Prayer for Unity).*

7. THINGS TO DO

Read: 1 Corinthians 12:12-31; John 18:28-38; John 15:1-17; John 17:1-26.

33. The Church of Jesus Christ

(Part 3)

The Ecclesiastical Office

1a. *"Peace be with you," he said again.*
"As the Father has sent me,
so I send you" (John 20:21).

Jesus came forward and addressed them in these words:
"Full authority has been given to me
both in heaven and on earth;
go, therefore, and make disciples of all the nations.
Baptize them in the name
'of the Father,
and of the Son,
and of the Holy Spirit.'
Teach them to carry out everything I have commanded you.
And know that I am with you always, until the end of the world!"
(Matthew 28:18-20).

1b. *I for my part declare to you, you are 'Rock,' and on this rock I will build my church, and the jaws of death shall not prevail against it. I will entrust to you the keys of the kingdom of heaven. Whatever you declare bound on earth shall be bound in heaven; whatever you declare loosed on earth shall be loosed in heaven" (Matthew 16:18-19).*

When they had eaten their meal, Jesus said to Simon Peter, "Simon, son of John, do you love me more than these?" "Yes, Lord," he said, "you know that I love you." At which Jesus said, "Feed my lambs."

A second time he put his question, "Simon, son of John, do you love me?" "Yes, Lord," Peter said, "you know that I love you." Jesus replied, "Tend my sheep."

A third time Jesus asked him, "Simon, son of John, do you love me?" Peter was hurt because he had asked a third time, "Do you love me?" So he said to him: "Lord, you know everything. You know well that I love you." Jesus said to him, "Feed my sheep" (John 21:15-17).

1c. *To the elders among you I, a fellow elder, a witness of Christ's sufferings and sharer in the glory that is to be revealed, make this appeal. God's flock is in your midst; give it a shepherd's care. Watch over it willingly as God would have you do, not under constraint; and not for shameful profit either, but generously. Be examples to the flock, not lording it over those assigned to you, so that when the chief Shepherd appears you will win for yourselves the unfading crown of glory (1 Peter 5:1-4).*

2a. Institution needed. It is clear that perseveringly living up to what Jesus Christ stands for cannot be done alone. We need one another's inspiration and encouragement. According to the will of our Lord Himself and the oldest traditions, we live Christianity in groups or congregations. (See Chapter 31, no. 2c.) Consequently, wherever one establishes a group, one needs institution, rules and regulations as an alternative to chaos. Hence, authority (one or another form of government) becomes a necessity.

In Chapter 27, we have briefly discussed authority in the Catholic Church. From observations made there and elsewhere in this book we may summarize:

(1) Apostolicity. Foundation and source of the ecclesiastical office is the Apostolicity of the community. "Apostolicity" of a community implies the Apostolic Faith and the ecclesiastical office which originates from it as a necessity. It is in the *Apostolic* Church that the Spirit operates!

In normal circumstances the procedure of conveying the office is as follows: At the wish of the congregation (Church) and after acceptance by the candidate, the existing college of officials accepts him into their college by prayer and the imposition of hands. As it is now, usually bishops are chosen and appointed by the Pope and God's people accepts them. However, there is a demand on the part of some local Churches to go back to the ancient pattern of election by laity and clergy.

From this observation it is clear that the ecclesiastical office (bishop, presbyter, deacon) has a twofold dimension:

(a) **The official represents the congregation** to the world. When a bishop or priest makes a statement on television, speaks at an ecumenical gathering, or instructs an inquiry class, he does so representing the Church.

(b) **The official represents our Lord** to the congregation. In and through the Apostolic message and the confession of Faith, his authority comes from Christ, Who said to the first officials: "As the Father has sent me, so I send you." (See no. 1a and Chapter 27.) Once a bishop or pastor has been installed, he cannot be discharged by the congregation as a politician can be voted out by his constituency in a democracy. Some separated Churches have given up this original pattern, and the result has often been preachers who just preach what the congregation wants to hear in order to keep their job.

(2) **Brotherly overtones.** As to the way authority is exercised, it seems feasible to adapt it to the circumstances of time and culture, as far as compatible with the basic structure which Christ Himself has given to His Church (see no. 1). Hence, in our democratic culture, Church authority should have not paternalistic but brotherly overtones, in order to function efficiently (see Chapter 27).

(3) **Service.** Authority should be seen as service to the people of God in a spirit of love. (See 1 Peter 5:1-4 in no. 1c.)

2b. The organization. At the bottom of the Church's structure we have the parish. The parish priests are ordained co-workers of the bishops.

The head of a parish is the pastor. His co-workers are called assistants or assistant priests (or associate pastors). Both pastor and assistants are addressed "Father." In 1967 the Holy Father restored the sacred order of deacons, who may also be assistants to the local pastor.

A group of parishes form a diocese, whose head is the bishop. A bishop is addressed "Your Excellency," or simply "Bishop."

Parish priests are either secular or religious. Secular priests are attached to a diocese; they are "prudent cooperators with the episcopal order" (*Constitution of the Church,* no. 28); they live in celibacy, as far as priests of the Latin rite of the Church are concerned, but do not take the vow of poverty. Religious priests take the three vows of poverty, celibacy, and obedience in a religious order and are placed by their religious superiors at the disposal of bishops. They can be moved from one diocese to another and be sent even to foreign countries as missionaries under the regulations of their particular religious society.

Some secular priests have the title of honor "Monsignor." In this time of renewal in the Church many Catholics look with criticism upon titles of honor and "promotion" for priests, since these practices represent deviations from the simplicity of the Bible. They exude medieval pomp and power, which are anything but evangelical. On the other hand we should not be too critical either. The Church is a wise Mother who knows her children.

An artist who observed the Second Vatican Council puts it this way: "In its wisdom the Church bestows playthings on its fools, gives medals to its vain, confers power on those who crave power incurably, provides magic for the naive [e.g., with regard to the exaggerated stress on the devotional in Latin America and southern European countries], reveals truth to its seekers, brings beatitude to its visionaries, and enlightenment to its Saints" (*Outsider in the Vatican,* p. 86).

This is the way an "outsider" sees things; but there is truth in his statement! The Church will always be a community of human beings, constantly in need of reform. If you think that the Church needs reforms, begin by reforming yourself into a better Christian and be gracious to fellow members!

2c. The office of Peter. In the set-up of the Church, we observe "the Office of Peter." According to the Bible (see no. 1b), Peter had a special position of leadership among the Twelve. He presided over meetings and made final decisions. (See Acts 15:1-12.) Peter went to Rome and died in that city as a martyr in 67 A.D. Since the Bishop of Rome is considered to be the successor of Peter, he now holds "the office of Peter." In other words, he is the head of the College of Bishops. During the Middle Ages, ever more power and authority was centralized in the office of Peter. The Popes made many decisions single-handedly! Nowadays, there is a demand to decentralize papal authority and bring it back to its early proportion of collegiality.

As for the College of Cardinals, it is composed of special advisers of the Pope. Several of them, in charge of the daily administration of the Church, live in Rome; others are bishops all over the world. When the Holy See becomes vacant, the cardinals choose a new Sovereign Pontiff.

2d. Division of tasks. There is no direct connection between the contemporary ecclesiastical offices (bishop, presbyter, deacon) and the founding act of the earthly Jesus. The Apostle was at once bishop and deacon, prophet and teacher. The office of Christ, which the Apostles shared, was established by God (see Matthew 28:18 in no. 1a), but its unfolding into that of bishop, presbyter (elder), and deacon was done by the Apostles guided by the Spirit.

3. Response in Faith. Essential to ecclesiastical office are the call of God to the individual, his response in Faith and his acceptance through the Church. Pray that those in office (deacons, priests, bishops, pope) may persevere in their response in Faith and serve the people of God as our Lord would have done. Moreover, assist them with your "creative fidelity!" (See Chapter 27 no. 3b.)

4. THINKING IT OVER

What is one of the reasons that Jesus Christ conceived of Christians as living in groups or congregations? Why is authority in the Church a necessity? Explain the foundation and source of ecclesiastical office! What does "Apostolicity" imply? How is office conveyed in the Catholic Church? Describe the twofold dimension of the ecclesiastical office! How should authority in the Church be exercised? What does the author of 1 Peter state about authority in the Church? Is your pastor a religious or secular priest? What does this mean? What is "the office of Peter" and who holds it now? What are Cardinals? Describe the origin of the ecclesiastical offices: bishops, presbyters (elders, priests), and deacons!

5. PRAY MEDITATIVELY

In your own words say Jesus' prayer for his Apostles and for the Church (see John 17:11-21).

6. THINGS TO DO

Many fine books with pictorial illustrations are available describing Rome and the Vatican. Ask your parish priest to recommend a book to you. Also, if possible, see a series of slides about this subject.

34. The Church Our Teacher

1. Peter proceeded to address them in these words: "I begin to see how true it is that God shows no partiality. Rather, the man of any nation who fears God and acts uprightly is acceptable to him. This is the message he has sent to the sons of Israel, the good news of peace proclaimed through Jesus Christ who is Lord of all. I take it you know what has been reported all over Judea about Jesus of Nazareth, beginning in Galilee with the baptism John preached; of the way God anointed him with the Holy Spirit and power. He went about doing good works and healing all who were in the grip of the devil, and God was with him. We are witnesses to all that he did in the land of the Jews and in Jerusalem. They killed him, finally, hanging him on a tree, only to have God raise him up on the third day and grant that he be seen, not by all, but only by such witnesses as had been chosen beforehand by God —by us who ate and drank with him after he rose from the dead. He commissioned us to preach to the people and to bear witness that he is the one set apart by God as judge of the living and the dead. To him all the prophets testify, saying that everyone who believes in him has forgiveness of sins through his name."

Peter had not finished these words when the Holy Spirit descended upon all who were listening to Peter's message (Acts 10:34-44).

2a. Commissioned to preach. Peter said: "Jesus commissioned us to preach to the people." The Church proclaims the good tidings (Gospel) of Jesus Christ to all nations. She teaches us by sermons, by instructions in school, in the confessional, in home visits, and in the rectory. Sometimes the Holy Father directly teaches his whole flock by sending an encyclical to all the bishops. Also, the bishop addresses his faithful, from time to time, by a letter that must be read in all the churches of his diocese. Moreover, the Church teaches us through books: the Bible, Catechism, Missal, prayer books and other spiritual books.

The "Imprimatur" ("Let it be printed") in this type of book is a guarantee that the contents are not in conflict with what is accepted as sound doctrine in the Church.

2b. Infallibility. Jesus has promised to be with His Church: "Teach them . . . I am with you always" (Matthew 28:20). The Church, God's own people, as a whole, anointed as she is by the Holy One (see John 2:20. 27), cannot err in matters of belief. When "the sense of the faithful," from the bishops down to the last member of the laity, shows universal agreement in matters of Faith and morals, the Church is infallible (*Constitution on the Church,* no. 12).

The guardians of the Church and of Christ's truth are the collective bishops. The infallibility of God's people results in their collective sense of Faith. That is why a Church Council is infallible when it expressly states it is speaking infallibly. The teaching Church is a living voice which interprets the Biblical values in any new time. This means that the interpretation of the Church can always be improved.

2c. Concerning revelation. The Church is infallible in proclaiming the Gospel of Jesus Christ and at certain significant moments of history in defending and explaining this Gospel. Infallibility always has to do with revelation. Aspects of natural morality which are not explicitly or implicitly contained in divine revelation do not belong to the area of the Church's infallibility.

At the same time, the Church teaches with authority in areas where she does not claim infallibility. When papal and ecclesiastical documents teach theological conclusions (a conclusion from revealed data), natural and social morality, norms for Biblical and theological research (see Chapter 14, no. 7), they are of the greatest authority for Catholics; but they are not infallible, hence reformable. The purpose of this teaching is disciplinary and pedagogical.

2d. Only interpreting. When "the sense of the faithful" is divided, it is the Bishop of Rome, the Pope, who speaks the last word. His task is the same as Peter's, his predecessor in the See of Rome, namely, keeping Christ's flock together in her unity of Confession. However, speaking the last infallible word does not mean that the Holy Father can proclaim dogmas without contact with the Church. He can only interpret what the Universal Church believes.

Moreover, only if the Pope expressly refers to his infallible teaching authority, must we accept his words as such. Over the course of the last century the Popes have taught in this manner only twice, namely, when they proclaimed the dogmas of Mary's Immaculate Conception and her Assumption into heaven. For such decision-making, see Acts 15, especially verse 12. Actually, when Catholics speak of infallibility of the Pope, they simply express strong belief in Christ's promise to His Church: "I am with you always" (Matthew 28:20).

2e. Public and private revelation. As Catholics we believe God's revelation as it comes to us through Christ, the Church and the Sacred Scriptures concerning which we follow the guidance of the Church. We call this public revelation. Besides this we know of private revelations, for example, of Mary at Lourdes, Fatima, Guadalupe, and of Jesus, showing His Sacred Heart to Margaret Mary, a cloistered nun in Paray-les-Monial, France.

Such private revelations, though approved by the Church as containing nothing that goes against her official doctrine, do not have the same authority as public revelation. Since so many have witnessed the remarkable events at the shrines in question, you may feel compelled to believe. But you are a Catholic in perfectly good standing if you do not believe in private revelations.

We must remember that our devotion to the Blessed Virgin and the Sacred Heart of Jesus does not depend merely on belief in these private revelations. It is founded in the very mystery of Public Revelation as it comes through us in Christ and the Church.

3. Housewives saintlier. Keep in mind that we do not follow our bishops simply because they are more learned or saintlier than other faithful. In any diocese there may be professors of theology who are more learned and housewives who are saintlier in God's eyes than the bishop. Rather we follow our bishops in matters of Faith or morals because we believe that "the sense of the faithful" culminates in them. Pray for our bishops and especially for the Bishop of Rome, the Holy Father, that they may always be faithful interpreters and teachers of God's revelation.

4. THINKING IT OVER

Why can God's people as a whole not err in matters of belief? Who are the guardians of the Church and Christ's truth? What does infallibility always concern? What is the purpose of the Church's non-infallible teaching regarding matters of natural and social morality? What is the task of the Holy Father? When only are his statements infallible? Name two of them! Speaking of infallibility, what do Catholics actually express by their belief in it? What is public and private revelation? Familiarize yourself with some of the famous papal encyclicals of this century (e.g., *Rerum Novarum* [on the social question], *Divini Illius Magistri* [on education], *Mystici Corporis* [on the Mystical Body], *Mater et Magistra* [Mother and Teacher], *Populorum Progressio* [on the Development of Peoples], *Humanae Vitae* [Human Life] and some of the documents of Vatican II).

5. READ ATTENTIVELY

How did Christ guarantee that He guides the Church in matters of belief?

Christ said to His Apostles: "He who hears you, hears me. He who rejects you, rejects me" (Luke 10:16).

6. PRAY MEDITATIVELY

The Profession of Faith [in your Missal].

7. THINGS TO DO

Read: Peter's Discourses: Acts 3:12-16; Acts 15:6-12; Paul's Discourse: Acts 20:17-38.

35. The Church, Custodian of Divine Tradition

1. Prophecy has never been put forward by man's willing it. It is rather that men impelled by the Holy Spirit have spoken under God's influence (2 Peter 1:21).

The Apostle Paul wrote to Timothy, who was consecrated bishop of Ephesus, as follows:

You have followed closely my teaching and my conduct. You have observed my resolution, fidelity, patience, love, and endurance, through persecutions and sufferings in Antioch, Iconium, and Lystra. You know what persecutions I have had to bear, and you know how the Lord saved me from them all. Anyone who wants to live a godly life in Christ Jesus can expect to be persecuted. But all the while evil men and charlatans will go from bad to worse, deceiving others, themselves deceived. You, for your part, must remain faithful to what you have learned and believed, because you know who your teachers were. Likewise, from your infancy you have known the sacred Scriptures, the source of the wisdom which through faith in Jesus Christ leads to salvation. All Scripture is inspired of God and is useful for teaching—for reproof, correction, and training in holiness so that the man of God may be fully competent and equipped for every good work (2 Timothy 3:10-17).

I charge you to preach the word, to stay with this task whether convenient or inconvenient—correcting, reproving, appealing—constantly teaching and never losing patience (2 Timothy 4:2).

2a. The start. After Christ's Resurrection, the Church started to "go into the whole world" to distribute the abundant riches given by Christ to her care.

Christ recognized and ratified the Old Testament (see Matthew 5:17-20). His Church continues to do so. "Prophecy has never been put forward by man's willing it. It is rather that men impelled by the Holy Spirit have spoken under God's influence" (2 Peter 1:21). The Church shows how the Old Testament is fulfilled in Christ. She does not destroy it but fulfills and perfects it with Christian Tradition.

Some of the early witnesses supplemented their preaching by writing. Thus did the Church become the Mother of the New Testament.

Writing, however, was only a small fraction of the early Church's world-wide activity of spreading the Gospel. She preached for the first decades without the New Testament, and during the first four centuries she used only parts of it along with other pious books. Do not forget that books were very scarce because each one had to be copied slowly by hand (printing was not invented until 1440), and they were available only to the few who had access to them and could read them.

2b. Genuinely Apostolic. Guided by the Spirit, only later did the Church reflect upon all the pious books in use and recognize some of them as genuinely Apostolic. These books were added to the series (canon) of sacred books already existing, namely, the Hebrew Bible (Old Testament), and considered as "Sacred Scripture." Both Old and New Testament writings then become the Apostolic rule of Christian Faith, to which both Office and Congregation are bound.

A Catholic Christian accepts *the Bible* (the core of Apostolic tradition), and with it *ecclesiastical tradition* (an ever-growing understanding of that Apostolic tradition) from the Church. Why? Because we believe that, as custodian of God's word, the Church is backed by Christ's promise. (See Vatican II, *Constitution on Divine Revelation,* no. 8 and Chapter 34, no. 2b—2d.)

2c. Binding authority. It is sad that in the 16th Century there were some men who though they could no longer accept Divine Tradition from the hands of the Church! From a long series, a few may be mentioned: In 1517, Martin Luther; in 1534, Henry VIII, King of England; in 1560, John Calvin, who started the Presbyterian Church in Switzerland; in 1560, Robert Brown, who established the Congregational and Christian Church in London; in 1611, John Smith and Thomas Helwys, who started the Baptist Church in England; in 1729, John and Charles Wesley and George Whitefield, who started the Methodist Church in Oxford, England; and in 1829, Joseph Smith, who established the Latter Day Saints (Mormons) in Palmyra, New York.

They have been followed by many others. About four hundred Protestant denominations are reading the Bible and interpreting it, but cannot accept it from the hands of the Church, who is its only lawful custodian and interpreter.

The King James Bible, widely read in our country, leaves out seven books which are unacceptable to many Protestants.

There is a difference between Bible reading by a Catholic and that by a Protestant: when faced with problems in reading his Bible, a Catholic studies of course the introductions to the individual books as well as the footnotes, both composed by serious Bible scholars, but he accepts the final explanation from the hands of the Church, not because the bishops and the Pope are learned men, but because their authority is backed by Christ (see no. 2b, above).

A Protestant Bible reader will also consult a Bible expert or his preacher when faced with difficult passages. Furthermore, even in the separated Churches Bible explanation is given with a kind of authority. But separated brethren do not look upon this authority as Catholics look upon the authority of the Church, namely, as binding, because it is ultimately Christ Who speaks in and through the Church. This lack of "binding" authority is the very reason why so many separated brethren reach divided opinions as to God's word in the Bible.

2d. Divided Christianity. The Catholic Church will be the last to deny that there were abuses in the Church of the 16th Century. If the Church had listened to Luther and other serious Reformers, who finally in utter disappointment left her, if Vatican II had taken place in 1500 instead of in the sixties of our century, a great part of the troubles of separation might very likely have been prevented. Who can tell?

As it is, we have a divided Christianity and the whole Church, divided as she is, stands guilty before God. We will discuss this sad event in Church history more extensively in Chapter 37.

2e. The "Imprimatur." The Church sees the Bible as a record of God's dealings with men. As the custodian of that precious record, the Church wants Catholics to read the entire Bible in a reliable translation with approved explanations of difficult parts. For this reason, Catholics read preferably publications approved by the Church. (See the "Imprimatur" in your Bible.)

3a. Hearts open to God. Catholics must gratefully and faithfully accept Christian Tradition from the hands of the Church, for, like Timothy, from their infancy they have "known the sacred scriptures" (see no. 1).

Non-Catholics who have become awakened to a "Catholic vision," and feel the call of God to full Faith and self-surrender, must not play with God's invitation. They must pray and keep their hearts open to God's guidance. A final decision should not be carelessly postponed, since the call of Almighty God to Faith implies the serious duty of grateful acceptance.

Praying together means staying together.

3b. Daily Bible reading. Every Catholic family should have a Bible and, along with family night prayers, should read daily a chapter from it. The head of the family may do the Bible reading himself, or he may have one of the older children read, after first preparing him well for this daily duty.

3c. Reverence. Standing in the church while the Gospel is read and the incensing of the book during a Solemn High Mass are signs of reverence for God's word in the Bible. The burning of candles at both sides of the book in Solemn High Mass symbolizes the light of Christ's good tidings.

4. THINKING IT OVER

See, in Matthew 5:17-20, how Christ ratified the Old Testament. See in the sermons of Peter, Stephen, and Paul (in the Acts of the Apostles) how the infant Church recognized and used the Old Testament. What was the main task of the Church in the beginning: writing or teaching? Describe how the New Testament came into being. Compare what a Catholic and a Protestant would do if faced with a problem in Bible reading. Why may we call the Church the "Mother of the Bible"? Read Acts 8:26-35 and apply its meaning to all the explanatory footnotes in your Bible. How are we to understand Genesis 1—11? (See Chapter 14.) How do we know whether the sacred writer is telling historical facts or is using a story merely to teach a religious truth? (See end of Chapter 14.)

5. PRAY MEDITATIVELY

God, Father in heaven, you have said "Not by bread alone does man live, but by every word that comes forth from the mouth of God." We ask you always to give us zeal in hearing and reading your word, that we may take it as food for our souls. Amen.

6. THINGS TO DO

Read in your Bible the Introduction to each of the four Gospels. Study number 17 of the section "How to Read Your Bible," p. 307.

36. The Church Continues Christ's Priesthood

1. You, however, are "a chosen race, a royal priesthood, a holy nation, a people he claims for his own to proclaim the glorious works" of the One who called you from darkness into his marvelous light. Once you were no people, but now you are God's people; once there was no mercy for you, but now you have found mercy (1 Peter 2:9-10).

2a. Worship. An important task of this "chosen race" is to make its public worship of God as worthy and as beautiful as possible. Through their public worship, Christians adore God, give thanks, ask for help, and make atonement for sin. The peak, or supreme act, of public worship is the Sacrifice of Christ's precious Body and Blood, present to Christians in the symbols of bread and wine.

When the holy people come together, Christ is in the midst of them. He is our High Priest. He stands between us and God to pray and to offer the Sacrifice in our name. Because Christ is the Mediator in our worship of God, we pray "through Christ our Lord."

Those ordained to the ministerial priesthood minister to their brethren by rendering present and effective Christ's saving action, especially the Eucharistic celebration.

2b. Sacred signs. As "a royal priesthood," the Church continues Christ's priesthood not only by praying and offering the Sacrifice, but also by administering the Holy Signs called "Sacraments."

In the name of the High Priest, the Church gives birth to God's children through Baptism, strengthens the life of grace by Confirmation, reestablishes the spiritual life through Penance, tends the life of grace through heavenly Food (Holy Eucharist), and gives her last help through the Anointing of the Sick. Moreover, the Church passes on Christ's priesthood (Holy Orders) to young men who will care for the spiritual life in our souls, and she gives Matrimony to those who serve God in the married state.

These Sacraments, Holy Signs conveying God's grace, will be discussed more thoroughly later on.

2c. Sacraments and sacramentals. Finally, the Church continues Christ's priesthood through her blessings. Our High Priest blessed the children. The Church also blesses children, the sick, mothers, bridegroom and bride, religious Sisters and Brothers, and all people (for example, at the end of the Mass).

The Church also blesses objects of devotion and places and things used in the service of God: medals, crucifixes, rosaries, images of Christ and the saints, scapulars, candles, holy water, palms, ashes, church buildings, altars, chalices, bells, cemeteries. She likewise blesses places and things used in daily life: houses, fields, food, cattle, cars, planes.

Because these blessings, holy actions and things, instituted by the Church, are in a way somewhat like the Sacraments, instituted by Christ, they are called "sacramentals." But they are not the same. Sacraments are Signs which convey God's grace infallibly, because Jesus Himself has attached to them His powerful prayer, which is always answered by the Father. Sacramentals, however, give benefits only because the Church accompanies their use with her prayers. These prayers are powerful also, but they do not have the special guarantee which Jesus attached to the Sacraments.

3a. Giving them a blessing. Laymen (non-priests) may also bless! It is a nice custom in Catholic families for the father, or mother, to make, with the thumb, a little cross on the forehead of the children, thus giving them a blessing before they go to bed. Parents and godparents are invited to trace the cross on the forehead of the child at Baptism.

We bless ourselves when we make the Sign of the Cross with holy water blessed by the priest.

3b. Polarization. You may use the sacramentals with Faith, but do not make them objects of superstition. There seems to be a polarization among Catholics concerning the use of sacramentals. Quite a few feel that they can do without them. Others feel that they need these symbols. Let us respect one another and enjoy the freedom of God's children!

Meanwhile it is interesting to observe that in the secular world, especially among the young, symbols and "sacred-rites" abound. Youth festivals have them, contemporary movies are filled with them!

4. THINKING IT OVER

Why do we often finish our prayers with "through Christ our Lord"? How does the Church continue the priesthood of Jesus Christ? What are Sacraments and what are sacramentals? How are sacramentals to be used?

5. READ ATTENTIVELY

How does the Church continue Christ's priesthood?

The Church continues Christ's priesthood by:

a. praying and offering the Sacrifice of the Mass;

b. giving birth to and tending the life of grace through the Sacraments;

c. dispensing the sacramentals (giving her blessing to persons, places, and things).

6. THINGS TO DO

Read: The official prayer of the Church: Mass of Rogation Day (three days before Ascension); the blessing of baptismal water on Holy Saturday; the blessing of candles on February 2; the blessing of the palms on Palm Sunday; the blessing of the ashes on Ash Wednesday.

37. Groping Toward Unity

1. It was resolved by the apostles and the presbyters, in agreement with the whole Jerusalem church, that representatives be chosen from among their number and sent to Antioch along with Paul and Barnabas. Those chosen were leading men of the community, Judas, known as Barsabbas, and Silas. They were to deliver this letter:

"The apostles and the presbyters, your brothers, send greetings to the brothers of Gentile origin in Antioch, Syria, and Cilicia. We have heard that some of our number without any instructions from us have upset you with their discussions and disturbed your peace of mind. Therefore we have unanimously resolved to choose representatives and send them to you, along with our beloved Barnabas and Paul, who have dedicated themselves to the cause of our Lord Jesus Christ. Those whom we are sending you are Judas and Silas, who will convey this message by word of mouth" (Acts 15:22-27).

Then, after fourteen years, I went up to Jerusalem again with Barnabas, this time taking Titus with me. I went prompted by a revelation, and I laid out for their scrutiny the gospel as I present it to the Gentiles—all this in private conference with the leaders, to make sure the course I was pursuing, or had pursued, was not useless (Galatians 2:1-2).

On the contrary, recognizing that I had been entrusted with the gospel for the uncircumcised, just as Peter was for the circumcised, and recognizing, too, the favor bestowed on me, those who were the acknowledged pillars, James, Cephas, and John, gave Barnabas and me the handclasp of fellowship, signifying that we should go to the Gentiles as they to the Jews. The only stipulation was that we should be mindful of the poor—the one thing that I was making every effort to do (Galatians 2:7.9-10).

2a. Keeping the flock together. From the above Bible passages which narrate a bit of early Church history, it is clear that Christ wants "men of authority" in His Church. The bond which keeps the Church together is, of course, primarily love. That is why authority should be exercised in love, and obedience to that authority exercised in the same way, in love. Christ intended His authority to teach, rule, and sanctify the Church in the Twelve Apostles; He also singled Peter out and gave him the keys of the Kingdom and the task to shepherd the flock in perfect unity. (See Chapters 27 and 33.)

We learn from the above Bible passages how the Apostles tried to keep the flock of Jesus Christ together. Paul kept constant contact with the body of the Apostles.

2b. Hopefully moving. With larger communities (Eastern Orthodox—Anglican—Protestant Churches) separated from full communion with the Catholic Church, we are not the Church as Christ wants her to be. A divided Church, as it is now, is sinful. It does not make sense to blame one another for these divisions. All of us are guilty (see Chapter 35).

A hopeful sign in our time is that there is a groping toward unity. There is something going on that we call an "ecumenical movement." Separated Churches have had their "World Council of Churches" for a couple of decades already. Pope John XXIII wanted Vatican II to be "an Ecumenical Council for the whole Church." He asked that observers be delegated by Protestant and Orthodox Churches; he had them seated in St. Peter's across the aisle from the Cardinals and he established a Secretariat for Promoting Christian Unity.

Vatican II: "The daily Christian life of these [separated] brethren is nourished by their Faith in Christ and strengthened by the grace of Baptism and by hearing the word of God. This shows itself in private prayer, their meditation on the Bible, in their Christian family life, and in the worship of a community gathered together to praise God" (*Decree on Ecumenism,* no. 23). The Spirit of God works also in the separated Churches; their members are truly reborn through Baptism and truly our brothers.

We are a "pilgrim Church," sinful by our divisions, but hopefully moving to a new oneness in Christ.

2c. The best available. Dedicated to Jesus of Nazareth and the philosophy of life He stands for, you have chosen to live your Christian commitment in the Catholic tradition, the best available as you see it. True, our "separated brethren" are Christians, but they have not incorporated a few precious elements, which we believe Christ has intended for His Church. Vatican Council II states: "Nevertheless, our separated brethren, whether considered as individuals or as Communities and Churches, are not blessed with that unity which Jesus Christ wished to bestow on all those who through Him were born again into one body, and with Him quickened to newness of life. . . . For it is only through Christ's Catholic Church, which is 'the all-embracing means of salvation,' that *the fulness of the means of salvation* can be obtained. We believe that our Lord entrusted *all* the blessings of the New Covenant to the Apostolic College alone, of which Peter is the head" (*Decree on Ecumenism,* no. 3).

3a. Candor essential. We should pray "that all may be one" (John 17:21). Vatican II states that Catholics should join in prayer with their separated brethren. Such joined prayer services are a very effective means of petitioning for the grace of unity. Moreover, the Church should cooperate in the field of charity and in solving the problems of modern society. (See *Decree on Ecumenism,* no. 8.)

But the Decree wisely warns against "a false irenicism [conciliatory approach]" (no. 11). Such an approach would be "foreign to the spirit of ecumenism." When we are really trying to see things through the eyes of another, we may be tempted to be so amiable that differences are obscured or blurred. For genuine and fruitful dialogue between the divided Churches candor is as essential as mutual respect.

3b. Common worship. "As for worship in common (*communicatio in sacris*) it is not to be considered as a means to be used indiscriminately for the restoration of Christian unity. There are two main principles governing the practice of such common worship: first, the bearing witness to the unity of the Church, and second, the sharing in the means of grace. Witness to the unity of the Church *very generally* forbids common worship to Christians, but the grace to be had from it *sometimes* commends this practice. The course to be adopted . . . is to be decided by local episcopal authority" (*Decree on Ecumenism,* no. 8).

4. THINKING IT OVER

How do the above Bible passages teach you about authority in the Church? How should authority and obedience be exercised? What signs of a groping toward Christian unity do you know? How is the Spirit of God also working in separated Churches? Why did you choose to live your commitment to Christ in the Catholic tradition? Where do we find the fullness of the means of salvation? What can be done for unity among Christians? What about common worship?

5. PRAY MEDITATIVELY

The Prayer for Unity found in Chapter 32, p. 129.

6. THINGS TO DO

Read Acts 2:37-47.

38. The Communion of Saints

(Part 1)

> 1a. Father, all-powerful and ever-living God,
> we do well always and everywhere to give you thanks
> through Jesus Christ our Lord.
> In love you created man,
> in justice you condemned him,
> but in mercy you redeemed him.
> Through Christ the choirs of angels
> and all the powers of heaven
> praise and worship your glory.
> May our voices blend with theirs
> as we join in their unending hymn:
> Holy, holy, holy Lord, God of power and might,
> heaven and earth are full of your glory.
> Hosanna in the highest (Preface to the Eucharistic Prayer).
>
> 1b. In union with the whole Church
> we honor Mary,
> the ever-virgin mother of Jesus Christ our Lord and God.
> We honor Joseph, her husband,
> the apostles and martyrs
> Peter and Paul, Andrew,
> and all the saints.
> May their merits and prayers
> gain us your constant help and protection (From the Roman Canon).

The Feast of All Saints is November 1.

> 1c. Remember, Lord, those who have died
> and have gone before us marked with the sign of faith. . . .
> May these, and all who sleep in Christ,
> find in your presence
> light, happiness, and peace (From the Roman Canon).

All Souls' Day is November 2.

2a. Helping one another. There is a union among the people of God on this earth because we are all brothers and sisters in Christ. We can help one another by our prayers and good works.

2b. Cleaving together. When the Lord comes in His Majesty, and all the angels with Him, death will be destroyed and all things will be subject to Him. This will be discussed more extensively in Chapter 67.

Meanwhile some are pilgrims here on earth. Some have left this life and are being purified. (See Chapter 66.) Others are in glory, beholding God clearly, as He is.

But in various ways and degrees we all partake in the same love for God and neighbor, and all sing the same hymn of glory to our God. (See nos. 1a and 1b.) For all who belong to Christ, having His Spirit, form one Church and cleave together in Him. Therefore, the union of the wayfarers with the brethren who have gone to sleep in the peace of Christ is not in the least interrupted. Meaningfully, the Church celebrates their days of death as the "birthdays" of those who gave an heroic example of virtue!

By reason of the fact that those in heaven are more closely united with Christ, they establish the whole Church more firmly in holiness, lend nobility to the worship which the Church offers on earth to God and do not cease to intercede with the Father for us.

2c. Our deceased. Very much aware of the bonds linking the whole Mystical Body of Christ (Chapter 32), the pilgrim Church cultivates with great piety the memory of the dead. Because it is "a holy and pious thought" to make "atonement for the dead that they might be freed from . . . sin" (2 Maccabees 12:45-46), we offer prayers for our deceased. (See no. 1c.)

3. With common rejoicing. It is supremely fitting that we love the friends and fellow heirs of Jesus Christ, who are also our brothers. We should invoke them and have recourse to their prayers, their power and help in obtaining benefits from God.

Our union with the Church in heaven is put into effect in its noblest manner when with common rejoicing we celebrate together the praise of the divine Majesty. This is especially the case in celebrating the Eucharistic Sacrifice. Be conscious of this as often as you participate at it. (See Vatican II: *Constitution on the Church* nos. 49 and 50.)

4. THINKING IT OVER

Do you pray regularly for your parents, brothers and sisters, your teachers, confessor, parish priest, bishop, and the Holy Father? Who is your patron saint and what you know about him? Who is the patron saint of your parish and your school? How should you honor the saints?

5. PRAY MEDITATIVELY

For ourselves, too, we ask
some share in the fellowship of your apostles and martyrs,
with John the Baptist, Stephen, Matthias, Barnabas,
and all the saints.

Though we are sinners,
we trust in your mercy and love
Do not consider what we truly deserve,
but grant us your forgiveness.

(From the Roman Canon)

6. THINGS TO DO

Read: the Mass for the Feast of All Saints, November 1; the Mass for All Souls' day, November 2.

39. The Communion of Saints

(Part 2)

Mary, Mother of the Redeemer and Our Mother

1. Thereupon Mary set out, proceeding in haste into the hill country to a town of Judah, where she entered Zechariah's house and greeted Elizabeth. When Elizabeth heard Mary's greeting, the baby leapt in her womb. Elizabeth was filled with the Holy Spirit and cried out in a loud voice: "Blest are you among women and blest is the fruit of your womb. But who am I that the mother of my Lord should come to me? The moment your greeting sounded in my ears, the baby leapt in my womb for joy. Blest is she who trusted that the Lord's words to her would be fulfilled" (Luke 1:39-45).

2a. The honor of our people. The most splendid of all saints is the Mother of the Redeemer, the Blessed Virgin Mary. She was taken up into heaven soul and body and is Queen of Heaven.

Mary stood close to the Cross of Jesus. She participated in the Sacrifice of Christ, saying "Amen," which means "So be it." That is why we also offer the Sacrifice of Christ's Body and Blood in union with Mary.

"You are the honor of our people"
(Mass of the Immaculate Conception)
Painting by Raphael (1483-1520).

2b. Loving presence. Mary is the Mother of Christ and therefore also the Mother of all who have put on Christ by Faith and Baptism: all Christians.

If a mother is taken to the hospital, the whole family feels lost and uncomfortable. Take Mary out of Christian doctrine and, in a way, the same thing would happen! She is indeed Mother most amiable, help of Christians.

Just as Christ realizes His Resurrection among us through His strong and efficient presence in the life of the world, so also is Mary present with her loving care, praying for us "now and at the hour of our death." It is true that the risen Christ and Mary have been "taken up into heaven"—the real Adam and Eve of Mankind. But we should not consider them to be far away, as if "heaven" were a big theater somewhere filled with souls—dim ghosts moving smoothly and silently—with only two seats occupied "bodily" by Christ and Mary!

We cannot visualize "heaven" with our concepts of space and time. (See Chapter 66.) The closeness of Christ and Mary can be experienced by speaking to them in prayer. The same can be said of other deceased. Some great Saints and good people are more intimately "present" than others. This is the Communion of Saints.

2c. Statues. Mary is an example for all of us. She is all-pure and never once was touched by the stain of sin. She is "the glory of Jerusalem," "the joy of Israel" and "the honor of our people" (see Mass of December 8). Great was Mary's Faith and self-surrender, though living the life of a simple rural housewife. She followed Christ to the very foot of the Cross.

Statues of Mary usually symbolize her virtues, her role, and her glory, e.g., her purity: Mary, the Virgin, crushing the head of Satan; her role as Mother: Mary carrying the Child Jesus or kneeling before the manger; her greatness as the sorrowful Mother: Mary standing at the foot of the Cross or holding on her lap the body of her Son; her glory as Queen of Angels and of All Saints: Mary with a gleaming crown on her head.

"By her maternal charity, Mary cares for the brethren of her Son who still journey on earth surrounded by dangers and difficulties until they are led to their happy homeland. Therefore, the Blessed Virgin is invoked by the Church under the titles of Advocate, Auxiliatrix, Adjutrix and Mediatrix. These, however, are to be so understood that they neither take away from nor add anything to the dignity and efficacy of Christ the one Mediator" (*Constitution on the Church,* no. 62).

3a. Continuing the tradition. In Luke's record, the angel honored Mary by saying: "Rejoice, O highly favored daughter! The Lord is with you." Filled with the Holy Spirit, Elizabeth said: "Blest are you among women and blest is the fruit of your womb." (See Luke, chapter 1.)

Describing the birth of our Lord, Luke records how beloved and esteemed Mary was in the early Christian communities. Christians of all ages have continued this beautiful tradition. They honor Mary when they pray the first part of the "Hail Mary." In the second part of the "Hail Mary," they ask Mary to help them.

Moreover, the people of God honor Mary by praying, three times a day, the "Angelus" (at Eastern time: *Regina Coeli*), by praying the Rosary, especially during the month of October, and by celebrating her feast days. They also go on pilgrimages to places made holy by our Lady. Well-known shrines of Mary are: Lourdes, Fatima, and Guadalupe. The grotto at Lourdes or the statue of Mary at some well-known shrine is often reproduced in the gardens of churches and convents, which become local centers of devotion to the Blessed Virgin. (For the authority possessed by private revelations, see Chapter 34, no. 2e.)

Pilgrims at Lourdes, France.

3b. An example. A good Christian will try to follow the example of the Blessed Mother in her purity, her faith, her devotion to duty, as described in no. 2c.

4. THINKING IT OVER

Who alone remained free from original sin? (See Chapter 14.) Why is Mary truly the Mother of God? (See Chapter 18.)

Why is Mary called "The Blessed Virgin"? (See Chapter 18.) Through Whose merits did Mary receive the fullness of grace? (See Chapter 18.) Mention the prayers in your Missal which we say in union with Mary. Why is Mary our Mother? Are the titles given to Mary all clear to you? Do you have a tasteful picture of our Lady in your home? Which titles of Mary are symbolized by statues of her in your church? How can Mary help us? How does Mary give an example to us? What are some Christian customs of honoring Mary?

5. READ ATTENTIVELY

The Angelus. (This is a prayer all Christians should know by heart.) See p. 291.

6. PRAY MEDITATIVELY

I. Praise

    Salutation of the Angel:

        Hail, Mary, full of grace! the Lord is with thee;

    Salutation of Elizabeth:

        Blessed art thou among women, and blessed is the fruit of thy womb, Jesus.

II. Request

        Holy Mary, Mother of God, pray for us sinners now and at the hour of our death. Amen.

Meditatively, pray Luke 1:46-55. It is a Hebrew song. "His servant in her lowliness" is "daughter Zion," who is Israel, God's people. Figuratively, Luke has put this song into the mouth of Mary. As a devout Jewess, Mary may have sung it when she took part in worship service. Hence, this song reflects beautifully

Mary's life of prayer. When you pray it, remember that you are God's "servant," His chosen people, and that God has done "great things" for you!

7. THINGS TO DO

Read: Masses of Our Lady of Guadalupe (December 12) and of Our Lady of Lourdes (February 11).

If circumstances permit, try to arrange for one of your parish organizations to show a series of slides about famous shrines.

Consider this book as a meditation book.

If you have time, read *The Song of Bernadette* by Weiszmantel.

"If anyone thirst, let him come to me; let him drink who believes in me."
(John 7:37).

CHRISTIAN INITIATION

Exploring how the early Church initiated (introduced-incorporated) new members into the community of Faith, we learn that the oldest traditions followed the sequence of Baptism-Confirmation-Eucharist. The Churches of the Eastern tradition have maintained this sequence, when they initiate new members into the Christian community. The Western Church has changed this sequence of rites: Children are baptized as babies. At the age of six or seven they take part in the Eucharist and only later they are confirmed by the bishop.

Suggestions. *Theologians propose to restore that sequence of Baptism-Confirmation-Eucharist and suggest various procedures.*

(1) Since infant Baptism has been a general custom from the 3rd Century on, many want to maintain this practice and suggest that the baptizing priest be authorized to confirm infants and give them the Eucharist all at the same time.

(2) Others suggest waiting to confer the three initiation rites till children are old enough to make their own decision. It is beyond the scope of this book to go into the details of this problem.

We will discuss first the initiation rites of Baptism and Confirmation (chapters 40-42), and later the Eucharist (chapters 47-49).

40. Baptism

(Part 1)

"The water I give shall become a fountain . . . leaping up to provide eternal life" (**John 4:14**).

The framework. Christianity is deeply rooted in Judaism. It originated in the homeland of Israel. Its Founder and His early co-workers were Jews. Its first theologians explained Christianity mainly with concepts from the Hebrew Bible (the Old Testament). In order to understand the Christian initiation rites of Baptism and Confirmation, we should first have a look at the frame-work in which they came into being, namely, the Jewish religion and society.

> 1. *Thus the word of the Lord came to me: Son of man, make known to Jerusalem her abominations. Thus says the Lord God to Jerusalem: By origin and birth you are of the land of Canaan; your father was an Amorite and your mother a Hittite. As for your birth, the day you were born your navel cord was not cut; you were neither washed with water nor anointed, nor were you rubbed with salt, nor swathed in swaddling clothes. No one looked on you with pity or compassion to do any of these things for you. Rather, you were thrown out on the ground as something loathsome, the day you were born.*
>
> *Then I passed by and saw you weltering in your blood. I said to you: Live in your blood and grow like a plant in the field. You grew and developed, you came to the age of puberty; your breasts were formed, your hair had grown, but you were still stark naked. Again I passed by you and saw that you were now old enough for love. So I spread the corner of my cloak over you to cover your nakedness; I swore an oath to you and entered into a covenant with you; you became mine, says the Lord God. Then I bathed you with water, washed away your blood, and anointed you with oil. I clothed you with an embroidered gown, put sandals of fine leather on your feet; I gave you a fine linen sash and silk robes to wear. I adorned you with jewelry: I put bracelets on your arms, a necklace about your neck, a ring in your nose, pendants in your ears, and a glorious diadem upon your head. Thus you were adorned with gold and silver; your garments were of fine linen, silk, and embroidered cloth. Fine flour, honey, and oil were your food. You were exceedingly beautiful, with the dignity of a queen. You were renowned among the nations for your beauty, perfect as it was, because of my splendor which I had bestowed on you, says the Lord God (Ezekiel 16:1-14).*

Bathing with water. The Bible passage tells about the Jewish custom of bathing the bride before the wedding ceremony. Jerusalem (the capital) stands for the chosen people, whom the writer considers as living in a Covenant (sacred partnership) with Almighty God. In Ezekiel, this partnership has marital overtones. Hence, Jerusalem is God's spouse. Figuratively, God says: "I bathed you with water . . . anointed you with oil . . . I clothed you with an embroidered gown . . . put a glorious diadem on your head." Think here of the Christian initiation rites, which will be discussed later and of Christians, through Baptism and Confirmation, living with God in a sacred partnership (Covenant), which has marital overtones!

Read Ephesians 5:25-29 (especially v. 26) and relate it to the above Bible passage!

2. A newborn child. From non-Biblical documents we know that at the beginning of the Christian era the Jews practiced a baptism for the proselytes (converts to Judaism). Actually, this initiation rite consisted of three parts: the circumcision, the bath of water, and a sacrifice. Since in the diaspora (dispersion— territories outside the Jewish homeland) the sacrifice was substituted for by an offering of money and the circumcision referred only to the males, often the bath of water remained the only rite of initiation into the Jewish religion.

At this Jewish baptism, disciples of the scribes recited the commandments, which were repeated by the candidate. The Talmud (the body of Jewish law) states: "A proselyte, who joins the Jewish religion, is like a newborn child." Think here of the baptized Christian as "begotten of water and Spirit!" Notice: Water was not only used for cleansing. Water was seen as life-giving. As such it was a very clear symbol in a land surrounded by deserts. (See picture with text of John 4:14.)

Read John 3:1-5 and relate it to the above statement from the Talmud.

3. "This is the rite you shall perform in consecrating them as my priests. Procure a young bull and two unblemished rams. Aaron and his sons you shall also bring to the entrance of the meeting tent, and there wash them with water. Take the vestments and clothe Aaron with the tunic, the robe of the ephod, the ephod itself, and the breastpiece, fastening the embroidered belt of the ephod around him. Put the miter on his head, the sacred diadem on the miter. Then take the anointing oil and anoint him with it, pouring it on his head" (Exodus 29:1.4-7).

Consecrating priests. This Bible passage tells us about the rites used to consecrate the Jewish priests. Pay attention to the following details: Wash them with water . . . clothe them with a robe . . . put on them the symbols of priestly dignity (ephod, breastpiece, embroidered belt, miter) . . . anoint them. At Baptism similar rites are used to signify that Christians share the royal priesthood of our Lord.

Read: 1 Peter 2:9-10 and relate it to the above Bible passage!

4. When they heard this, they were deeply shaken. They asked Peter and the other apostles, "What are we to do, brothers?" Peter answered: "You must reform and be baptized, each one of you, in the name of Jesus Christ, that your sins may be forgiven; then you will receive the gift of the Holy Spirit. It was to you and your children that the promise was made, and to all those still far off whom the Lord our God calls."

In support of his testimony he used many other arguments, and kept urging, "Save yourselves from this generation which has gone astray." Those who accepted his message were baptized; some three thousand were added that day (Acts 2:37-41).

A certain man named Simon had been practicing magic in the town and holding the Samaritans spellbound. He passed himself off as someone of great importance. People from every rank of society were paying attention to him. "He is the power of the great God," they said. Those who followed him had been under the spell of his magic over a long period; but once they began to believe in the good news that Philip preached about the kingdom of God and the name of Jesus Christ, men and women alike accepted baptism. Even Simon believed. He was baptized like the rest and became a devoted follower of Philip. He watched the signs and the great miracles as they occurred, and was quite carried away (Acts 8:9-13).

Sealing the budding Faith. The above Bible passages tell us about what is supposed to go ahead of Baptism. It is the preaching of the good news of our Lord (the Gospel). Consequently Faith and penance follow. (You must reform . . . those who accepted the message . . . they began to believe the good news.) The budding Faith and penance are sealed and perfected by Baptism.

5. Later Jesus, coming from Galilee, appeared before John at the Jordan to be baptized by him. John tried to refuse him with the protest, "I should be baptized by you, yet you come to me!" Jesus answered: "Give in for now. We must do this if we would fulfill all of God's demands." So John gave in. After Jesus was baptized, he came directly out of the water. Suddenly the sky opened and he saw the Spirit of God descend like a dove and hover over him. With that, a voice from the heavens said, "This is my beloved Son. My favor rests on him" (Matthew 3:13-17).

What, then, are we to say? "Let us continue in sin that grace may abound?" Certainly not! How can we who died to sin go on living in it? Are you not aware that we who were baptized into Christ Jesus were baptized into his death? Through baptism into his death we were buried with him, so that, just as Christ was raised from the dead by the glory of the Father, we too might live a new life. If we have been united with him through likeness to his death, so shall we be through a like resurrection (Romans 6:1-5).

Immersion-infusion. Besides the baptism of proselytes (no. 2, above) and Jewish customs as described in nos. 1 and 3, we know also initiation rites of the baptismal sects during the time of Jesus and the Apostles. Known are the Essenes and the congregation of Qumran. (See Chapter 16, no. 2.)

The baptism of John (no. 5) and that of the early Church must be understood in this framework. Whether John's baptism consisted of a total immersion or whether the candidate stood in the Jordan with John pouring water over him is unknown. The same must be said about Baptism in the early Church. Acts 2:41 tells about 3000 people baptized at Pentecost and Acts 16:30 about the Baptism of the jailer and his household "at a late hour of the night" and in the jail house! In these cases "immersion" must be excluded.

However, we assume that as a rule the early Church baptized by some form of descending into the water and rising from it. Only in the 4th Century was Paul's comparison of Baptism (no. 5), described as being buried with Christ (in the tomb of water) and raised with Him to a new life, used as a reason to baptize by total immersion.

In the Western Church, Baptism by immersion was probably customary, at least for children, up to the 15th Century. Later on, Baptism by infusion became the lawful custom. The new baptismal rite of 1970 provides the option for either immersion or infusion for the Baptism of children.

6. *Husbands, love your wives, as Christ loved the church. He gave himself up for her to make her holy, purifying her in the bath of water by the power of the word (Ephesians 5:25-26).*

Each one of you is a son of God because of your faith in Christ Jesus. Jesus. All of you who have been baptized into Christ have clothed yourselves with him. There does not exist among you Jew or Greek, slave of freeman, male or female. All are one in Christ Jesus. Furthermore, if you belong to Christ you are the descendants of Abraham, which means you inherit all that was promised (Galatians 3:26-29).

A signifying word. In number 1, we have explained the bath of water (Baptism) as the ritual bath through which Christians are initiated into that sacred partnership (Covenant) with God, which has such clear marital overtones in Scripture. Christians are related to God in an intimate love that may be compared with the love of husband and wife in marriage.

Here we want to discuss the addition: "by the power of the word" (no. 6). There is no doubt that a signifying word belonged to the rite of Baptism (bath-immersion-infusion). There were so many baptisms: The baptism of the proselytes (no. 2), baptism as initiation to sects (no. 5), the baptism of John (no. 5). Somehow it should be expressed with whom one was united by Baptism.

Into Christ. The Bible tells us that Christians were baptized into Christ (no. 6). They belong to Christ. The Acts of the Apostles (2:38; 8:16; 10:48; 19:5) tells us of baptizing "in the name [person] of Jesus"—a better translation would be "*into* the name [person] of Jesus." Only in the 4th Century did the formula "In the name of the Father, and of the Son, and of the Holy Spirit" become customary.

Although the Church of the Apostolic era did not know the trinitarian baptismal "word" (in the name of the Father . . .) but only the Christological one (into the name of Jesus Christ), this does not exclude the fact that every Christian Baptism is actually a Baptism into communion with the Father, the Son, and the Holy Spirit. Faith in Jesus is implicitly Faith in the Father: "He who acknowledges the Son can claim the Father as well" (1 John 2:23). And the early Church had a firm belief that through Baptism one was sealed with the Holy Spirit. "He saved us through the Baptism of new birth and renewal of the Holy Spirit." (See Titus 3:5-7.)

7. Existential reading. The above Bible quotations on Baptism are so rich that you should read them more than once "existentially," in other words, relating them to your own existence or life situation, thanking God and renewing the commitment of your Baptism.

8. THINKING IT OVER

From Ephesians 5:25-29, explain how Paul sees a baptized person's relationship with God. To what Jewish custom as in Ezekiel 16:1-14 does Paul refer in Ephesians 5:25-29? (No. 1.) To what Jewish custom would you relate Baptism as mentioned in John 3:1-5? (No. 2.) What Jewish background do you see in "the royal priesthood" of God's people through Faith and Baptism? (See 1 Peter 2:9-10 and no. 3.) What were the conditions for being baptized in the early Church? (No. 4.) How did the Church baptize during the ages of her existence? (No. 5.) What baptisms were known at the beginning of the Christian era? Explain the history and meaning of the formula that accompanies the act of baptizing! (No. 6.)

9. THINGS TO DO

Write down the symbols, used in the Bible passages of this chapter, to explain man's special relttionship with God through Baptism.

41. Baptism

(Part 2)

1. Now in Caesarea there was a centurion named Cornelius, of the Roman cohort Italica, who was religious and God-fearing. The same was true of his whole household. He was in the habit of giving generously to the people and he constantly prayed to God.

The following day, he arrived in Caesarea. Cornelius, who was expecting them, had called in his relatives and close friends.

Peter had not finished these words when the Holy Spirit descended upon all who were listening to Peter's message.

Peter put the question at that point, "What can stop these people who have received the Holy Spirit, even as we have, from being baptized with water?" So he gave orders that they be baptized in the name of Jesus Christ. After this was done, they asked him to stay with them for a few days (Acts 10:1-2. 24. 44. 47-48).

2a. The setting. In the previous chapter, we discussed Baptism from the setting in which it came into being, namely, Judaism, the religion and culture of Jesus of Nazareth. We studied how Baptism results in a special relationship of man to God, as described in the Bible with various figures of speech.

Moreover, we saw how the early Church baptized: First the anouncement of the Gospel . . . consequently Faith and penance, which were sealed and perfected by Baptism "into the name [person] of Jesus Christ." Hence, we are called Christians, which means people related in a special way to Christ. Later, "into the name of Jesus" was elaborated and became "in[to] the name of the Father, and of the Son, and of the Holy Spirit."

2b. Baptism of children. Up till now, we have studied the Baptism of adults. What about the Baptism of children, who cannot yet listen to the Gospel, nor yet profess Faith, neither be sorry for sins? There are only indirect indications that the early Church baptized children. It seems that they were children who were already living when their parents converted to Christianity. They were baptized with them. (See no. 1.) However, from the 3rd Century on, the Baptism of children has been the normal practice of the Church.

2c. In the Faith of the Church. How to explain the Baptism of children? First, we should observe that the doctrine of original sin did not yet play an important role when the Baptism of children was generally accepted in the 3rd Century. (See Chapters 13 and 14.) Little children are innocent. God loves them. Christ died for all. Read Mark 10:13-16 and Matthew 18:1-4. Parents whose children die before Baptism for some reason or other should not worry.

The reason why children are baptized is not that some "stain" has to be washed away. The **new** *Rite of Baptism for Children* mentions "original sin" once, **not** as "a stain to be washed away" nor as "guilt to be remitted," but as "some situation to be set free from." The priest says: "We pray—set him (her) free from original sin." (See Ch. 14, no. 2.) Theologians tell us that we should see Baptism for children mainly as a rite of initiation (incorporation) into the Church of God. Faith and penance are required from adults. For children the Faith of parents and the Church, the environment in which the child will grow up, is sufficient. "Children are baptized in the Faith of the Church." *(Rite of Baptism of Children)*

2d. Reasonable chance. From the above explanation it becomes clear that the Church should baptize children only if there exists a reasonable chance that these children will grow to a personal attitude of Faith in a Christian life situation. That is why the baptizing minister (priest, deacon) addresses the parents as follows: "You have asked to have your child baptized. In doing so you are accepting the responsibility of training him (her) in the practice of the faith. It will be your duty to bring him (her) up to keep God's commandments as Christ taught us, by loving God and neighbor. Do you clearly understand what you are undertaking?"

The parents answer: "We do."

Then the minister turns to the godparents: "Are you ready to help the parents of this child in their duty as Christian parents?"

The godparents answer: "We are."

Moreover, the minister speak to the parents and godparents: "If your faith makes you ready to accept this responsibility, renew now the vows of your own Baptism. Reject sin; profess your faith in Christ Jesus." Parents and godparents renew the commitment of their own Baptism.

Then the minister baptizes the child saying: "N., I baptize you in the name of the Father *(He immerses the child or pours water upon it)* and of the Son and of the Holy Spirit."

It should be mentioned that everybody, even an unbeliever, can baptize a child in danger of death, as long as he is willing to do what Christ and the Church want to be done in such a case.

2e. Ancient customs. The ceremonies which surround Baptism should be seen as somehow related to ancient customs. (See Chapter 40, nos. 1 and 3.) We mention the anointing with chrism (oil) and the words: "God the Father of our Lord Jesus Christ has freed you from sin, given you a new birth by water and the Holy Spirit, and welcomed you into his holy people. He now anoints you with the chrism of salvation. As Christ was anointed Priest, Prophet, and King, so may you live as a member of his body, sharing everlasting life."

We also mention the clothing with the white garment: "N., you have become a new creation, and have clothed yourself in Christ. See in this white garment the outward sign of your Christian dignity. With your family and friends to help you by word and example, bring that dignity unstained into the everlasting life of heaven."

Finally, one of the family lights the child's candle from the Easter candle. The minister says: "Parents and godparents, this light is entrusted to you to be kept burning brightly. This child of yours has been enlightened by Christ. He (she) is to walk always as a child of light. May he (she) keep the flame of faith alive in his (her) heart."

"May he keep the flame of faith alive in his heart" (The Rite of Baptism).

2f. Joining the Church. To enrich the relationship between godparents and godchildren, it is a good practice for godchildren to remember their godparents on special occasions (at Christmas, for example), to let them know when they are going to receive their first Holy Communion and Confirmation, when they graduate from school, and when they plan to marry.

It is a praiseworthy custom for parents or godparents to prepare special baptismal clothing and also to furnish the baptismal candle for the child, to be used again for First Communion and the celebration of anniversaries.

A separated brother who has with certainty been validly baptized may join full communion in the Catholic Church merely by a profession of Faith. Because it is often difficult for a priest to determine whether or not such a previous Baptism was real (some denominations, for example, just sprinkle the baptismal candidates), persons joining the Catholic Church are often encouraged to be baptized again. The baptizing priest will then say: "If you are not baptized, I baptize you . . ."

3. Christian education. Parents and godparents should pay attention to the words addressed to them at the Baptism of a child. The problems of Christian education are serious in our changing world. There are no ready-made answers, but the serious duty to maintain a deeply Christian atmosphere in the home may not be taken lightly.

4. THINKING IT OVER

What are the prerequisites for an adult Baptism? How to explain the Baptism of children, who cannot meet these prerequisites? What are the conditions for the Baptism of children as far as the parents are concerned? What do godparents have to do with the Baptism of children? What about children who died before Baptism? Describe the meaning of some ceremonies that surround Baptism and relate them to ancient customs mentioned in Chapter 40, nos. 1 and 3.

5. READ ATTENTIVELY

How would you administer an emergency Baptism?

Pour the water on the head (if that is not possible, on another part of the body) while saying: "I baptize you in the name of the Father, and of the Son, and of the Holy Spirit."

6. PRAY MEDITATIVELY

"O God, you have made the different nations one in professing your name. Let those who have been born again through Baptism be of one mind in Faith and holiness" *(Prayer from the Mass of Thursday in Easter week).*

7. THINGS TO DO

Read: Acts 8:26-39; John 4:1-45.

Chapters 25, 28, 40 and 41 in this book describe your rebirth in Christ. This reading will embrace the "heart of the matter." Take your time for a "summing-up" meditation upon it.

42. Confirmation

1a. But once they began to believe in the good news that Philip preached about the kingdom of God and the name of Jesus Christ, men and women alike accepted baptism. Even Simon believed. He was baptized like the rest and became a devoted follower of Philip. He watched the signs and the great miracles as they occurred, and was quite carried away.

When the apostles in Jerusalem heard that Samaria had accepted the word of God, they sent Peter and John to them. The two went down to these people and prayed that they might receive the Holy Spirit. It had not as yet come down upon any of them since they had only been baptized in the name of the Lord Jesus. The pair upon arriving imposed hands on them and they received the Holy Spirit (Acts 8:12-17).

1b. While Apollos was in Corinth, Paul passed through the interior of the country and came to Ephesus. There he found some disciples to whom he put the question, "Did you receive the Holy Spirit when you became believers?" They answered, "We have not so much as heard that there is a Holy Spirit." "Well, how were you baptized?" he persisted. They replied, "With the baptism of John." Paul then explained, "John's baptism was a baptism of repentance. He used to tell the people about the one who would come after him in whom they were to believe—that is, Jesus." When they heard this, they were baptized in the name of the Lord Jesus. As Paul laid his hands on them, the Holy Spirit came down on them and they began to speak in tongues and to utter prophecies. There were in the company about twelve men in all (Acts 19:1-7).

2a. Subsequent stage. We have discussed Baptism as the initiation (incorporation) into the people of God that considers itself as living with God in a sacred partnership (Covenant). But Baptism, the initiation rite as the Western Church knows it now, lacks its subsequent stage, which is called Confirmation. During the first eleven centuries, Confirmation, along with Baptism, was part of the solemn rite of initiation celebrated at the Easter and Pentecost vigils.

The Churches of Eastern tradition still see Baptism, Confirmation and the Eucharist as three parts of the one initiation into

God's people. Hence, all three of them are given to the infant. Only toward the 11th Century does Confirmation take on a liturgy of its own in the Western tradition, where the bishop is the ordinary minister. However, though separated by time and rite, Confirmation perfects (consummates-completes) Baptism and as such it is part of Christian initiation.

We might say that the Western Church has divided the roles. The priest performs the first stage of initiation (Baptism), the bishop, as chief shepherd of the flock, performs the subsequent stage (Confirmation). This is a regulation of the Church. When baptizing a person in danger of death, or baptizing adults, the priest performs both stages of initiation, administering both Baptism and Confirmation. When already baptized adults join the church the Church by their confession of Faith, the priest may confirm them, during the same ceremony.

To stress the fact that Confirmation is in a sense the continuation of the baptismal rites, candidates renew their baptismal promises before they kneel before the bishop, who lays hands on them.

2b. Guided by the Spirit. Considering Christian initiation, we observe that the communication of the Spirit is a very important element in these rites. In Chapters 27-29, we discussed the presence of the Spirit with God's people. Reading "The Acts of the Apostles," one gets the impression that this presence was in high esteem in the early Church (see no. 1a). God's people, baptized "in[to] the name [person] of Jesus" and as such belonging to Him, is guided (filled-animated) by the Spirit.

2c. Symbols. Confirmation stresses this guidance of the Spirit. The symbols used to communicate the Spirit are the imposition of hands (see no. 1b) and the anointing with chrism (oil, consecrated by the bishop), accompanied by the words of the bishop: "N. . . . receive the seal of the Holy Spirit, the Gift of the Father."

It seems that the first symbol (the imposition of hands) is the oldest one (see no. 1b). The anointing with chrism was added later. Its symbolism is rooted in customs of Hebrew culture. (See Chapter 40, nos. 1 and 3 and 1 Samuel 16:13.) Kings and priests and prophets were anointed for their sacred duties. The Spirit of the Lord was upon them. (Read also Isaiah 61:1-3.) The Spirit of the Lord was upon our Savior. He was figuratively "anointed" for His supreme task. His name is Christ, i.e., the "Anointed." From this setting we should understand the symbolism of anointing at Confirmation. You are anointed for your sacred duty of being a Christian in this word—courageous, willing, and ready to be a witness of Christ.

The Church suggests that the holy oils of Confirmation should be perfumed as a reminder that Christians are "the good scent of Christ everywhere."

Finally, the bishop prays: "God our Father, you sent the Holy Spirit upon the apostles and through them and their successors you give the Spirit to your people May the faith and love that spread everywhere when the gospel was first preached continue to grow through the hearts of all who believe."

3. Meditate. Baptized into Christ and as such "clothed with him" (Galatians 3:27), moreover guided by the Spirit, stressed so much when the bishop fully initiated you into the community of the faithful (Confirmation), you should meditate on what this means for you by prayerfully reading Paul's words in Romans 8:1-13. See your Bible!

4. THINKING IT OVER

Explain the relation between Baptism and Confirmation! How do the Churches of Eastern tradition handle the fact that Baptism, Confirmation, and the Eucharist are actually three parts of the one Christian initiation? How is the unity of Baptism and Confirmation expressed in the Confirmation rite of the Western Church? Make some remarks on how Christian tradition sees the presence of the Spirit in God's people (Chapters 27-29). Name the symbols used in Confirmation to communicate the Spirit.

Explain the symbolism of anointing. What does all of this mean to you according to Paul in Romans 8:1-13?

5. PRAY MEDITATIVELY

The same prayer as in Chapter 27, no. 5, p. 108.

6. THINGS TO DO

Read John 16.

43. Christian Virtues

Faith, Hope, and Love

1. *As he drew near Jericho a blind man sat at the side of the road begging. Hearing a crowd go by the man asked, "What is that?" The answer came that Jesus of Nazareth was passing by. He shouted out, "Jesus, Son of David, have pity on me!" Those in the lead sternly ordered him to be quiet, but he cried out all the more, "Son of David, have pity on me!" Jesus halted and ordered that he be brought to him. When he had come close, Jesus asked him, "What do you want me to do for you?" "Lord," he answered, "I want to see." Jesus said to him, "Receive your sight. Your faith has healed you." At that very moment he was given his sight and began to follow him, giving God the glory. All the people witnessed it and they too gave praise to God (Luke 18:35-43).*

2a. Inspired psychology. Early theologians describe the new life of a Christian and discover in it certain dispositions. Their observations could be called a kind of inspired psychology of what our new life in Christ is all about. In human life psychologists discover certain dispositions, habits, qualities, aptitudes, abilities: for example, an aptitude for business, language, music, or a more than usual disposition for communicating with others. In similar fashion, our new life in Christ is qualified by a number of new dispositions or abilities, which are called "virtues."

We mention the "theological virtues": Faith, Hope, and Charity (Love), which have God (*Theos* in Greek) as their object. Then there are the "seven gifts of the Holy Spirit": wisdom, understanding, counsel, fortitude, knowledge, piety, and fear of the

Lord (see Isaiah 11:2-3). Some of the effects of these gifts in us are called the "fruits of the Holy Spirit": charity, joy, peace, patience, benignity, goodness, long-suffering, mildness, faith, modesty, continency, chastity. All these virtues are so many new dispositions, given with your new life in Christ.

2b. Faith. Of special importance are the three theological virtues. Faith, sealed and perfected by Baptism, may be called a new consciousness or a new awareness. Theologians of the early Church described it with the aid of the miracle story above (no. 1). Faith is a new awareness, which makes us experience things in a different way. Abraham had this experience (see Chapter 1); ours is similar and sealed with the sacred sign of Baptism.

"I want to see" (Luke 18:41).

2c. Hope. Another disposition is Hope, "which draws authority from a hidden vision" (Gabriel Marcel). Hope is given to man with his rebirth from water and the Spirit. For the man without hope, time is closed. Life is a pure repetition. He chooses to remain in the dark and so avoid risk. The person who hopes, however, is like an inventor, an artist, or a discoverer. Hope allows a man to pierce through to a real future, to something new.

2d. Special dimension. The Marxist philosopher Ernst Bloch defines hope as "the pioneer existence which we humans lead on the foremost frontier of the world-process." For Bloch the Marxist, there is no God. The world is sufficient for itself. Christians should share that same Hope with all their fellowmen, but for them it has a special dimension, namely, the Ultimate Reality, God. Their Hope is the one the Christian philosopher Gabriel Marcel describes. Marcel sees Hope somehow linked with God.

He writes: "Hope and Faith are intimately connected. Faith in the Absolute Thou (God) makes me look upon despair as a kind of betrayal."

2e. Challenge to search. Hope, as Marcel describes it, is the Hope we find on almost every page of the Bible. The Hebrews suffered one political disaster after another. Yet they never lost that tenacious expectation and hope in a future! A Messiah will come to restore human dignity for them. A savior will come, but . . . sent by God! As such, reading about this experience of the Hebrews in your Bible is so valuable. While reading, you feel the challenge to search for meaning in your own situation, never to give up, to hope always.

Like Bloch, we Christians have Hope in this life. We accept full responsibility for a better world and we do this in constant dialogue with all men, always trying to achieve the best possible and to realize ourselves ever more (see Chapter 37, no. 3b). But our Hope has a Christian dimension, it is Hope with the help of God and with an outlook on a hereafter, where full self-realization is promised (see Chapter 45, no. 2c: the sign value of celibacy).

2f. Love. The virtue of Charity (Love) is a gift of God that enables you to love God above all things with your whole heart and soul. God is worthy to be loved. He is all-good! God loved you first and makes you able to love Him.

> The symbol of Faith is a cross.
> The symbol of Hope is an anchor, often combined with Christ's monogram.
> The symbol of Love is a heart.

3a. Given dispositions. Nobody is able through his own power to believe, to hope, or to love God. These three Christian virtues are dispositions given with your new life in Christ.

3b. Your candle burning. At Baptism you received a lighted candle, which symbolizes the Light of Faith. You can keep your candle (Light of Faith) burning by listening to sermons, reading daily from the Bible, and further, by reading spiritual books and Catholic magazines.

Pray for an increase of Faith. It is a gift which God will not withhold if you seek and ask for it.

3c. Develop Hope. When you are in trouble, you as a Christian must not despair. You know that God is with you. Develop the virtue of Hope so that you will always place your trust in God. Follow the example of Job who was a pagan, but who hoped in God (see no. 6).

3d. Return love. Because God's love became perfectly visible in His Son Jesus Christ, you should love Christ with a fervent love. In many works of art, the open Heart of Jesus, the symbol of Divine Love, is shown. Return that Divine Love!

Every good tree bears good fruit. By their fruits you will know them. The fruits of the tree of Life (your new life in Christ) are: Faith, Hope and Love. By these fruits your fellowmen will know whether you are a real Christian or not.

4. THINKING IT OVER

What is Faith? (See Chapter 1.) With what may you compare Faith? (See Chapter 17, no. 2.) How does God reveal Himself to you? (See Chapter 3.) What is the meaning of the baptismal candle? What should you do to keep that candle burning? What religious books are there in your home? Do you have a subscription to one or more Catholic magazines or newspapers, or do you buy such literature every Sunday, if available, as you leave your parish church? Do you know the Catholic bookshop in your parish or city? How can guests in your home see that you are a Catholic? How does Ernst Bloch describe hope? Should we share it? What is Christian Hope? How does Gabriel Marcel describe Hope? Regarding Hope, why is Bible reading so valuable? How does Chapter 7, no. 3b, motivate Hope? Why must you never despair?

What is the virtue of Love? Are you by your own power able to love God? Why is God worthy to be loved? How did God's love become perfectly visible? How should you show your devotion to the Sacred Heart of Jesus? How do others know whether or not you are a good Christian?

5. PRAY MEDITATIVELY

Meditatively, apply to yourself: "We keep thanking God for all of you and we remember you in our prayers, for we constantly are mindful before our God and Father of the way you are proving your faith, and laboring in love, and showing constancy of hope in our Lord Jesus Christ" (1 Thessalonians 1:2-3).

6. THINGS TO DO

Read about Faith in John 9. Note: (a) the attitude of the parents who were unwilling to face the problem, so that they would not be disturbed in their peaceful tranquility (do you know of similar cases in your environment?); (b) the attitude of the Pharisees, unbelievers who would not see (if you know of similar people, pray for them); (c) the attitude of the blind man who cooperated with God's grace. (Follow his example!)

Read about Hope in Job 2; and about Love in 1 Corinthians 13.

44. Love of Neighbor

1. On one occasion a lawyer stood up to pose him this problem: "Teacher, what must I do to inherit everlasting life?" Jesus answered him: "What is written in the law? How do you read it?" He replied:

> *"You shall love the Lord your God*
> *with all your heart,*
> *with all your soul,*
> *with all your strength,*
> *and with all your mind;*
> *and your neighbor as yourself."*

Jesus said, "You have answered correctly. Do this and you shall live." But because he wished to justify himself he said to Jesus, "And who is my neighbor?" Jesus replied: "There was a man going down from Jerusalem to Jericho who fell prey to robbers. They stripped him, beat him, and then went off leaving him half-dead. A priest happened to be going down the same road; he saw him but continued on. Likewise there was a Levite who came the same way; he saw him and went on. But a Samaritan who was journeying along came on him and was moved to pity at the sight. He approached him and dressed his wounds, pouring in oil and wine. He then hoisted him on his own beast and brought him to an inn, where he cared for him. The next day he took out two silver pieces and gave them to the innkeeper with the request: 'Look after him, and if there is any further expense I will repay you on my way back.'

"Which of these three, in your opinion, was neighbor to the man who fell in with the robbers?" The answer came, "The one who treated him with compassion." Jesus said to him, "Then go and do the same" (Luke 10:25-37).

2a. Basic option. Love for God cannot be separated from love for your neighbor. That is what Moses taught under God's inspiration. This oneness between love of God and love of neighbor was stated again through Christ and His Apostles.

The Apostle John said that we must love God, that even though no one has ever seen God, we can love Him in our neighbor!

"If we love one another
God dwells in us,
and his love is brought to perfection in us" (1 John 4:12).

Of course nobody can be forced to love. Love is a free thing. But once you have accepted God's invitation and chosen Christianity as your way of life, your basic option is "love," and your constant quest must be: "What is the loving thing to do in this, my situation?

2b. Your enemies. In accord with Christ's teachings, we must love even our enemies: "Love your enemies, pray for your persecutors" (Matthew 5:44). Moreover, Christ's teaching on brotherly love is explained clearly in the above Bible story (no. 1). Remember, Jews did not associate with Samaritans (see John 4:9).

2c. As we forgive? If you get angry now and then, make peace with your neighbor as soon as possible. The Apostle Paul said: "The sun must not go down on your wrath" (Ephesians 4:26). And Christ Himself said to His followers: "If you bring your gift to the altar and there recall that your brother has anything against you, leave your gift at the altar, go first to be reconciled with your brother, and then come and offer your gift" (Matthew 5: 23-24).

Ch. 44   Love of Neighbor

If you are resentful, do not pray: "And forgive us our trespasses, as we forgive those who trespass against us"! You have to *mean* what you pray!

2d. Household of the Faith. There are gradations in love of our neighbor. St. Paul says: "Let us do good to all men—but especially those of the household of the faith" (Ephesians 6:10). You should especially love your parents, brothers and sisters, friends, benefactors, and your country. If your parents are old and lonesome, do you visit them?

3a. Christianized. You must extend your love to everybody, with a warm human heart. Be kind, be good to everyone, regardless of race, religion, or social standing! Human love must be Christianized in order to be strong and durable. The Act of Love says: "I love my neighbor as myself for the love of You." This chief motive should always be present in the background of your actions. This one motive makes the difference between Christian charity and humanitarianism without God. We must realize that every human being is the offspring of God.

Because love of neighbor is also a gift of God, you must often pray: "Lord, increase my love!"

"And who is my neighbor?" (Luke 10:29).

As you have already learned, you must develop your new life in Christ, with its good habits, within you. You develop your ability to love "by loving"!

3b. Love—justice. Have the courage to translate the word "charity—love" into "justice," e.g., underpaying labor or denying jobs just because of race and soothing one's Christian conscience by donating some used clothes or left-over food is hypocrisy.

Love of Neighbor

By their fruits you will know them:

"This is how all will know you for my disciples:
your love for one another" (John 13:35).

Take Christ's words seriously in your daily contacts and relationships with your fellowmen! This characteristic will always make you recognizable everywhere as a practicing Christian.

4. THINKING IT OVER

Why should you opt for love as a basic attitude in the first place? How can you love the invisible God? What does Christ tell you about love for your enemies and people you do not like? How and where did Christ give an example of love for His enemies? What should you do after a burst of anger? While in a resentful state of mind, may you receive Holy Communion? (See 1 Corinthians 11:17-19 and 27.) What does Christ say about making peace before taking part in the Sacrifice of the Mass? Why cannot a resentful person possibly pray the "Our Father"? Apply Jesus' doctrine of love to your own circumstances: at home, at work, while driving, toward your subordinates, etc. Are you taking a fair share in the charitable work of your parish? (See Chapters 32 and 20.) What should be the main motive for love of your fellowmen? In what way are Sisters who work in hospitals, institutions for lepers, foreign missions, and our Catholic schools fulfilling Christ's command? What must you constantly do in order to increase the ability to love your neighbor, which is a gift of God? What is the best way of developing the virtue of Love? What makes Christian love differ from humanitarianism? What is the relation between Christian charity and justice?

5. READ ATTENTIVELY

What characteristic did Jesus emphasize about His disciples?
Jesus characterized His disciples as follows:

"This is how all will know you for my disciples:

"Your love for one another" (John 13:35).

6. PRAY MEDITATIVELY

Lord, increase my constant awareness to see You in my fellowmen. Give me the courage to do the loving thing in all situations of my life!

7. THINGS TO DO

Read the Gospel of Holy Thursday and "The Washing of the Feet." Read: Matthew 5:1-12; 1 John 4:7-21; 1 John 5:1-5; Matthew 25:31-42.

Listen, if possible, to a recording of the last part of the *Ninth Symphony* of Beethoven.

45. Prayer

1a. I will bring holocausts to your house;
  to you I will fulfill the vows
Which my lips uttered
  and my words promised in my distress.
Holocausts of fatlings I will offer you,
  with burnt offerings of rams;
  I will sacrifice oxen and goats.
Hear now, all you who fear God, while I declare
  what he has done for me.
When I appealed to him in words,
  praise was on the tip of my tongue.
Were I to cherish wickedness in my heart,
  the Lord would not hear;
But God has heard;
  he has hearkened to the sound of my prayer.
Blessed be God who refused me not
  my prayer or his kindness! (Psalm 66:13-20).

1b. "When you are praying, do not behave like the hypocrites who love to stand and pray in synagogues or on street corners in order to be noticed. I give you my word, they are already repaid. Whenever you pray, go to your room, close your door, and pray to your Father in private. Then your Father, who sees what no man sees, will repay you. In your prayer do not rattle on like the pagans. They think they will win a hearing by the sheer multiplication of words. Do not imitate them. Your Father knows what you need before you ask him. This is how you are to pray:

> 'Our Father in heaven,
> hallowed be your name,
> your kingdom come,
> your will be done
> on earth as it is in heaven.
> Give us today our daily bread,
> and forgive us the wrong we have done
> as we forgive those who wrong us.
> Subject us not to the trial
> but deliver us from the evil one.'

"If you forgive the faults of others, your heavenly Father will forgive you yours. If you do not forgive others, neither will your Father forgive you" (Matthew 6:5-15).

2a. Secret suspicion. There is no doubt that "how to pray" is a problem for many Christians. To begin with, one must get rid of the secret suspicion that prayer is nothing else but a good psychological means of comfort by talking persuasively to oneself, as it is for the man who cannot see God transcending creation as an Absolute You (see Chapter 5, no. 2b). Following the inspired experience of the Hebrews and especially Jesus' example *in Faith,* we know that the ground of our being, the Ultimate Reality, God, is a "You," really related to us as a person.

2b. Prayer—dialogue. The great philosopher and devout Jew, Martin Buber, has said: "All real life is meeting." When you meet a good person and become his friend, your meeting him will enrich your life. Whenever you experience person-to-person contact, a dialogue, you live more fully. This is very evident in the encounter of two persons in love.

"Let my prayer come before you" (Psalm 88:3).

Buber describes such an intimate relationship as possible also between man and God. And it is possible because of our radical elevation in Christ. By Faith and Baptism you share in this elevation of human nature. You share in God's life by your rebirth from water and the spirit (see Chapter 28, no. 2b, c).

"Prayer" is that encounter or meeting between you and God, of which Buber is speaking. Prayer is a dialogue between you and God. You speak and you listen when you meet God in your Bible, in a good sermon, in the Eucharistic celebration, in any good person, in any event of your life. If real life is "meeting," this certainly applies to your meeting God in prayer.

Read some of the first Bible passages of Sunday Masses in your Missal or Missalette and pray the responsorial Psalms following those first readings. Praying is something you learn by doing!

2c. He needs to say it. We describe prayer as encounter, meeting, dialogue or conversation with God. This dialogue or direct encounter is a necessity. Today, there is a great emphasis on meeting God as immanent in your fellowmen. "As often as you did it for one of my least brothers . . ." (Matthew 25:40) makes headlines. Religious sisters leave their convents to dedicate themselves to the poor of the ghettos. A life of dedication to fellowmen is even called "prayer"—in fact "prayer of engagement," in which "prayer of withdrawal (disengagement)" must be rooted.

We might liken this to a family man telling his wife: "Honey, don't ask me anymore whether I love you. I told you that when we married ten years ago. I provide for the family, pay the notes on the new refrigerator and the mink I gave you for Christmas. Isn't that enough?" The fact is it is not! She wants to hear that he loves her over and over again, and he needs to say it. If this is not done, these two people will drift apart and jeopardize their marriage.

Your relationship with God is that of a sacred partnership (Covenant) which has clearly marital overtones (see Chapter 7). Of course, no comparison is adequate. God does not feel unhappy when you do not encounter him directly in prayer or say that you love him and appreciate what he is doing for you. But you need to do so! And if you do not, you will drift away, regardless of your charity to fellowmen. An atheistic humanitarianism which consists of total, durable, and indiscriminate dedication is a rare exception. We need to set apart time for prayer.

2d. More than functional. But prayer is more than just functional, an aid to make our commitment to God and the world more fruitful and lasting. Confining it to merely boosting our morale would rob prayer and worship of their real joy and beauty. Prayer has also meaning in itself. In the Judaeo-Christian tradition, we speak of joyfully praising God, admiring him, thanking him. Pray meditatively Psalm 33 and you will learn about the intrinsic meaning of prayer.

2e. Surprising initiatives. The prayer of request (petition) offers neither more nor less difficulties than prayers of adoration, praise, or thanksgiving. The common soil on which all prayer flourishes, the prayer of request included, is the realization that everything is a gift. Nothing is obvious. The request for forgiveness indeed means that we question the obviousness of forgiveness. To ask for bread and health is to question the obviousness of our well-being and our welfare. Asking God for help is related to our Christian Hope, which is always "a Hope with the help of God" (see Chapter 43, no. 2e).

We must take the dialogue between God and man so seriously that we also accept the fact that God Himself, too, is active, even though we have no idea about the way in which He channels His personal care for us. "If we accept, in Faith, a real interpersonal relationship between God and man, it is not necessarily absurd that God really takes totally surprising initiatives" (E. Schillebeeckx).

2f. Frequent symbolization. Prayer in the Hebrew Bible (Old Testament) is frequently related to sacrifice. Together they constitute the cult or community worship (see no. 1a). Prayer and sacrifice signify man's self-dedication to the Almighty (see Chapters 8 and 22,23). The Catholic Church continues this tradition by attributing sacrificial characteristics to the Lord's supper, as celebrated in our churches (see Chapter 47). It is all in line with the Judaeo-Christian tradition to join the congregation in this frequent symbolization of your dedication in love to God and fellowmen. Figuratively, God says in Psalm 50:

"Not for your sacrifices do I rebuke you,
for your holocausts are before me always . . .

"Offer to God praise as your sacrifice
and fulfill your vows to the Most High."
(Psalm 50:8. 14).

2g. How to pray? Praying is something you must learn. How do we acquire and develop a sense for music or poetry? The study of notes or grammar may well lead us to the threshold, but the real sense of music or poetry will only come when we cross that threshold and surrender ourselves to that peculiar world of music and poetry. Hence, just pray, and you will find out that prayer has meaning! And study the examples and lessons of our Lord. How should I pray? Read the Bible passage in no. 1b.

Read the parable of the Pharisee and the publican in Luke 18:9-14. Read also Matthew 7:7-11; Luke 11:5-13; Luke 18:1-8. And read our Lord's prayer in distress in Luke 22:39-46.

2h. Guide and inspiration. Prayer formulas reflect the prayer experience of others. Many of the Psalms in the Bible are beautiful prayers. Prayer formulas are apt as songs and community prayers. From the early beginning, Christans have been praying and singing together. We need one another's inspiration. Prayer formulas are also a guide and inspiration for private use and as such they are valuable. See our Lord's prayer in no. 1b.

Traditionally, quite a few Christians depend heavily on prayer formulas: the rosary, the way of the cross, prayers composed by a beloved saint. It is their perfect right to do so! However, there is a trend away from standard formulas of prayers for private use. If still used, they serve more as a source of inspiration for private prayer and meditation than as a text that must be recited in its entirety. Let freedom reign!

2i. Supple rhythm. Should we pray only when we feel the urge to do so? There are religious who have given up daily Masses and meditation. There are lay people, too, who do not pray regularly anymore. Prayer should be spontaneous! It is noteworthy, however, that after research and experimentation quite a few become convinced of the positive value of a supple yet regular rhythm in our life of prayer, which is not determined simply by the personal urgency of the moment.

2j. The family that prays together . . . It is a Christian custom to say some morning and night prayers. At least night prayers, with daily Bible reading, should be said together by the family. Find time for it (after supper, perhaps) when the whole family is together. A short prayer before and after meals expresses our belief that all good gifts come from God! (See p. 292.)

3. Stammering words. How to pray, can be a problem. You might start from your own situation, which could lead you to prayer: A cry of despair, a "yes" in the face of a difficult decision, the acknowledgment of grave guilt, quiet satisfaction in some good deed, gay rejoicing at an unexpected happiness! Stammering words in such a situation are prayer already. And it is through this kind of implicit mental prayer that explicit prayer comes. Moreover, you should cultivate "a supple yet regular rhythm" of prayer, especially by prayerfully reading your Bible daily.

4. THINKING IT OVER

What has prayer to do with your concept of God? (See no. 2a and Chapter 5, no. 2b.) Why is prayer necessary? Describe how prayer can have meaning in itself. What is common soil on which all prayer should flourish? Explain this for the prayer of request (petition)! What has Hope to do with the prayer of request? (See Chapter 43, no. 2b.) Name the two elements which constitute the cult. How do we Christians in the Catholic tradition practice cult? How does one learn to pray? What about prayer formulas? Should one pray only when one feels the urge to do so? Find the relationship (response!) of any responsorial psalm to the first Bible reading of Sunday Masses! Then pray them!

5. READ ATTENTIVELY

What does Jesus say about praying together?

Jesus says: "Where two or three are gathered in my name, there am I in their midst."

6. PRAY MEDITATIVELY

"Lord, teach us to pray, as John taught his disciples" (Luke 11:1).

7. THINGS TO DO

Read: Acts 2:42-47.

A splendid prayer in music is the *Symphony in D Minor* of Cesar Franck. If you have an opportunity, listen to it.

46. The Sign Value of Marriage and Celibacy

1a. Follow the way of love, even as Christ loved you. He gave himself for us as an offering to God, a gift of pleasing fragrance.

Husbands, love your wives, as Christ loved the church. He gave himself up for her to make her holy, purifying her in the bath of water by the power of the word, to present to himself a glorious church, holy and immaculate, without stain or wrinkle or anything of that sort. Husbands should love their wives as they do their own bodies. He who loves his wife loves himself. Observe that no one ever hates his own flesh; no, he nourishes it and takes care of it as Christ cares for the church—for we are members of his body.

> *"For this reason a man shall leave his father and mother,
> and shall cling to his wife,
> and the two shall be made into one."*

This is a great foreshadowing: I mean that it refers to Christ and the Church (Ephesians 5:2.25-32).

1b. Some Pharisees came up to him and said, to test him, "May a man divorce his wife for any reason whatever?" He replied, "Have you not read that at the beginning the Creator made them male and female and declared, 'For this reason a man shall leave his father and mother and cling to his wife, and the two shall become as one'? Thus they are no longer two but one flesh. Therefore, let no man separate what God has joined." They said to him, "Then why did Moses command divorce and the promulgation of a divorce decree?" "Because of your stubbornness Moses let you divorce your wives," he replied; "but at the beginning it was not that way. I now say to you, whoever divorces his wife (lewd conduct is a separate case) and marries another commits adultery, and the man who marries a divorced woman commits adultery."

His disciples said to him, "If that is the case between man and wife, it is better not to marry." He said, "Not everyone can accept this teaching, only those to whom it is given to do so. Some men are incapable of sexual activity from birth; some have been deliberately made so; and some there are who have freely renounced sex for the sake of God's reign. Let him accept this teaching who can" (Matthew 19:3-12).

2a. Pointing to love. Our Lord wants the Church to be like yeast in dough (Matthew 13:33). He never promised that the whole world would become yeast. The world is the dough in which Christians are present with their always uplifting impact. Wherever Christians are, their presence should point in a certain direction.

A very important area where the presence of Christians should point in a certain direction is the area of human relations. There is no doubt that our Lord emphasized love as one of the most basic elements in the relationship of human beings and that he wants His congregation to do the same in word and example. Motivated by these ideas of Jesus of Nazareth, Christians therefore have a particular outlook on marriage and abstinence from it (celibacy). How do both marriage and "celibacy for the sake of God's Reign," as lived by Christians, point in a certain direction, namely, to love as the basic characteristic of all human relations—in other words, to God's Reign of love, peace, and justice?

2b. Married Christians a sign. As far as marriage is concerned, we refer to the first Bible passage of this chapter (no. 1a). Christians see the relationship of love between husband and wife lived as the mystery of Christ and the Church. This does not mean that Christians do not live marriage as an earthly reality. They enjoy sound sex as a sign of their mutual love just as all human beings should. They may incorporate into their lives the wisdom of contemporary psychology and consult marriage counselors to solve their problems. In Chapter 56, we will discuss marriage more extensively.

But Christian couples know that in the earthly reality of marriage they are called to signify the intimate mystery of Christ and the Church (no. 1a), in other words, to express the fact that the Reign of God (a Reign of justice, love, fidelity, and peace) has been initiated already in our history. And as such, married Christians are a sign, a light on the mountain top, the salt of the earth or, as mentioned above, yeast in dough, having an uplifting impact on world where values such as justice, love, peace, and fidelity are often not brought into existence.

2c. Celibacy a sign. Marriage lived as the mystery of Christ and the Church is one way in which Christians are a sign of the Reign of God in our history. "Celibacy for the sake of God's Reign" is another one (see no. 1b). Though there is no consensus among Bible scholars concerning how to explain verse 12: "Some men are . . .," it is often related to the status of our priests, religious sisters, and laybrothers, who "have freely renounced sex for the sake of God's Reign."

2d. Related to the other. Psychology and other behavioral sciences tell us that a human being does not exist as person before he becomes related to others. Only in relation to others, parents, brothers and sisters, teachers, friends, etc., do we become persons. Both marriage and celibacy are fundamental ways in which man decides on his relationship to the other.

(1) Marriage. In marriage man and woman relate themselves to the other exclusively, and become the persons whom we call husband and wife. They relate themselves not to many people but to one. Their mutual self-surrender in love is exclusive in such a way that it cannot be universal.

(2) Celibacy. The Christian who chooses "celibacy for the sake of God's Reign" chooses to relate his openness to the other not to one person but to the human community as a whole. His outlook is universal. The celibate keeps himself free from exclusive relations in order to be free to live on that level on which everybody, man and woman, can relate to one another. The celibate keeps himself free to dedicate himself entirely to the establishment of universal human relations. His way of life, cultivating the universal brotherhood of all people, expresses the fact that the Reign of

God (a Reign of justice, love, fidelity, and peace) has been initiated already in our history.

2e. Another dimension. Basically, both celibates and married people point to the same reality, namely, the presence of God's Reign in our history. Both intend to make visible God's unfathomable love for man. But celibacy points to more than just values in this world. While Christian marriage as an earthly reality points to the Reign of God as initiated in this world, "celibacy for the sake of God's Reign"—in addition to doing the same—also points to another dimension of God's Reign, namely, its full realization in the hereafter. Celibacy does this:

(1) by its dedication to universal brotherhood as it will be fully realized in the world to come (see 1 Corinthians 15:28),

(2) and by its abstinence from sex. By freely renouncing the very normal way of self-realization in marriage, the celibate signifies clearly that self-realization of man on the level of this life is not the final goal of human existence.

The very way of life in "celibacy for the sake of God's Reign" is the constant reminder of this to all. The celibate is a sign. He is like a light on a mountain top, the salt of the earth, yeast in dough. Consecrated celibacy is an imitation of the life-style of our Lord Himself. (See Chapter 43, no. 2c, d, e on Hope!)

2f. God's folly. From the above observations, it is clear that life in "celibacy for the sake of God's Reign" is a special vocation or call by Almighty God. The same is true of marriage lived as the mystery of Christ and the Church. Both are closely related to Faith, sealed by Baptism. To outsiders, all this sounds like pious nonsense. We could call it "God's folly." But this folly is wiser than the wisdom of man! (See 1 Corinthians 1:18-25.)

2g. Three vows. Since celibacy is the most obvious characteristic in the lives of our religious sisters and laybrothers, we have discussed it more extensively. Traditionally, a religious (not every priest—see Chapter 33, no. 2b) takes three vows: voluntary poverty (dependence on superiors), perfect obedience, and perpetual celibacy. By doing so, he surrenders himself, his heart, and all he possesses totally to God in his fellowmen and becomes a living sign of God's Reign.

2h. Male and female personality. From this explanation it will be clear that a monastery (convent) is not a refuge for people who are unable to perform their task in life. In a convent there are people who were fully conscious of their ability and freedom to remain in the world and to establish a family, but who followed Christ's invitation, hoping, with His special help, to be faithful to their freely chosen kind of life: "All should realize that the profession of the evangelical counsels, though entailing the renunciation of certain values which undoubtedly merit high esteem, does not detract from a genuine development of the human person" (*Constitution on the Church,* no. 46).

Renouncing marriage does not mean renouncing one's male or female personality. Although sex is not practiced, it must exist in a person in order to make him or her a real man or woman. No quality of body or heart is superfluous. As a mature man or woman a religious dedicates himself or herself to God and fellowmen.

"I dedicate myself to You in perpetual poverty, celibacy and obedience."

3. Christian witness. The special charisma (gift) of celibacy is given to the people of God perhaps not always in the same abundance. There was a time that many volunteered for the celibate priesthood and religious life. Nowadays, we see many defections and few who want to join this life of witness for the Reign of God. Perhaps lack of appreciation of God's gift and confusion in a changing world have something to do with it.

The same can be said about Christian marriage lived as the mystery of Christ and the Church. In our permissive society there is a breakdown of family life and authority. (Authority is exercised differently today than in the past, and it does not mean "no more authority.") Where parents are no longer witnesses of God's Reign in the earthly reality of their marriage (no. 2b, f), one cannot expect children to be interested in a life of witness either!

Perhaps there is also a shift of Christian witness to the area of social justice and love by all, and not just by our religious and priests!

Meanwhile, you should be a witness of God's Reign in your situation! Perhaps some youthful ways of witness, bizarre as they may be, might inspire you to genuine dedication.

4. THINKING IT OVER

What symbols does the Bible use to indicate that the Christian life should be a sign? What should Christian life be a sign of in regard to human relations? Describe the sign-value of marriage lived as the mystery of Christ and the Church. How does one realize his relationship to the other in marriage and how in "celibacy for the sake of God's Reign"? Describe the sign-value of "celibacy for the sake of God's Reign!" How does "celibacy for the sake of God's Reign" signify something more than does "marriage lived as the mystery of Christ and the Church"? What have Faith and Baptism to do with all of this? What three vows does a religious take? Describe how renunciation of marriage does not detract from a genuine development of the human person! Mention reasons for lack of interest nowadays in "celibacy for the sake of God's Reign!"

5. PRAY MEDITATIVELY

Adapting John 17:9-19, pray for priestly and religious vocations.

6. THINGS TO DO

Read: Matthew 19:16-22; Luke 18:28-30; Matthew 5:13-16.

47. The Eucharist

(Part 1)

Eucharist originally meant "Great Prayer of Thanksgiving and Adoration." The Eucharist (or Eucharistic Prayer), the center or main part of the Mass, begins with "The Lord be with you." It ends with

> "Through him,
> with him,
> in him,
> in the unity of the Holy Spirit,
> all glory and honor is yours,
> almighty Father,
> for ever and ever."

The congregation answers: "Amen" (So be it).

"I have greatly desired to eat this Passover with you . . ." (Luke 22:15).

The Eucharist

1a. "Observe the month of Abib by keeping the Passover of the Lord, your God, since it was in the month of Abib that he brought you by night out of Egypt. You shall offer the Passover sacrifice from your flock or your herd to the Lord, your God, in the place which he chooses as the dwelling place of his name. You shall not eat leavened bread with it. For seven days you shall eat with it only unleavened bread, the bread of affliction, that you may remember as long as you live the day of your departure from the land of Egypt; for in frightened haste you left the land of Egypt. Nothing leavened may be found in all your territory for seven days, and none of the meat which you sacrificed on the evening of the first day shall be kept overnight for the next day.

"You may not sacrifice the Passover in any of the communities which the Lord, your God, gives you; only at the place which he chooses as the dwelling place of his name, and in the evening at sunset, on the anniversary of your departure from Egypt, shall you sacrifice the Passover. You shall cook and eat it at the place the Lord, your God, chooses; then in the morning you may return to your tents. For six days you shall eat unleavened bread, and on the seventh there shall be a solemn meeting in honor of the Lord, your God; on that day you shall not do any sort of work" (Deuteronomy 16:1-8).

1b. The day of Unleavened Bread arrived on which it was appointed to sacrifice the paschal lamb. Accordingly, Jesus sent Peter and John off with the instruction. "Go and prepare our Passover supper for us." They asked him, "Where do you want us to get it ready?" He explained to them: "Just as you enter the city, you will come upon a man carrying a water jar. Follow him into the house he enters, and say to the owner, 'The Teacher asks you: Do you have a guest room where I may eat the Passover with my disciples?' That man will show you an upstairs room, spacious and furnished. It is there you are to prepare." They went off and found everything just as he had said; and accordingly they prepared the Passover supper (Luke 22:7-13).

1c. When the hour arrived, he took his place at table, and the apostles with him. He said to them: "I have greatly desired to eat this Passover with you before I suffer. I tell you, I will not eat again until it is fulfilled in the kingdom of God."

Then taking a cup he offered a blessing in thanks and said: "Take this and divide it among you; I tell you, from now on I will not drink of the fruit of the vine until the coming of the reign of God."

Then, taking bread and giving thanks, he broke it and gave it to them, saying: "This is my body to be given for you. Do this as a remembrance of me." He did the same with the cup after eating, saying as he did so: "This cup is the new covenant in my blood, which will be shed for you" (Luke 22:14-20).

I received from the Lord what I handed on to you, namely, that the Lord Jesus on the night in which he was betrayed took bread, and after he had given thanks, broke it and said, "This is my body, which is for you. Do this in remembrance of me." In the same way, after the supper, he took the cup, saying, "This cup is the new covenant in my blood. Do this, whenever you drink it, in remembrance of me." Every time, then, you eat this bread and drink this cup, you proclaim the death of the Lord until he comes! This means that whoever eats the bread or drinks the cup of the Lord unworthily sins against the body and blood of the Lord (1 Corinthians 11:23-27).

2a. Two themes. In Chapters 22 and 23, we have seen that mainly two themes were used to explain the expiatory character of our Lord's cruel Death, which seemingly was just the death of another civil rights worker.

(1) The Servant-of-the-Lord theme. We cited our Lord Himself and Luke. One just man suffered vicariously to make up for evil done by many (Chapter 22).

(2) The identification of our Lord's Death with the ritual sin-offerings of Jewish worship: Christ is both the offering High Priest and offered victim, offering Himself as a spotless lamb on the altar of the cross to make up for the sin of the world. We cited especially the Letter to the Hebrews (Chapter 23).

In the framework of this second theme (Christ's Death as an antitype of ritual sacrifices), we observe in Sacred Scripture a special identification of our Lord with the paschal (passover) lamb. "Christ, our Passover, has been sacrificed" (1 Corinthians 5:7).

2b. "Personally gone out of Egypt." For the setting of the first Bible reading (no. 1a), you might read again Chapter 6. Note that when Jews commemorate the deliverance from their slavery in Egypt, they do much more than just look back to the past. At the Passover, the Jews who celebrate the exodus from Egypt identify themselves with those who actually did leave Egypt. Past and present coincide. As Jewish tradition has it: "From generation to generation everyone must consider himself as having personally gone out of Egypt. Therefore we must thank him [God] and praise him who led our fathers *and us* through these wonderful things out of slavery to freedom" (*Mishna Pes.* 10:5).

2c. "I am that passover lamb." This is exactly what Jesus and His disciples did in the upper room on the night before His Death. (See no. 1b.) We must keep this in mind in order to understand the third Bible passage (no. 1c). What Jesus did was to give this ancient sacrifice and sacred meal (the Jewish Passover) a new meaning by saying in other words: "I am that passover lamb, sacrificed to deliver you figuratively from the slavery in Egypt and actually from all evil. Do this as a memorial of Me!" It is important to take note of the words added in 1 Corinthians 11:26: "Every time, then, you eat this bread and drink this cup, you proclaim the death of the Lord until he comes." What is called forth in this "memorial" is the Death of the Lord, i.e., the Redemption by God in the Lord Jesus, in which the partakers of the meal share.

3. The Mass and the Passover. The memorial of our Lord, the Mass, is a Jewish Passover with a new meaning. "Christ, our Passover, has been sacrificed" (1 Corinthians 5:7). That is the reason why we should celebrate it as the Jews still celebrate their Passover. Celebrating our collective exodus from evil, we identify ourselves with all men redeemed by Christ's sacrifice (Death on the Cross) and believe that this sacrifice is made present to us in the symbols of bread and wine. And we thank God in the Eucharist (Great Prayer of Thanksgiving and Adoration) and praise Him Who led us out of the slavery of evil to freedom.

4. THINKING IT OVER

Explain the two main themes used in the Bible to clarify the expiatory meaning of our Lord's Death! With which ritual sacrifice especially do Biblical theologians identify our Lord's Death? Explain how Jews see the annual celebration of their Passover. Describe how Jesus gave a new meaning to the Jewish Passover! How should we celebrate the Christian Passover, the Eucharist? (Briefly describe both the traditional and the new approach of reasoning about the Lord's presence in the Eucharist: See no. 6b, above.)

5. PRAY MEDITATIVELY

Lord, look upon this sacrifice which you have given to your Church;
and by your Holy Spirit, gather all who share this bread and wine
into the one body of Christ, a living sacrifice of praise *(Eucharistic Prayer IV).*

6. THINGS TO DO

a. For the meaning of sacrifices, read: 1 Chronicles (Paralipomenon) 29:10-18. For identification of Christ with the paschal lamb, read: John 1:29.36; John 19:36 (the passover lamb's bones should not be broken: Exodus 12:46); 1 Peter 1:17-21 (especially 18-19).

b. For an opinion on the real presence of our Lord in the Eucharist, the following observation may help:

(1) The traditional approach. The old and more traditional approach distinguishes in a thing its so-called *substance* (its real essence) and its *appearances* (the non-essential properties, such as, what you can see, smell, feel, taste). In relation to the Eucharist it is said that the substance of bread and wine is changed into the Body and Blood of Christ, but the appearances (namely taste, color, weight, shape, etc.) remain. Hence, the word "Transubstantiation" in our traditional catechisms.

(2) A new approach. Contemporary theologians try to approach the mystery of Christ's presence in the Eucharist in the following way. We know of two kinds of presence: *a local presence*: two bodies, two things, which are close or even touch one another, and a *personal presence:* the manner in which two friends are together, sharing their personalities.

You can be *locally* present somewhere and nevertheless *personally* far away, e.g., persons are locally very close together in an overcrowded bus, but at the same time personally far away. You do not share anything with the fellow who bumps against you in that bus!

However, you can be *locally* absent and nevertheless *personally* present, e.g., in a letter or a present you have sent to your husband or wife. That present, though it may be a simple necktie or ring, is not just a piece of material! It is a symbol (token) of yourself and therefore valuable to the beloved person. Your heart, you yourself are present in it. What really matters, then, and has the most value is primarily a *personal presence*.

Personal presence. God and persons who are glorified (Jesus, Mary) cannot be present locally. That is the reason why we must see Jesus' presence in the Eucharist as a personal presence. Jesus is present in the bread and the wine as the giver is present in his gift, with all His ardent love, understanding and surrender of Himself; but even more intimately than that, since this comparison does not exhaust the mystery of Christ's presence.

The Consecration does not bring down Christ from heaven in a local way. The Lord's presence in signs is not a repetition of His local presence formerly in Israel. Neither is there a physical or chemical change of bread and wine. What happens at the Consecration is a "trans-signification," a sign-change.

Modes of Christ's Presence. "To accomplish so great a work, Christ is always present in His Church, especially in her liturgical celebrations. He is present in the sacrifice of the Mass, not only in the person of His minister . . . *but especially under the Eucharistic species*. By his power He is present in the sacraments, so that when man baptizes it is really Christ Himself who baptizes. He is present in His word, since it is He Himself who speaks when the holy Scriptures are read in the Church. He is present, finally, when the Church prays and sings, for He promised: 'Where two or three are gathered together for my sake, there am I in the midst of them'" (Matthew 18, 20)—Vatican II, *Constitution on the Sacred Liturgy,* no. 7.

A Sacred Sign. Jesus, really present in "the bread of life and the cup of eternal salvation," wants this food to be a sign of Himself in order to suggest that He wants you to be united *(communion)* with the all-perfect Victim which you have offered with Him to God, symbolizing your oneness with His Sacrifice in total surrender to the Father, and at the same time to undergo the mystical strength of that sacrificial repast.

Summary. Meanwhile, we are conscious that both ways of reasoning (nos. 1 and 2) do nothing more than approach this tremendous mystery of Faith, since we cannot adequately understand how God and Jesus Christ are present and communicate with us. The first approach (1) was made by the Council of Trent (1545-1563) with the philosophical concept of "substance and appearances" then in vogue. The second one (2) is contemporary and must await acceptance or rejection eventually by the Church.

48. The Eucharist

(Part 2)

1. Moses called all the elders of Israel and said to them, "Go and procure lambs for your families, and slaughter them as Passover victims. Then take a bunch of hyssop, and dipping it in the blood that is in the basin, sprinkle the lintel and the two doorposts with this blood. But none of you shall go outdoors until morning. For the Lord will go by, striking down the Egyptians. Seeing the blood on the lintel and the two doorposts, the Lord will pass over that door and not let the destroyer come into your houses to strike you down.

"You shall observe this as a perpetual ordinance for yourselves and your descendants. Thus, you must also observe this rite when you have entered the land which the Lord will give you as he promised. When your children ask you, 'What does this rite of yours mean?' you shall reply, 'This is the Passover sacrifice of the Lord, who passed over the houses of the Israelites in Egypt; when he struck down the Egyptians, he spared our houses.'"

Then the people bowed down in worship, and the Israelites went and did as the Lord had commanded Moses and Aaron (Exodus 12:21-28).

2a. Sacrifice and sacrificial repast. The Jewish Passover, as celebrated and given a new meaning by Jesus on the night before His Death, was both a sacrifice and a sacrificial repast. Only after the destruction of the Temple (70 A.D.) did the Passover become just a Jewish family celebration without the paschal victim and hence a less spectacular observance.

Since the Mass is a Jewish Passover with a new meaning, we must have a close look at the Jewish Passover in order to understand better our own Eucharistic worship service.

How was the Jewish Passover celebrated in Jesus' days? The slaughter of the animals began within the Temple precincts. It could only be done in the Temple of Jerusalem and nowhere else. The blood was dashed against the altar and parts of the animals were burned on it as at the "communion sacrifices" (see Leviticus 3).

The sacrificed meat was eaten by families or small groups in their homes or in rented rooms. During the Passover, tourist business thrived in Jerusalem. Jesus and His disciples were not the only pilgrims! Unleavened bread, bitter herbs, and wine were part of the menu. The father explained the symbolical meaning of the dishes.

2b. Meaning. We are interested in what the Jews meant by this Passover ritual, first as far it was a sacrifice and secondly as far as it was a sacred meal.

(1) As a sacrifice. Ethnology teaches that, with slight differences, mankind has considered sacrifices as symbols of self-surrender to their deities or to God. Something of man (animals or part of his harvest) stands for himself, his heart, his good-will, submission, love. It is more or less the same symbolism as we still possess in our Christmas presents. A gift stands for something! The reasons for offering gifts to the deity may be to ask for blessings, to make up for sins (in the Bible "sin-offerings"), or to give thanks. As far as the Jewish Passover was a sacrifice, it was first of all a sacrifice of thanksgiving for the deliverance of Israel from slavery to freedom, and besides that also a reminder to their God of His promises.

(2) As a meal. The Jews certainly felt that this sacred meal brought them into communion not only with one another—think of our family turkey dinner at Thanksgiving!—but also and especially with the divinity. Exactly how they thought this communion with their God was effected is not clear. Whatever the precise reason, Israelites, eating together the sacrificed meat, recognized this rite as a means of communion with God.

2c. New meaning. Our Lord gave this Jewish Passover a new meaning and told His Church to celebrate it in its renewed form. "Do this as a memorial of me!" (See Chapter 47, no. 2c.)

(1) As a sacrifice. How do we see the sacrificial character of the Christian Passover, our Eucharistic celebration, the Mass? Our Lord said: "This is my body, to be given for you . . . this cup is the new covenant in my blood which will be shed for you" (Luke 22:19-20). In his report, Paul adds: "Every time, then, you eat this bread and drink this cup, you proclaim the death of the Lord" (1 Corinthians 11:26). These words refer to Christ's Death on the Cross, which Christians see as a sin-offering, a sacrifice. (See Chapters 23 and 47, no. 2a.) The Christian Passover is Christ's Sacrifice of the Cross, made present (called forth) in the signs of bread and wine. It is not a new sacrifice. It is a dramatic representation: Christ, our Passover, sacrificed, present in signs! The Eucharistic Prayer—Great Prayer of Thanksgiving and Adoration—is the setting.

(2) As a meal. Besides being a sacrifice, the Christian Passover is also a sacrificial repast or sacred meal. We call it Holy Communion. This sacred meal brings us into communion not only with one another, but also and especially with God in Christ, our Lord. Bread and wine (like coffee, tea or a "coke" in our culture) are symbols related to the human condition as such. The meaning is clear: Our Lord, meeting us in these symbols, wants to "feed" us, wants to enrich us by sharing his personality.

3a. Sacrifice. Seeing the Christian Passover as a sacrifice, a symbol of self-surrender to God in submission and love, you should always make it a symbol of your self-surrender to your Maker. Void symbols are meaningless. As far as you are concerned, you must give meaning to the symbolical representation of our Lord's sacrifice in your church. The Eucharistic Prayer ends:

> "Through him,
> with him,
> in him,
> in the unity of the Holy Spirit,
> all glory and honor is yours,
> almighty Father,
> for ever and ever."

It should always be your prayer, which you emphasize with your "Amen," so be it.

3b. Meal. (1) We see our Christian Passover meal as communion with one another. A meal together! Table fellowship is still an oriental virtue. We have our banquets, Thanksgiving and Christmas meals. They are symbols which have only as much meaning as you give to them! The handshake of peace precedes the Christian Passover meal. Make all of this symbolism meaningful!

(2) We see the Christian Passover meal as communion with God in Christ, our Lord. It is communion in a symbol, a sacrificial repast. But communication with our Lord is only possible, if you "open up," if you want to communicate. Every time you go to the sanctuary, there should be a real encounter of a person to a person, a more intimate "I-Thou" relation between you and the Lord Jesus. (For our Lord's presence in the signs of bread and wine, see Chapter 47, no. 6b.)

4. THINKING IT OVER

Describe how the Jews of our Lord's day celebrated the Passover. What is the meaning of the Jewish Passover as a sacrifice? as a meal? What did our Lord do to this Jewish Passover on the night before His Death? How do we see the sacrificial character of the Christian Passover? How do we see it as a meal? What does the Christian Passover both as a sacrifice and a meal mean to you? What are you supposed to do to make these symbolisms meaningful? Which prayer before Holy Communion reminds you of the Eucharist as a Passover meal?

5. PRAY MEDITATIVELY

Parts of the Eucharistic Prayers. Discuss them with your instructor if there are parts which are not clear to you.

6. THINGS TO DO

The Roman Canon (Eucharistic Prayer I) refers to the sacrifices of Abel, Abraham, and Melchizedek. Read Genesis 4:1-5; 22:9-12; 14:18-20, Read also John 6:48-59 and note the symbolism: "He who eats my flesh . . ." Communion—communicating with a person!

Read also Genesis 22:1-19. Bible scholars see in this tradition the constitution of all sacrificial worship, namely, God accepts sacrifices only if they symbolize our total surrender in love and obedience to our Maker.

49. The Eucharist
(Part 3)

1a. *This boasting of yours is an ugly thing. Do you not know that a little yeast has its effect all through the dough? Get rid of the old yeast to make of yourselves fresh dough, unleavened loaves, as it were; Christ our Passover has been sacrificed. Let us celebrate the feast not with the old yeast, that of corruption and wickedness, but with the unleavened bread of sincerity and truth (1 Corinthians 5:6-8).*

1b. *What I now have to say is not said in praise, because your meetings are not profitable but harmful. First of all, I hear that when you gather for a meeting there are divisions among you, and I am inclined to believe it. There may even have to be factions among you for the tried and true to stand out clearly. When you assemble it is not to eat the Lord's Supper, for everyone is in haste to eat his own supper. One person goes hungry while another gets drunk. Do you not have homes where you can eat and drink? Would you show contempt for the church of God, and embarrass those who have nothing? What can I say to you? Shall I praise you? Certainly not in this matter!*

I received from the Lord what I handed on to you, namely, that the Lord Jesus on the night in which he was betrayed took bread, and after he had given thanks, broke it and said, "This is my body, which is for you. Do this in remembrance of me." In the same way, after the supper, he took the cup, saying, "This cup is the new covenant in my blood. Do this, whenever you drink it, in remembrance of me." Every time, then, you eat this bread and drink this cup, you proclaim the death of the Lord until he comes! This means that whoever eats the bread or drinks the cup of the Lord unworthily sins against the body and blood of the Lord. A man should examine himself first; only then should he eat of the bread and drink of the cup. He who eats and drinks without recognizing the body eats and drinks a judgment on himself (1 Corinthians 11:17-29).

1c. *What care I for the number of your sacrifices?*
　　says the Lord.
I have had enough of whole-burnt rams
　　and fat of fatlings;
In the blood of calves, lambs and goats
　　I find no pleasure.
When you come in to visit me,
　　who asks these things of you?
Trample my courts no more!
　　Bring no more worthless offerings;
　　your incense is loathsome to me.
New moon and sabbath, calling of assemblies,
　　octaves with wickedness: these I cannot bear.
Your new moons and festivals I detest;
　　they weigh me down, I tire of the load.
When you spread out your hands,
　　I close my eyes to you;
Though you pray the more,
　　I will not listen.
Your hands are full of blood!
　　Wash yourselves clean!
Put away your misdeeds from before my eyes;
　　cease doing evil (Isaiah 1:11-16).

2a. The old dough. During the 3rd Century B.C., when the ancient traditions concerning the Exodus from Egypt were edited, the Passover and the Feast of the Unleavened Bread were fused together. (See Deuteronomy 16:1-8 and Chapter 48, no. 2b.) Jesus observed this feast as such. Jews ate and still eat the Passover meal with unleavened bread.

To understand the symbolism of eating unleavened bread you must remember that yeast (leaven, old fermenting dough) was regarded as a principle of decay. (See Matthew 16:5-12.) Jews were supposed to do away with the old dough (leaven) on the eve of the Feast of the Unleavened Bread, symbolizing that they wished to celebrate the Passover without the decay of sin. Christians should have the same sentiments when they celebrate the Passover in its renewed form. (See no. 1a.)

Paul says: "He who eats and drinks without recognizing the body [of the Lord] eats and drinks a judgment on himself" (no. 1b). To receive the Body of the Lord (being intimately united with Him in Love) in a state of deliberate aversion from Him (serious sin—"divisions among you": no. 1b.) is an obvious discrepancy.

2b. Undivided Christ. Until the Middle Ages, Christians usually received Holy Communion under both signs. This is still customary in Churches of the Eastern tradition. There are 700,000 Eastern Rite Catholics in this country! But from the beginning, Holy Communion was also given under the sign of bread only: for example, to the sick and to prisoners. It is now customary in the Church of the Western tradition to receive Holy Communion under one sign only. The whole and undivided Christ is present under each sign. Since Vatican II, Communion under both signs is permitted on special occasions. Western Catholics who occasionally attend Mass in an Eastern Rite may also receive Holy Communion under both signs.

2c. Active participation. "In liturgical celebrations each person, minister or layman, who has an office to perform, should do all of, but only, those parts which pertain to his office by the nature of the rite and the principles of liturgy . . .

"To promote active participation, the people should be encouraged to take part by means of acclamations, responses, psalmody, antiphons, and songs, as well as by actions, gestures and bodily attitudes . . ." (*Constitution on the Sacred Liturgy,* nos. 28, 30).

2d. "The solemn." As a reaction against those who denied the real presence of Christ in the Holy Eucharist the Church has paid much attention to it in the recent past by public devotions, processions and Forty Hours Devotions. But Vatican II (*Constitution on the Sacred Liturgy*) asserts that our Lord is present in manifold ways. (See Chapter 47, no. 6b.)

Guided by the Spirit, the Church wants us to place Christ's presence as food back again into the context of Christ's total presence in the liturgy, as described in Chapter 47, no. 6b. Hence, there is a growing consciousness among God's people that "the solemn" and "the splendid" with reference to the Eucharist must be chiefly the Eucharistic Celebration (Mass). Perhaps devotion to Jesus' mysterious presence in the sign of bread will be expressed ever more in future by our private prayer in church.

3. To be honest. We can regard the above Bible passages as a plea for truthfulness and honesty. Symbolize only reality! To do otherwise is fake, void, meaningless, and, if done consciously, hypocritical. At the table of the Lord, symbolizing your oneness with fellow Christians but having "divisions among you" (no. 1b) is hypocrisy. Likewise, symbolizing self-surrender to God in and through the Lord's sacrifice, called forth in the symbols of bread and wine, but not living up to your commitment, may direct to you the words Isaiah put figuratively into the mouth of God: Isaiah 1:11-16, above, no. 1c. Read meditatively and apply it to your own situation!

4. THINKING IT OVER

Explain the symbolism of the Jewish Feast of Unleavened Bread. How does Paul apply this Jewish symbolism to the Christian Passover? What guidelines does the *Constitution on the Sacred Liturgy* give for active participation in the Eucharistic Celebration? Does Isaiah 1:11-16 (no. 1c) condemn sacrifices as such? Explain!

5. READ ATTENTIVELY

What did our Lord promise as the result of partaking in the Eucharist?

Our Lord said: "He who feeds on my flesh and drinks my blood has life eternal, and I will raise him up on the last day. He ... remains in me, and I in him" (John 6:54. 56).

6. PRAY MEDITATIVELY

"O Lord our God, you are worthy to receive glory and honor and power! For you have created all things; by your will they came to be and were made!" (Revelation 4:11).

7. THINGS TO DO

Read: 1 Corinthians 10:14-22; Psalm 66:13-20; Matthew 5:23-24. Apply this to the Christian Passover and your own situation!

SACRED SIGNS

50. The Sacrament of Penance

(Part 1) Temptation and Sin

1. Then Jesus was led into the desert by the Spirit to be tempted by the devil. He fasted forty days and forty nights, and afterward was hungry. The tempter approached and said to him, "If you are the Son of God, command these stones to turn into bread." Jesus replied, "Scripture has it:

> 'Not on bread alone is man to live
> but on every utterance that comes
> from the mouth of God.' "

Next the devil took him to the holy city, set him on the parapet on the temple, and said, "If you are the Son of God, throw yourself down. Scripture has it:

> 'He will bid his angels take care of you;
> with their hands they will support you
> that you may never stumble on a stone.' "

Jesus answered him, "Scripture also has it:

> 'You shall not put the Lord your God to the test.' "

The devil then took him up a very high mountain and displayed before him all the kingdoms of the world in their magnificence, promising, "All these will I bestow on you if you prostrate yourself in homage before me." At this, Jesus said to him, "Away with you, Satan! Scripture has it:

> 'You shall do homage to the Lord your God;
> him alone shall you adore.' "

At that the devil left him, and angels came and waited on him (Matthew 4:1-11).

2a. Tempted and harassed. Jesus was confronted with the idea of being a political Messiah with all the wealth, glory, and power this entailed (See Chapter 19, no. 2b.) His followers expected him to be one. (See Luke 24:21; 19:11; Matthew 20:20-21.) The idea of Jesus going to the desert to pray is equally acceptable. (See Matthew 14:23.) This may be the core of this tradition. The way it is presented to us is parabolic. And as such, a parable, the Gospel writers use it to describe the temptations of the early Church. The people of God was tempted and often harassed by opponents. The sacred writer identifies God's people with its Founder and lets Him give the answers in name of the Church. Hence, this parable describes the temptations all of us have to cope with and suggests how we should handle them.

2b. Clouded vision. A Christian has made a basic choice for love. (See Chapter 44, no. 2a.) But maturity in love is rather rare. Humbly we must acknowledge this. The reality of temptation and evil does cloud our vision. Sin may approach us under the guise of reason. Sin could make us prone to rationalize ourselves out of a situation where the loving thing should be done!

As it is, "the sin of the world" (Chapter 13) is a reality. We are born into this situation and must learn to live with it. We are out of balance, we are as it were infected by evil. The Bible mentions the devil. Evil surrounds us as an extremely contagious disease. But the Bible states also that God is faithful and does not permit you to be tempted beyond your strength. If a child holds the hand of his father, he cannot possibly fall!

2c. Thing or relationship? The Bible describes sin and sinners. Traditional catechisms classified sins as mortal (serious, deadly) and venial (less serious) sins. Mortal sin was primarily explained in terms of an external act, thereby viewing sin more as a thing than as a relationship. These catechisms frequently classified the catalogues of actions which were mortal sins. One missed Mass on Sunday three times, hence three mortal sins!

Contemporary theologians emphasize the fact that mortal sin is not just an external action viewed in itself, but more a change of heart. In order to get a clear picture, we must keep in mind that the Bible sees man as God's partner. This sacred partnership (Covenant) has clearly marital overtones. (See Chapter 7.) As a Christian, you have accepted God's invitation to this intimate relationship of love. Love for God and fellowmen is your basic or fundamental option. (See Chapter 44, no. 2a.) Against this background, sin is seen as breaking this fundamental relationship of love with God and neighbor.

2d. Injury to personal love. The malignancy of serious sin does not consist in trespassing impersonal laws on the books, as, for example, running through a red traffic light. It consists in the injury to personal love, the love of God.

Serious sin is an aversion from God as you meet Him in your fellowmen and in your conscience. This does not necessarily mean that you hate God. It can also mean that you refuse something that is essential to love and fidelity—just as you hurt your wife not only by hatred but also by infidelity in something that is essential to love.

Some acts indicate that there must be something seriously wrong with a man's relationship to God and His loving care. The person himself, guided by his conscience, knows best what his motives were and whether deliberate aversion and diehard indifference were in the picture or not.

2e. Plank and speck. Paul speaks of sins that exclude you from the Kingdom of God. (See Galatians 5:19-21; 1 Corinthians 6:9-11.) We must realize that if a man deliberately perseveres in his aversion from God, and keeps himself till the moment of death in a diehard situation of total indifference with relation to God and His loving care, he creates hell for himself! Read in what direction Jesus points in Mattthew 25:31-46.

When sin does not come from the very center of our person, but is more or less peripheral, theologians speak of venial sin, which could be "the speck" our Lord speaks about in Matthew 7:3. Venial sin remains an action which does not involve the core decision of the person (total aversion from God); it rather illustrates the condition of man who constantly falls short of the total love union with God and fellowmen to which he is called.

2f. Community involved. By sinning, you turn yourself away from God as you meet Him in your conscience and in your fellowmen. This aversion from God in your fellowmen may do visible harm to the welfare of the community; for example, a divorced wife with children to rear alone, drunkenness and gambling causing unhappiness at home, children that fail in life because they did not get an adequate education.

Sin always harms, invisibly though no less truly, the Christian community of which you are a member by Faith and Baptism. You believe that you are a branch of the Vine. One dead branch may deface the whole Vine and make it less pleasing to the heavenly Vinedresser! Paul compares the Church, of which you are a member, to a bride. Your sins stain her wedding garment! You believe that the supreme task of the Church is joining in the heavenly worship of the angels and the saints. But your sins are the dissonance in the choir! One black sheep makes the whole family ashamed! These metaphors will impress you if you have "team" spirit and a "community" sense.

Through sinning, you are guilty in the eyes of God and His Church. It is important to mention this "community" aspect of sin in order to understand the attitude of the Church toward sin and the sinner.

3. Realistic. As a reaction against an over-pessimistic theology that saw sin and reason for guilt everywhere, we are at the present time witnessing an over-optimistic view of the goodness of the Church, the world, and the individual. A certain kind of psychology tries to do away with moral evil (sin) and guilt as pathological symptoms of the past. This is not realistic. Even Christ's first elected ones failed! Read Galatians 2:11-14: Paul and Peter at loggerheads because Peter was backing down and rationalizing before the delegation of Judaizers. Read Acts 15:36-40: Paul and Barnabas, long-time companions as missionaries to the pagans, unable to get along. What would have been the loving thing to do? Sin and failure to live up to the beautiful ideals of Jesus Christ is found in the highest echelons of the Church as well as daily in and around us.

3b. Christianity—Christians. Do not be shocked when you see fellow Christians, even those who are leaders, fail to live up to what they should stand for. There is nothing wrong with Christianity, but too often there is something wrong with Christians! All of us, the Pope and you included, pray before Mass: "I confess that I have sinned in what I have done and in what I have failed to do." The Church and the world need constant reformation. Each of us should start reforming himself daily. Evil should be resisted (Bible reading no. 1, above). The traditional means such as prayer, meditative Bible reading, self-control, mortification, avoiding idleness, interest in work, hobbies, and healthy recreation will still effect this reformation. We should not do away too easily with the wisdom of Christians before us.

4. THINKING IT OVER

Explain the literary form of Matthew 4:1-11 in no. 1. How was sin defined traditionally and how do contemporary theologians define sin? How would you explain serious sin and venial sin? What has the community to do with sin? Explain it! What are the means to resist temptation and to avoid sin?

5. PRAY MEDITATIVELY

I confess to almighty God,
and to you, my brothers and sisters (see 2f),
that I have sinned through my own fault
in my thoughts and in my words,
in what I have done,
and in what I have failed to do;
and I ask blessed Mary, ever virgin.
all the angels and saints,
and you, my brothers and sisters,
to pray for me to the Lord our God.

(Penitential Rite before Mass)

6. THINGS TO DO

Read: Genesis 3: temptation of "Everyman"; 2 Samuel 12; John 8:1-11 Luke 7:36-50; Matthew 7:1-5 (the speck and the plank); Galatians 5:16-26; 1 Corinthians 6:9-11 (sins which exclude from the Kingdom of God).

51. The Sacrament of Penance

(Part 2)

Contrition, Guilt, and Forgiveness

1a. They led him away under arrest and brought him to the house of the high priest, while Peter followed at a distance. Later they lighted a fire in the middle of the courtyard and were sitting beside it, and Peter sat among them. A servant girl saw him sitting in the light of the fire. She gazed at him intently, then said, "This man was with him." He denied the fact, saying, "Woman, I do not know him." A little while later someone else saw him and said, "You are one of them too." But Peter said, "No, sir, not I!" About an hour after that another spoke more insistently: "This man was certainly with him, for he is a Galilean." Peter responded, "My friend, I do not know what you are talking about." At the very moment he was saying this, a cock crowed. The Lord turned around and looked at Peter, and Peter remembered the word that the Lord had spoken to him, "Before the cock crows today you will deny me three times." He went out and wept bitterly (Luke 22:54-62).

1b. Hence, declare your sins to one another, and pray for one another, that you may find healing.

The fervent petition of a holy man is powerful indeed. Elijah was only a man like us, yet he prayed earnestly that it would not rain and no rain fell on the land for three years and six months. When he prayed again, the sky burst forth with rain and the land produced its crop.

My brothers, the case may arise among you of someone straying from the truth, and of another bringing him back (James 5:16-19).

1c. As long as I would not speak, my bones wasted away
    with my groaning all the day,
For day and night your hand was heavy upon me;
    my strength was dried up as by the heat of summer.
Then I acknowledged my sin to you,
    my guilt I covered not.
I said, "I confess my faults to the Lord,"
    and you took away the guilt of my sin.
For this shall every faithful man pray to you
    in time of stress.

> Though deep waters overflow,
> they shall not reach him.
> You are my shelter; from distress you will preserve me;
> with glad cries of freedom you will ring me round
> (Psalm 32:3-7).

1d. Then Judas, who had handed him over, seeing that Jesus had been condemned, began to regret his action deeply. He took the thirty pieces of silver back to the chief priests and elders and said, "I did wrong to deliver up an innocent man!" They retorted, "What is that to us? It is your affair!" So Judas flung the money into the temple and left. He went off and hanged himself (Matthew 27:3-5).

2a. On the human level. Proper understanding of sin and guilt is necessary for the contemporary Christian to appreciate the gift of God in Christ by which we have been saved from sin and death. In the previous chapter we defined sin as *aversion* from God as you meet Him in yourself (your conscience) and in your fellowmen. Hence, contrition (repentance) should be seen as *conversion* to God in yourself and fellowmen.

Our Lord taught us to pray: "[Father-God] forgive us our trespasses, as we forgive those who trespass against us." Only insofar as you have an awareness of guilt and forgiveness on the human level, can you be aware of guilt toward God and His abundant mercy and willingness to forgive. Peter met God on the human level, in our Lord Whom he had denied. "The Lord turned around and looked at Peter . . . and Peter wept bitterly" (no. 1a). The reading from James (no. 1b) hints in the same direction of confession of guilt and forgiveness on the human level, and even today we still pray before Mass: "I confess to Almighty God, *and to you, my brothers and sisters,* that I have sinned."

2b. New attitude. The Bible testifies that conversion of spirit (heart-attitude) is the most fundamental demand made on mankind. The Bible is not interested merely in repentance and reparation for each individual transgression of the divine law, but in a new attitude of man toward God. The psalmist prays:

> "A clean heart create for me, O God,
> and a steadfast spirit renew within me."
> (Psalm 51:12)

2c. Always forgiving. God is willing to forgive always. Judas knew Psalm 32 (no. 1c), but did not apply it to his own case (no. 1d).

2d. By his wounds. Chapters 22—24 have shown us that forgiveness, as Christians see it, is always forgiveness "through Christ our Lord." As Peter states: "In his own body he brought your sins to the cross, so that all of us, dead to sin, could live in accord with God's will. By his wounds you were healed" (1 Peter 2:24). Whether it was your first reconciliation with God, sealed by Baptism, or a subsequent one through a heartfelt contrition, sealed by the prayer of the Church (Sacrament of Penance, Chapters 53,54), forgiveness is granted by God because of our Lord's vicarious suffering, Death, and constant pleading for us "at God's right hand."

3. As we forgive. You should keep in mind the necessity to be aware of guilt and forgiveness on the human level. At this very moment, can you pray honestly: "Forgive us our trespasses as we forgive those who trespass against us"?

4. THINKING IT OVER

How would you define contrition? Why is awareness of guilt and forgiveness on the human level so important? Explain this from the Bible passages! What is more important than repentance for each individual transgression of the divine law? What was wrong in Judas' repentance? What has Jesus Christ to do with contrition and forgiveness? What does the parable of the Pharisee and the tax collector teach you about awareness of guilt and forgiveness on the human level? (See Luke 18:9-14.)

5. PRAY MEDITATIVELY

And forgive us our trespasses as we forgive those who trespass against us, and lead us not into temptation, but deliver us from evil. Amen.

6. THINGS TO DO

Read meditatively: Psalm 51 and the Liturgy of Ash Wednesday.

52. The Sacrament of Penance

(Part 3) Authority to Forgive Sins

1a. *Then he reentered the boat, made the crossing, and came back to his own town. There the people at once brought to him a paralyzed man lying on a mat. When Jesus saw their faith he said to the paralytic, "Have courage, son, your sins are forgiven." At that some of the scribes said to themselves, "The man blasphemes." Jesus was aware of what they were thinking and said: "Why do you harbor evil thoughts? Which is less trouble to say, 'Your sins are forgiven' or 'Stand up and walk'? To help you realize that the Son of Man has authority on earth to forgive sins"—he then said to the paralyzed man—"Stand up! Roll up your mat, and go home." The man stood up and went toward his home. At the sight, a feeling of awe came over the crowd, and they praised God for giving such authority to men (Matthew 9:1-8).*

1b. *"If your brother should commit some wrong against you, go and point out his fault, but keep it between the two of you. If he listens to you, you have won your brother over. If he does not listen, summon another, so that every case may stand on the word of two or three witnesses. If he ignores them, refer it to the church. If he ignores even the church, then treat him as you would a Gentile or a tax collector. I assure you, whatever you declare bound on earth shall be held bound in heaven, and whatever you declare loosed on earth shall be held loosed in heaven.*

"Again I tell you, if two of you join your voices on earth to pray for anything whatever, it shall be granted you by my Father in heaven. Where two or three are gathered in my name, there am I in their midst" (Matthew 18:15-20).

1c. *On the evening of that first day of the week, even though the disciples had locked the doors of the place where they were for fear of the Jews, Jesus came and stood before them. "Peace be with you," he said. When he had said this, he showed them his hands and his side. At the sight of the Lord the disciples rejoiced. "Peace be with you," he said again.*

> *"As the Father has sent me,*
> *so I send you."*

Then he breathed on them and said:

> *"Receive the Holy Spirit.*
> *If you forgive men's sins,*
> *they are forgiven them;*
> *if you hold them bound,*
> *they are held bound" (John 20:19-23).*

2a. Giving such authority. The Bible passage in no. 1a conveys a clear invitation to the Christian community to thank God for the authority which dwells in men to whom it has been confided by Jesus Himself. "A feeling of awe came over the crowd, and they praised God for giving such authority [as to forgive sins in God's name!] to men."

In the same light you must understand the other Bible readings (nos. 1b and 1c). Whence comes this certitude of divine ratification of the community's decisions with regard to sin? It flows from the mysterious presence of the redeeming Christ in His Church. "Where two or three are gathered in my name, there I [Christ] am in their midst" (Matthew 18:20). Forgiveness of sin was usually exercised in the form of prayer!

2b. An appeal. In order to have a clear picture, we make the following observations:

(1) Through sinning, man is guilty in the eyes of God and the Church. Included is Jesus Christ, Who is head of the Church. (See Chapter 50, no. 2f.)

(2) Forgiveness, as Christians see it, is granted by God through Christ our Lord, because of His vicarious suffering, Death, and constant pleading for man. (See Chapter 51, no. 2d.)

(3) The early Christian communities were aware of the fact that authority to forgive sins (in the name of Jesus Christ-God!) was given to them. (See no. 1a, b, c.)

(4) This authority to forgive sins was exercised not first of all juridically (as in a courtroom!), but in the form of prayer. And praying together, the comunity believed that our Lord was in their midst! (See Matthew 18:20.) Hence, every confession of sin was an appeal to that powerful prayer of our Lord and the Church. And remember that along with this powerful prayer was given God's reponse, the bestowal of grace, which man needs so much to be released from human lethargy and to go on growing in love.

2c. Various rites. The Church of Jesus Christ has not always exercised that authority to forgive sins in the same way. There were various rites of penance. Theologians do not agree about which ones were the Sacrament of Penance proper and which ones were just pious exercises, as, for example, our penitential rite at the beginning of Mass.

(1) Only very serious sins. It seems certain that the Sacrament of Penance proper was used only in the case of very serious sins—sins that excluded from the Kingdom of God. Hence, during the first centuries probably most Christians did not receive this Sacrament at all.

(2) Public affair. Penance was a public affair. Sins were confessed privately to the bishop or his substitute. This was the condition, for one to be received into the class of the penitents. Works of penance (fasting, prayer, wearing a hairshirt, etc.) and a time of penance (from three weeks to a lifetime!) were imposed publicly. Penitents were considered as excommunicated (excluded from the community). Ashes were sprinkled over their heads. Also the reconciliation with the Church was public. From the 4th Century on, the Church of Rome had its reconciliation rites on Holy Thursday.

(3) Privately. Only from about 670 A.D. do we have indications on the British Isles that people confessed their sins privately to a priest once a year before Christmas and received their penance right away. A century later, this was also done in France at the beginning of Lent.

(4) Changing formulas. Until about 1000 A.D., reconciliation by bishop or priest was always given in the form of a prayer. Only later do we see that those prayer forms become "wish" formulas, as our "May almighty God have mercy on us, forgive us our sins . . ." at the beginning of Mass. In the 13th Century the indicative form "I [the priest] absolve you from your sins in the name of the Father . . ." became the custom which still exists today.

But whatever the wording of the reconciliation rite, sins are forgiven because the power of our Lord and the prayer of the Church are present in the rite. (See p. 145, 2c, par. 3, sacraments.)

2d. Open mind. This bird's-eye view of the history of penance may help you to understand the changes which are proposed in this time of renewal after Vatican II. This should not shock you. The awareness that the Church has God-given authority concerning penance and the forgiveness of sin has always been there. Only the way it should be exercised was seen differently over the centuries.

There is a tendency to make penance a community affair once again. Sooner or later some kind of penitential rite may be introduced in your parish. This chapter may help you to accept this new way of penance with an open mind.

3a. Through fellowmen. We have discussed awareness of guilt and forgiveness on the human level (Chapter 51, no. 2a). God approaches us in our human selves (your conscience) and in our fellowmen. Whenever you encounter genuine love, care, and understanding, somehow you meet God. God forgives us in and through fellowmen: Our Lord Jesus Christ and the community which He established. This is the basis for the confession of sins, as we practice it in the Catholic tradition. It is so important to be human and to communicate with fellow human beings, especially when wrong or injustice has occurred. (Read again Chapter 50, no. 2f.)

3b. Wish to encounter. Go regularly to confession. All kinds of liturgical and personal moments in life can be meaningful for receiving the Sacrament of Penance: Easter, Christmas, or any feast; also before a marriage, giving birth, serious surgery, or when you are about to do some important work. Finally, confession is especially for moments when man is conscious of his sins, that is, when he lives in serious sin.

There are Christians who like to receive the Sacrament of Penance often. If they do so merely because they are afraid, they should not continue to receive so often. But if they do so because they wish to encounter Christ and appeal to His powerful prayer, it can be very evangelical for them. They should discuss their problems and again include any sins of their past for which they are especially sorry.

4. THINKING IT OVER

What lesson does the first Bible passage (no. 2a) try to bring out? Whence comes this certitude of divine ratification of the community's decisions with regard to sin? Why are sins always forgiven in the Sacrament of Penance? (See nos. 2c, 4.) Describe how the authority to forgive sins was exercised over the centuries! Why is it so important to be aware of guilt and forgiveness on the human level?

5. PRAY MEDITATIVELY

Psalm 38: "O Lord, in your anger . . ." Make it an existential Bible reading, in other words, relate the text to your existence or life situation!

6. THINGS TO DO

Read: Romans 1:1-7; 5:1-11.

53. The Sacrament of Penance

(Part 4) **Confession of Sins**

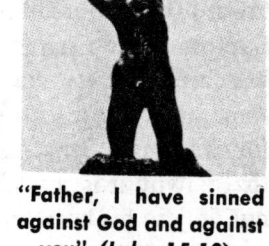

"Father, I have sinned against God and against you" (Luke 15:18). The Prodigal Son. Sculpture by Rodin.

1. Jesus said to them: "A man had two sons. The younger of them said to his father, 'Father, give me the share of the estate that is coming to me.' So the father divided up the property. Some days later this younger son collected all his belongings and went off to a distant land, where he squandered his money on dissolute living. After he had spent everything, a great famine broke out in that country and he was in dire need. So he attached himself to one of the propertied class of the place, who sent him to his farm to take care of the pigs. He longed to fill his belly with the husks that were fodder for the pigs, but no one made a move to give him anything. Coming to his senses at last, he said: 'How many hired hands at my father's place have more than enough to eat, while here I am starving! I will break away and return to my father, and say to him, Father, I have sinned against God and against you; I no longer deserve to be called your son. Treat me like one of your hired hands.' With that he set off for his father's house. While he was still a long way off, his father caught sight of him and was deeply moved. He ran out to meet him, threw his arms around his neck, and kissed him. The son said to him, 'Father, I have sinned against God and against you; I no longer deserve to be called your son.' The father said to his servants: 'Quick! bring out the finest robe and put it on him; put a ring on his finger and shoes on his feet. Take the fatted calf and kill it. Let us eat and celebrate because this son of mine was dead and has come back to life. He was lost and is found.' Then the celebration began" (Luke 15:11-24).

2a. Real contrition. The parable (no. 1) illustrates what your attitude should be when you go to confession. The most important thing is not an exact account of sins committed. More attention should be paid to real contrition or conversion to God.

2b. Also to the Church. The reason why Christians confess sins that are already forgiven by God because of contrition is that sinning results in your being guilty not only toward God but also toward the Church, of which you are a member by Faith and Baptism. (See Chapter 50, no. 2f.) From the very beginning there has been a keen awareness that the Christian community has something to do with sin and guilt. It has God-given authority to forgive sins. (See Chapter 52, nos. 2b (3), (4), and 3a.) And that is why it is reasonable for a sinner to confess himself as such not only in his heart to God but also to the Church of Christ.

2c. Confessing venial sins. It is not necessary to confess your venial sins, but it is advisable to do so. When you have offended a fellowman, even if the matter was not serious, you apologize. Jews and Moslems set aside a special day each year on which they settle all irregularities with their fellowmembers. Christians should do this by regular confession, in which they seek peace with Christ and the Church.

Note this well: In the Sacrament of Penance there is present the powerful prayer of Jesus and the Church. Jesus' pleading for you, time and again, will help to release you from human lethargy and thus make you love God more fervently. Every confession of your sins, even of venial sins and sins of your past life, is a humble appeal to this powerful prayer of our Lord and the Church.

2d. Family doctor. Confess your sins to a regular confessor. A family doctor, who knows his patient for a long time, is usually more capable of giving good advice than a doctor who sees the patient for the first time!

There is no reason for being ashamed to confess your sins. The confessor is Christ's representative. And Christ loves the sinner! Moreover, the priest is bound by the seal of the Sacrament of Penance. He is forbidden to reveal anything that has been confessed to him. Think, for example, of St. John Nepomucene, confessor of the Queen of Bohemia, who gave his life rather than break the seal of confession.

2e. First confession. A Protestant who joins the Catholic tradition usually makes his first confession at his Profession of Faith or conditional Baptism. Since a first confession is usually not easy for a person not used to it from childhood on, one could tell the confessor that his is a first confession and be sure that the priest is willing to help.

3. Doing it. Before you enter the confession booth, pray for guidance to the Holy Spirit, examine your conscience, and try to arrive at a real contrition, which includes the intention to avoid the occasions of sin as well as possible and the serious effort to do better.

The priest will generally give you a short spiritual instruction and finally a penance. The penance given by the priest is usually rather easy (consisting of a few brief prayers or some effort related to your faults). This small penance should be the beginning of a life of penance, always and everywhere!

Upon leaving the confessional you should thank God for the grace He has given you through this Sacrament, perform your penance, and think a moment about the instruction the priest gave you. A good thanksgiving prayer is to make the Stations of the Cross. Through Christ's Passion you received forgiveness of sin. Meditation upon the Passion is therefore one of the best ways to thank Him.

4. THINKING IT OVER

Confessing your sins, what is most important in connection with the Bible passage of this chapter? What is the reason to confess sins even after God has forgiven them through personal "conversion"? Why is it good to go to a regular confessor? Why is it advisable to confess also your venial sins? What is the procedure concerning confession when a Protestant Christian joins the Catholic Church? Of what should penance, given by a confessor, be the beginning?

5. PRAY MEDITATIVELY

Psalm 32: "Happy is he . . ."

6. THINGS TO DO

Read Luke 7:36-50. Make it an existential Bible reading, which means, apply the text to your own existence or life situation!

54. Anointing of the Sick

1a. Then Jesus went with them to a place called Gethsemani. He said to his disciples, "Stay here while I go over there and pray." He took along Peter and Zebedee's two sons, and began to experience sorrow and distress. Then he said to them, "My heart is nearly broken with sorrow. Remain here and stay awake with me." He advanced a little and fell prostrate in prayer. "My Father, if it is possible, let this cup pass me by. Still, let it be as you would have it, not as I" (Matthew 26: 36-39).

1b. Since Jesus was aware that they wanted to question him, he said: "You are asking one another about my saying, 'Within a short time you will lose sight of me, but soon after that you will see me.'

"I tell you truly:
you will weep and mourn
while the world rejoices;
you will grieve for a time,
but your grief will be turned to joy.
When a woman is in labor
she is sad that her time has come.
When she has borne her child,
she no longer remembers her pain
for joy that a man has been born into the world.
In the same way, you are sad for a time,
but I shall see you again;
then your hearts will rejoice
with a joy no one can take from you" (John 16:19-22).

1c. Is there anyone sick among you? He should ask for the presbyters of the church. They in turn are to pray over him, anointing him with oil in the Name [of the Lord]. This prayer uttered in faith will reclaim the one who is ill, and the Lord will restore him to health. If he has committed any sins, forgiveness will be his (James 5:14-15).

2a. The power of demons. James (no. 1c) tells us about the Christian custom of anointing the sick. We should try to understand this anointing of the sick and accompanying prayer from its original setting.

In ancient times, oil, penetrating the skin, was frequently used for healing. However the ancients, including the Hebrews of Jesus' time, did not see a scientific relation between medication and healing, as we do. Their understanding of medication was mainly a magical one. Sickness and death were considered as signs and consequences of sin. A sick person was seen as delivered into the power of demons. Helpless, he turned first of all to the priest for help.

Hence, the ministry of healing the sick is one of the signs of the messianic era, the time of salvation from the power of satan and of God's Reign on earth. God, made present in His Messiah, overcomes the power of sin and demons! "He [Jesus] taught in their synagogues . . . and he cured every sickness and disease" (Matthew 9:35). "They [the Apostles] expelled many demons, anointed the sick with oil, and worked many cures" (Mark 6:13).

The problem is that we no longer regard sickness as caused by demons and sin. Sick people send for the doctor, not for the priest. Only when medical science and skill fail do they ask for the Sacrament of the Sick.

2b. Still meaningful? Nevertheless, the primitive outlook on sickness, as caused by demons and sin, gives us the clue to discover the purpose of anointing with oil in the minds of Jesus and His contemporaries. That purpose was to overcome the power of sin and demons, since they were thought to cause sickness and disease.

Can this ancient custom of "anointing with prayer" still have meaning for us who do not see sickness as caused by the power of sin and demons? Yes it can, since evil, sin, and guilt are still realities in our lives, even though they are not related to sickness. Sin and guilt are also realities in the lives of people who suffer from serious and terminal sickness. Seriously sick people need the presence of God in a special way to overcome the evil of loneliness, helplessness, sin, guilt, and whatever may cause them anguish.

2c. Making God present. Who should make God present to a terminal or seriously ill patient? (We have discussed the meaning of presence in Chapter 28, no. 3. Read it again!)

(1) Doctor and nurses. Those involved are first of all the doctor and the nurses. As professionals, they know that they should practice a psychosomatic approach to their patients, in other words, an approach not just to the patient's body (surgery, "shots," food, etc.), but to the total person, who is a oneness of mind and body. The patient's outlook on life and his religion are part of his personality. Hence, if he is a Christian, doctors and nurses should treat the patient as such, certainly when his sickness is very serious and terminal. Christian doctors and nurses cannot be indifferent to a patient's religious outlook without giving up their professional psychosomatic approach. In their way, they should make God present to the patient.

An inquiry shows that four out of five (potential) patients want to be informed about death drawing near and that a great number of physicians is not willing to give that information. Another inquiry shows that 56 out of 60 terminal patients, to whom apt counseling was given, were able to die their own death. A terminal patient has the right to know his situation, unless it is very certain that mentally he is not able to accept it. Whether or not the doctor will give this information directly to the patient or through the minister, a good friend, or relative, should be considered in each individual case.

(2) Relatives and friends. Others involved are relatives and close friends of the terminal patient. All depends here on sound judgment and genuine love. We should be really concerned and even to a certain extent involved in an often tragic situation. Usually a patient has a keen feeling as to whether he is approached as a person or just treated as a case!

(3) The priest. Last but not least, we mention the priest. He should be notified in time. The priest represents the congregation that is concerned about a fellow Christian who is going to depart from this world. Christians pray for their suffering fellow members.

The priest is also in a special way the man of God. He comes to make God present to the patient and as such he represents Christian Hope. (See Chapter 43, no. 2c.)

Atheists define death as "the transition from being to nothingness." They can see death only as an absurdity. For the Christian, it is different. Death is not only a sad and inevitable necessity; it has a positive meaning. Christians see death as the optimum opportunity for accepting God and for full realization of one's self. Dying with Christ, a Christian believes that he will arise with Him! This is done in the semidarkness of faith, which needs to be strengthened in the difficult hours of transition.

The priest tries to strengthen that Faith by counseling the patient (part of it could be the sick person's Confession), by helping him to see death from the framework of Scripture, and by mediating God's grace through prayer underlined by the sacred sign of the anointing. Symbols, when well understood, speak a language of their own and make God more tangibly present than words can do. And only that presence of God, experienced in Faith, is man's consolation in the lonesome hours of dying.

2d. Wounded by sin. From ancient times, oil has stood for healing. The anointing with oil symbolizes spiritual healing! A Christian figure of speech calls man "wounded" by sin. A terminal patient's wounds may be loneliness, helplessness, the darkness of Faith, sin and guilt because of missed chances to be the person he should be. Prayer underlined by the symbol of anointing asks God to be present to a suffering fellowman and to heal his wounds with His infinite mercy.

2e. Anointing the senses. The rites of this sacrament are as follows: The priest anoints the sick person on the forehead and on the hands, saying: "Through this holy anointing and his great love and kindness, may the Lord fill you with the power of his Holy Spirit. In his goodness may he ease your suffering and extend his saving grace to you, freed from all the power of sin."

Christians see Holy Communion as the bread of life everlasting. A terminal patient should encounter our Lord often in the sign of bread. It is He Who taught us how to die. (See no. 1a, b.) He also will strengthen us.

2f. Adaptation. The purpose of the Sacrament of the Sick seems to have been originally the restoration of health, both physical and spiritual (of course, by overcoming the power of sin and demons!) rather than preparation for death (no. 2c). Later on it became the custom to confine this Anointing of the Sick to those in danger of death. Hence, the name "Extreme Unction." The documents of Vatican Council II speak of "Anointing of the Sick," which is more in accordance with the ancient pattern.

2g. Bodily recovery? Can the "Anointing of the Sick" be related to bodily recovery? James and the early Christians who saw sickness as caused by the power of demons did so! Of course, God can take totally surprising initiatives as an answer to our prayers. (See Chapter 45, no. 2e.) Whether God will do so in a case declared terminal by a physician in our time of advanced medical science is another question. Perhaps in such terminal cases Christians should pray as our Lord taught us, "Thy will be done!"

3. All responsible. In no. 2c. we have stressed concern and involvement in our care for sick people. All Christians should feel responsible for the suffering members of God's people.

In this time of Church renewal and updating, with the Sacrament seen as the "Anointing of the Sick," modern man should be encouraged to receive the Sacrament in time of illness and not wait until the illness is extreme. Likewise older folk and the aged should receive the anointing of the sick from time to time.

4. THINKING IT OVER

Describe the original setting of the "Anointing of the Sick." Why did sick people of Jesus' time first of all go to the priest? How does the primitive outlook on sickness give us the clue to the purpose of anointing with oil in the minds of Jesus and His contemporaries? How does "Prayer with Anointing" still have meaning for sick people of our time and culture? Describe the role of doctors and nurses with reference to a seriously ill person. What can friends and relatives do? What is the priest's task in the case of a terminal patient? Describe the meaning of "Prayer with Anointing." Can the Anointing of the Sick be related to bodily recovery?

5. THINGS TO DO

How would you discuss death with a good friend (terminal cancer patient), presupposing that he is willing and able to do so?

55. Holy Orders

1a. Even Christ did not glorify himself with the office of high priest; he received it from the One who said to him,

> *"You are my son;*
> *today I have begotten you";*

just as he says in another place,

> *"You are a priest forever,*
> *according to the order of Melchizedek."*

In the days when he was in the flesh, he offered prayers and supplications with loud cries and tears to God, who was able to save him from death, and he was heard because of his reverence. Son though he was, he learned obedience from what he suffered; and when perfected, he became the source of eternal salvation for all who obey him, designated by God as high priest according to the order of Melchizedek (Hebrews 5:5-10).

1b. Under the old covenant there were many priests because they were prevented by death from remaining in office; but Jesus, because he remains forever, has a priesthood which does not pass away. Therefore he is always able to save those who approach God through him, since he forever lives to make intercession for them (Hebrews 7:23-25).

1c. In the presence of God and of Christ Jesus, who is coming to judge the living and the dead, and by his appearing and his kingly power, I charge you to preach the word, to stay with this task whether convenient or inconvenient—correcting, reproving, appealing—constantly teaching and never losing patience. For the time will come when people will not tolerate sound doctrine, but, following their own desires, will surround themselves with teachers who tickle their ears. They will stop listening to the truth and will wander off to fables. As for you, be steady and self-possessed; put up with hardship, perform your work as an evangelist, fulfill your ministry (2 Timothy 4:1-5).

2a. Aspects of Christ's office. Meditating on the great mystery of Christ, early theologians considered all the aspects of Christ's office. They described our Lord as King (Ruler), Prophet, Servant of the Lord, Rabbi (Teacher), Son of Man (representing the people of God) and finally as Priest and simultaneously the sacrificial Lamb, offered to God. These qualifications were partly used by our Lord Himself. But there is a clear elaboration of the mystery of Christ in New Testament literature. For example, though our Lord referred to His Death as a sin-offering, He never called Himself a priest. It is mainly the Epistle to the Hebrews which brought out this aspect of Christ's office, comparing our Lord with the Jewish High Priest and his sacrificial function on the Day of Atonement.

2b. Priest-mediator. In Jewish tradition, the priest was the man of the sanctuary. His main task was the offering of the sacrifice. As such he was a mediator. He offered God the gifts of His faithful and conveyed to them God's blessings. Using this example, the author of Hebrews describes Christ as the unique Mediator between God and man. On the Cross, Jesus offered Himself as a sacrificial Lamb to God and conveyed God's blessings and salvation to men. (See no. 1a.) And our Lord remains our unique High Priest, since he lives on making intercession for us. (See no. 1b.)

2c. Shared by all. As for this priestly aspect of Christ's office, we observe that the New Testament sees this shared first of all by the whole Christian people. "You . . . are a chosen race, *a royal priesthood,* a holy nation, a people he claims for his own to proclaim the glorious works of the One who called you from darkness into marvelous light" (1 Peter 2:9). Christians are, properly speaking, priests. Sharing in Christ's priesthood, they worship God with Him. (See Chapter 36.)

Through the Sacrament of Orders, some Christians are singled out to exercise a special ministry in this priestly people. This priesthood conferred by the Sacrament of Orders (prayer and imposition of hands) is related to the baptismal priesthood of all believers precisely as service. We regard the presbyter as a Christian who ministers to his brethren by rendering present and effective Christ's saving action. (See also Chapter 33, no. 2a.)

2d. Changing role. The principal service which the presbyter renders to the community is the Eucharistic Celebration (making present Christ's Sacrifice in the signs of bread and wine) and conveying God's blessings through the sacred signs (Sacraments) which our Lord gave us. As such the priest is the man of the sanctuary.

Is this all the presbyter does to render present and effective Christ's saving action to his brethren? Indeed, it is the reason why we call the presbyter "priest," since for centuries he confined himself almost solely to this service. But we have seen that the priesthood is only one aspect of Christ's office. There are many more! (See no. 2a.)

In this time of Church renewal, there is much to do about the changing role of the priest. Many refer to his work now as "active ministry." This brings out the fact that the "minister" does not share only our Lord's priesthood (merely having a cultic function in church), but also many other aspects of His office.

The modern minister (presbyter-priest) is not only a man of the sanctuary who presides over the Eucharistic Celebration and conveys God's blessings through the Sacraments. The modern minister preaches and teaches religion and in so doing he also shares Christ's office. (See no. 1c.) The office of Christ is so inexhaustible and the needs of God's people are so manifold! There are ministers who work in education; others specialize in sacred theology, or sociology and social work; some become civil rights workers (prophets!); some work as professional psychiatrists and counselors; some are mainly administrators (rulers!). Any one of these or other tasks is acceptable as long as it is done as a sharing and continuation of our Lord's unique office in a spirit of love and service to the "brethren."

But let us be fair! Do not expect one minister to be an expert in all the aspects of Christ's office. The early Church understood this when she divided the office and gave special tasks to bishops, presbyters, and deacons. (See Chapter 33, no. 2d.) A reshuffling of tasks will be necessary now and then because of the constantly changing needs of God's people.

A recent example of reshuffling tasks in the ecclesiastical office is the revival of the permanent diaconate, an office that over the centuries has been reduced to little more than a name. The deacons are officials upon whom hands are imposed not for the priesthood, but for a ministry of their own. Deacons are able to officiate at Baptisms, marriages, funerals and burials, to distribute Communion, to read the Scriptures, to preach, and to assist in the administration of a parish and work with the lay apostolate. They cannot offer Mass or hear confessions. Deacons are chosen from both unmarried and married members of God's people.

2e. Celibacy. Priests of the Latin Rite live in celibacy in order to be more free and ready for their task of service and moreover to signify certain Christian values by their very way of life. (See Chapter 46.) The Eastern Rites have not only priests living in celibacy but also married priests. Bishops are elected solely from unmarried priests. There is a demand in the Latin Church to change this law of obligatory celibacy for priests.

2f. In the midst of the world. "The priest: To live in the midst of the world without wishing its pressures; to be a member of every family, yet belonging to none; to share all sufferings; to penetrate all secrets; to heal all wounds; to go from men to God and offer Him their prayers; to return from God to men to bring pardon and hope; to have a heart of fire for charity and a heart of bronze for chastity; to teach and to pardon, console and to bless.

"My God, what a life!
"And it is yours, O priest of Jesus Christ" (Lacordaire).

3. Challenge. Boys in high school and college should pray that the Lord may enlighten their hearts. As mentioned in Chapter 33, no. 3, essential to ecclesiastical office are God's call to the individual, his response in faith, and his acceptance through the Church (in present practice, through the bishop or his representative in the name of the Church).

Every Catholic should pray often for many and good priests. He should create in his home a soundly religious atmosphere, the usual condition for a vocation to the priesthood. A mother should consider it an honor to have God call her boy to the altar. (See also Chapter 46, no. 3.)

4. THINKING IT OVER

Recall some aspects of our Lord's office. What was the priest's task in the Jewish tradition? How does the Epistle to the Hebrews qualify Christ as a priest? How do our priests share in Christ's priesthood? What is the principal service the presbyter (priest) renders to the community? What else do priests do to continue Christ's office in the contemporary Church? Why cannot one priest be an expert in all the aspects of Christ's office? How do a bishop, a presbyter (priest, minister), and a deacon share in Christ's office? Why do priests live in celibacy? In Chapter 46, no. 3, what was mentioned as a prerequisite for a vocation to the priesthood? What is the religious atmosphere (i.e., regular family prayers, daily Bible reading, mutual love, decency of conversation, jokes, behavior) in your home? How would you react if God were to call your son (if you have one) to the sacred priesthood? Where are the minor and major seminaries of your diocese located?

5. PRAY MEDITATIVELY

Apply this prayer of our Lord and pray it for your priests:

"O Father most holy,
protect them with your name which you have given me . . .
I gave them your word,
and the world has hated them for it . . .
I do not ask you to take them out of the world,
but to guard them from the evil one. .
They are not of the world,
any more than I belong to the world . . .
As you have sent me into the world,
so I have sent them into the world;
I consecrate myself for their sakes now,
that they may be consecrated in truth."   (John 17:11-19)

6. THINGS TO DO

Read: Mark 6:6-13; Luke 9:1-11; Matthew 18:10-14; Luke 22:19-20; John 20:19-23; Mark 16:14-18; John 21:15-19.

Read the novels: *The Devil's Advocate* (Dell Publishing Co.) and/or *The Shoes of the Fisherman* (Morrow), both by Morris L. West. These novels give you, in addition to entertainment, a good picture about the life of priests and the organization, customs, etc., of the Church.

56. Marriage in Christ

1a. Happy the husband of a good wife,
   twice-lengthened are his days;
A worthy wife brings joy to her husband,
   peaceful and full is his life.
A good wife is a generous gift
   bestowed upon him who fears the Lord;
Be he rich or poor, his heart is content,
   and a smile is ever on his face.
A gracious wife delights her husband,
   her thoughtfulness puts flesh on his bones;
A gift from the Lord is her governed speech,
   and her firm virtue is of surpassing worth.
Choicest of blessings is a modest wife,
   priceless her chaste person.
Like the sun rising in the Lord's heavens,
   the beauty of a virtuous wife is the radiance of her home
                                    (Sirach 26:1-4.13-16).

1b. "As the Father has loved me,
so I have loved you.
Live on in my love.
You will live in my love
if you keep my commandments,
even as I have kept my Father's commandments,
and live in his love.
All this I tell you
that my joy may be yours
and your joy may be complete.
This is my commandment:
love one another
as I have loved you.
There is no greater love than this:
to lay down one's life for one's friends" (John 15:9-13).

2a. Love is basic. In chapter 46, we have discussed the sign value of marriage. Read it again and pay attention to the Christian outlook on marriage: the relationship of love between husband and wife, lived as the mystery of Christ and the Church. A Christian husband is supposed to love his wife in the same way and (assuming he knows what love is) be willing to surrender himself, that is, to do everything possible to make his wife happy.

God's people are supposed to be subject to Christ in a very intimate love. Likewise, a Christian wife should be subject to her husband in a very intimate love.

Inspired by the Holy Spirit, the Apostle Paul impressed these supreme ideals upon mankind, inclined to egotism. A wise man, knowing that God created the human heart, love, sex, and marriage, will, first of all, investigate the Creator's design about these matters, rather than accept the risky statements of magazines, books, and movies. God, being a loving Father, wants your happiness in love and sex as in all other phases of life.

So, following God's revelation, as quoted above, you see that only a partner who knows how to love, that is, knows how to forget himself to make the other partner happy, will become happy himself in marriage. Young people who want to be truly happy later on should, from their early youth, learn how to love. If a teenager constantly wants to concentrate both his own and others' attention upon himself, he is being a selfish egotist! ("Ego" means "I.") He will never be capable of love later on in marriage! "Love" means "giving in order to make another person happy." Basic to Christianity and to marriage is this attitude of love. All of us must be converted daily from egotism to a more perfect love. As long as a person is an egotist, he is neither a good Christian nor a good husband or wife.

'This is a great foreshadowing: I mean that it refers to Christ and the Church" (*Ephesians 5:33*).

2b. The rites of marriage. People who intend to marry should inform the priest at least a month before the wedding. It should be the usual procedure for Catholics to marry at a special wedding Mass (the Nuptial Mass).

The rite of marriage is briefly as follows: The priest invites the couple to declare their consent: "I, N., take you, N., for my lawful wife (husband), to have and to hold, from this day forward, for better, for worse, for richer, for poorer, in sickness and in health, until death do us part."

Receiving their consent, the priest says: "You have declared your consent before the Church. May the Lord in his goodness strengthen your consent and fill you both with his blessings. What God has joined, men must not divide."

The priest blesses the rings, which bridegroom and bride place on one another's ring finger. They may say: "N., take this ring as a sign of my love and fidelity." More prayers and blessings follow in the framework of the Eucharistic celebration.

2c. Marriage and law. As Church law stands now, Catholics must express their consent to live as husband and wife in the presence of three witnesses, one of whom is a Catholic priest. As a rule, this must be done also in the case of a mixed marriage, though the bishop can permit the ceremony to be performed by the minister of the non-Catholic party.

Non-Catholics may follow their own customs to make their marriage lawful. Hence, a non-Catholic Christian who decides to join the Catholic tradition does not have to be remarried in the Catholic Church.

There is a tendency among modern theologians to regard marriage once again as a social and civil affair, more or less as was done before the 11th Century when marriage was not under the jurisdiction of the Church. These theologians state also that the classical Bible texts on the indissolubility of marriage should be interpreted as an appeal to Christian perfection rather than as juridical principles. Let us pray that the Spirit may guide God's people in its constant search for what the Maker of the human race wants for our benefit!

2d. Marriage a Sacrament. For Christians, their oneness as two persons is raised to the level of a Sacrament, which means "a title that appeals constantly to the powerful prayer of our High Priest Jesus Christ." And God the Father, Who always hears the prayer of His Son, uninterruptedly pours out His abundant help and blessings on those who are married in Christ. This is true also for the lawful marriage of two Protestants who through Baptism are members of the one Church of Christ!

2e. Innocent party. As a rule *only death* can separate a married couple and give freedom to marry another partner. A lawful marriage of two Protestants is also subject to this law (see no. 2d).

See 1 Corinthians 7:39; Mark 10:2-12; Romans 7:2-3; Matthew 19:3-9.

The law was given for the common good, although an individual can possibly suffer when her (his) spouse is not faithful to the marriage vows. Nevertheless, God foresaw this and you can be sure He is a loving Father to any unhappy and lonely wife or husband, deserted by her (his) mate (see Chapter 14, no. 3). Sometimes divorce is granted. If you have problems, ask your priest for further information. Referring to the traditional interpretation in the Eastern Orthodox Church of Matthew 5 and 19, the question was raised at the Second Vatican Council whether the Church has the power to permit remarriage of the so-called "innocent party," i.e., the party innocently deserted. For the opinion of modern theologians, see no. 2c. Pray that the Spirit of all truth may guide the Church concerning this very important pastoral problem!

2f. Catholic partner, or mixed marriage. Choosing a partner for life is your own task, and you alone must make the decision by following your heart, your mind, your common sense, and last, but not least, the principles of your religion.

Your heart: You must love each other. The time when young persons of opposite sex associate with one another before marriage is for the purpose of finding this out. But you will find out only if you have clear ideas about love! (See no. 2a.)

Your mind, your common sense, your religion: That is why young persons, who cannot possibly have the experience and wisdom of life that comes with maturity, should listen to the advice of their parents, priests, and educators. Do not marry too young. Choose a good Catholic who attends Mass regularly, goes to confession and receives Holy Communion; who is serious about having children; who really wants to establish a home; who is not a selfish, immature, "much-promising and nothing-giving" egotist. Girls should respect themselves, realizing that even the man guilty of seducing and abusing girls ultimately wants a good and faithful girl as his partner for life.

A marriage between close relatives is not allowed. A mixed marriage is discouraged by the Church. The reason is that in a mixed marriage a certain division is introduced into the living cell of the Church, the family. The Church is most desirous that Catholics in matrimony be able to attain to perfect union of mind and full communion of life. Nevertheless, the Church also recognizes the natural right of man to marry and to exercise this right free from undue pressure. Thus the Church makes special arrangements for mixed marriages.

(1) Catholic and other Christian pastors should jointly do all they can to prepare couples for a mixed marriage.

(2) A common life of prayer in the home should be developed by these couples.

(3) Prior to marriage they should reach a common mind concerning the religious education of their children. Otherwise, they most likely will find a severe strain later that can subject them to well-meaning but tension-building pressures from relatives on both sides.

(4) Neither party may abdicate the fundamental responsibility of parents to see that their children are instilled with deep and abiding religious values.

(5) The non-Catholic partner must be informed that the Catholic shall make the following promise: "I reaffirm my faith in Jesus Christ and, with God's help, intend to continue living that faith in the Catholic Church. I promise to do all in my power

to share the faith I have received with our children by having them baptized and reared as Catholics."

(6) For the legal procedure of a mixed marriage, see no. 2c.

2g. Love, sex and children. The question may be asked: why do man and woman marry, have intercourse, and stay together? Is it to give themselves to one another, finding fulfillment in conjugal love, or is it to beget and rear children? This question separates what is one and should remain one. Fertility is something that proceeds naturally from love, and love is always—also in other human values—life-giving. Wherever love is, there originates more intense and more human life!

Very meaningfully we say that animals mate, but that human beings make love. Having intercourse only, or mainly, because of passion is degrading oneself and one's partner to the level of animals. It means disregarding the ideals of love and endangering your marriage. Overemphasis on passion will arouse the desire for ever stronger impulses, and may finally lead to infidelity. Wise couples will foster mutual love, for they know that as they grow older passion will decrease while mutual love will continue to increase. Elderly couples who happily share an intimate unity of mind will say spontaneously: "My wife and I think . . ." An egotist will never achieve this ideal!

The Hebrews protected family life by figuratively putting into the mouth of God the commandments: "You shall not commit adultery . . . you shall not covet your neighbor's wife."

Consider briefly, against this background, why it is wrong to refuse intercourse, granted the request is reasonable (see 1 Corinthians 7:3-4). Are adultery and divorce serious sins? Examine also such problems as: irresponsible and overly long separations (e.g., because of both partners working and living in different places); overemphasized emancipation and independence of the female partner; legal separation (not one granted by the Church); the presence of a boarder in the family group for a long time, and slighting the importance of the family meal by seldom having meals together.

2h. Your personal problems. Marriage problems of Catholics who want to do God's will usually center around sex and planned parenthood.

The Church cares and tries to approach your problems with a broadminded understanding. But remember that her priests did not make the laws of marriage. The Church is only God's interpreter! And God is all-wise, all-good, all-understanding. So, in discussing the physical and psychological problems of sex, you must first adapt your vision to God's vision, as interpreted to you by the Church.

A catechism is not a marriage instruction book. Read a good Catholic book about physical and psychological questions in marriage. There are serious and good non-Catholic books too, but often these overstress the role of technique and passion, thereby giving a distorted or wrong picture. (See also Chapter 46, no. 2b.)

You may also discuss privately your questions and personal problems with any priest, if you wish. He will give you literature on request and, if necessary, will direct you to a reliable sexologist. Make it a rule of life to discuss rising problems in the family with your priest. Discussing and facing them as adults may prevent a good deal of trouble. Not the lawyer but the priest is the first who should be consulted!

2i. Responsible parenthood should be the guiding principle for Christian couples. As for the number of children, this will be the fruit of their mutual love. Always considering their responsibility to the Creator, society, and the children to come, they should discuss together what can be done physically (health of the mother), financially (education), and emotionally. The method of rhythm is the approved way of exercising responsible parenthood. But there are many cases in which this method does not work for physical or psychological reasons (or both). This creates a serious problem for "the sons of the Church" who are forbidden from using contraceptives (the pill and other means) by Church teaching.

The recent encyclical *On Human Life* states the official position of the Church and must be taken into consideration when forming one's conscience in this matter. For further information, see Bibliographical Notes, p. 327, no. 84.

2j. Young couples constantly in state of grace? The following quotation from a priest-professor in Moral Theology, undoubtedly written down after discussing problems with reliable sexologists, may be a guide to Christian couples:

"You have to consider tenderness as belonging to the whole of married life and not only to sexual intercourse.

"Tenderness is a modest expression of love and respect; it is an element which expresses love and keeps it alive. Tenderness does not kill passion, but permeates and ennobles it. Really affectionate couples can more easily abstain from complete sexual intercourse and satisfaction, when the occasion demands, because for them passion cannot be separated from tenderness and roughly pushed forward.

"Therefore, a husband must not consider every tenderness and desire for tenderness from his wife as a request for intercourse.

"Tenderness, even sensual tenderness, as an expression of mutual love is permissible without the purpose of directing it toward sexual intercourse. Nor do such tendernesses become illicit when they are, now and then, involuntarily and unexpectedly accompanied by complete satisfaction.

"Couples with a delicate conscience possibly go too far now and then with abstinence from conjugal tenderness, especially when one partner pays too much attention only to his (her) own task to keep himself (herself) safe from the power of passion. By doing so these couples defraud themselves of the joy of mutual love, and deprive themselves of the soothing effect it has on the appeasement of passion.

"An allowed conjugal caress, perhaps necessary to comfort the partner or to prove one's love, may unexpectedly cause an emission, especially during the days when the natural discharge is due. In those days, these tendernesses are often more fervently desired by one or both partners. Tactful and attentive love should make one aware of the partner's distress and help him (her) either by avoiding or by giving tenderness, as the occasion dictates. The danger of an unwilled emission is less than the danger of dampening mutual love.

"If conjugal attraction is to be constant, it cannot, from the very beginning, be confined to the field of sex alone. Married people should make themselves attractive and desirable to each other in every respect. In this way the common struggle for a strongly controlled purity will become easier. Married people are also capable, with God's help, of even longer periods of abstinence when circumstances make it necessary." (From *Das Gesetz Christi* [The Law of Christ], *Dargestellt fuer Priester und Laien* [Explained to Priests and Laymen] by Bernhard Haring, CSSR, pp. 1096-1097, 1109—English edition available from Newman Press.)

3. Conscience. If you are married, discuss this quotation of Father Haring with your partner. And do not look for sin where there is none. Both an overly narrow conscience and one that is too easy going are wrong!

4. THINKING IT OVER

Describe the sign value of a Christian marriage as in Chapter 46. What could a Christian couple learn from 1 Corinthians 13? What is the best preparation of young people for marriage? Describe the rite of a Catholic marriage! In choosing a partner, what should be observed? Why does the Church discourage a mixed marriage? What arrangements has the Church made for mixed marriages? How are love, sex, and children related? Why should a person who has problems in marriage consult first a priest rather than a lawyer? As regards responsible parenthood, to whom are Christian couples responsible? What is the role of tenderness in marriage?

5. THINGS TO DO

Read Ephesians 5:1-2. 25-32. Note that Paul refers to the patriarchal marriage pattern of his time and culture, in which the wife was "submissive in love" to her husband. Our culture has outgrown this and stresses more that the wife is a companion equal to the husband—in love!

Read also 1 Corinthians 7. What would you consider as conditioned by time and culture (hence not binding anymore) and what as timeless (hence binding also now)?

57. The Sacraments

1. When he came down from the mountain, great crowds followed him. Suddenly a leper came forward and did him homage, saying to him, "Sir, if you will to do so, you can cure me." Jesus stretched out his hand and touched him and said, "I do will it. Be cured." Immediately the man's leprosy disappeared (Matthew 8:1-33).

Before Jesus had finished speaking to them, a synagogue leader came up, did him reverence, and said: "My daughter has just died. Please come and lay your hand on her and she will come back to life." Jesus stood up and followed him, and his disciples did the same.

When Jesus arrived at the synagogue leader's house and saw the flute players and the crowd who were making a din, he said, "Leave, all of you! The little girl is not dead. She is asleep." At this they began to ridicule him. When the crowd had been put out he entered and took her by the hand, and the little girl got up. News of this circulated throughout the district (Matthew 9:18-19. 23-26).

As he walked along, he saw a man who had been blind from birth. His disciples asked him, "Rabbi, was it his sin or that of his parents that caused him to be born blind?"

> "Neither," answered Jesus:
> "It was no sin, either of this man
> or of his parents.
> Rather, it was to let God's works show forth in him.
> We must do the deeds of him who sent me
> while it is day.
> The night comes on
> when no one can work.
> While I am in the world
> I am the light of the world."

With that Jesus spat on the ground, made mud with his saliva, and smeared the man's eyes with the mud. Then he told him, "Go, wash in the pool of Siloam." (This name means "One who has been sent.") So the man went off and washed, and came back able to see (John 9:1-7).

2a. Saving presence. For the miracle stories in the Gospels, read "How to Read Your Bible," no. 13e, p. 303. In the miracle stories, the early Church expresses her Faith in the saving presence of our Lord, made tangible in symbols!

2b. The language of symbols. We should keep in mind that all man's activities are symbolic. It is through symbols that we communicate our thoughts, emotions, and experiences with one another. The spoken or written word is the most widely used symbol for communication. But we use many other symbols (e.g., a handshake, a kiss, a move of the hand, dance, music, a present, a meal together, etc.) which convey a message often more efficiently than the spoken word. See also "How to Read Your Bible," no. 13h, p. 304.

As a matter of fact, we adapt our symbols to the intelligence of our addressees. To a child one speaks the language a child can understand.

Observing these facts, we should try to understand the way Almighty God tries to communicate with man. The symbols He uses are adapted to human intelligence. He utilizes the experience of a people, as we possess it in its sacred literature, the Bible, and above all the most outstanding specimen that came forth from this people: Jesus of Nazareth. We see Him as the Sacrament (sign, symbol) of the encounter with God.

Likewise the Church, being the extension of our Lord in this world, is seen as a sign or Sacrament of God's loving presence. We experience this loving presence of God in symbols adapted to our intelligence. Some of these symbols received a special significance in the Christian tradition. They are the symbols known as Sacraments: a meal, washing, anointing, laying on of hands, marriage vows, all of them very fundamental elements in men's lives. Christ and the Church designated these elements as effective symbols of a sacred reality, namely, God present, giving Himself, communicating with man.

2c. Sacraments and grace. Viewing the Sacraments as means of communication of God with man, we should keep in mind that these symbols are not magic tricks to produce "something" in us which could be called "grace." (See Chapter 36, no. 2b, c.)

Communication is not a magic trick. It is a two-way, give-and-take, affair between two persons. God approaches you in a symbol and you respond in Faith. Moreover, grace is not "something." Grace is that interpersonal relationship with God, analogous to the relationship between friends. (See Chapter 28). When grace is an interpersonal relationship with God, we should be careful in attributing "special graces" to the different Sacraments, as has been done in traditional catechisms. One does not dissect friendship! Analysis only destroys an interpersonal relationship in its effort to know it. Such a relationship can be known only by respectful contemplation and description, as we have tried to do in Chapters 40-56. Of course, a repeated encounter with God in these symbols (the Sacraments) should change us, just as a constant relationship with a good friend makes us different persons.

3. Formalism deforms. A Bible, no matter how expensively bound and profusely illustrated, does not do any good unless you have a regular and faithful contact with God in and through that Bible. God communicates with you only if you open out to Him!

Other means of communication are the Sacraments, as we know them in the Catholic tradition. It is up to you! Meeting our Lord in the symbols of bread and wine entails the special danger of routine. It is done so often! How do you feel when somebody shakes your hand and meanwhile continues his conversation with somebody else? Such a handshake is a void and meaningless symbol. Formalism deforms religion. Avoid it as far as you are concerned!

4. THINKING IT OVER

How should we understand the miracle stories of the Gospels? Why is it necessary to adapt our symbols of communication to the intelligence of our addressee? What means did God choose to communicate with man? How would you define the concept "grace"? How does formalism deform religion?

5. THINGS TO DO

Read some of the miracle stories in the Gospels. Try to understand them as indicated in no. 2a and apply them to your own life situation as suggested in "How to Read Your Bible," no. 17, p. 307.

ETHICS IN THE KINGDOM OF GOD

"I will meditate on your precepts and consider your ways" (*Psalm 119:15*).
The Thinker. Sculpture by Rodin (1840-1917), France

58. On Appreciation

*1. See what love the Father has bestowed on us
in letting us be called children of God!
Yet that is what we are.
The reason the world does not recognize us
is that it never recognized the Son.
Dearly beloved,
we are God's children now;
what we shall later be has not yet come to light.
We know that when it comes to light
we shall be like him,
for we shall see him as he is.
Everyone who has this hope based on him
keeps himself pure, as he is pure (1 John 3:1-3).*

*We, for our part, love
because he first loved us.
If anyone says, "My love is fixed on God,"
yet hates his brother,
he is a liar.
One who has no love for the brother he has seen
cannot love the God he has not seen.
The commandment we have from him is this:
whoever loves God must also love his brother.
Everyone who believes that Jesus is the Christ
has been begotten of God.
Now, everyone who loves the father
loves the child he has begotten.
We can be sure that we love God's children
when we love God
and do what he has commanded.
The love of God consists in this:
that we keep his commandments—
and his commandments are not burdensome.
Everyone begotten of God conquers the world,
and the power that has conquered the world
is this faith of ours (1 John 4:19—5:4).*

2a. Free and loving. This Bible passage is a theological reflection on the Christian experience from the school of St. John. Bible scholars attribute the three Epistles of John as well as the fourth Gospel to John "the disciple Jesus loved," though John's disciples may have edited and published them later.

John's point is: "We are to love then, because he [God] loved us first" (4:19). God has called you (Chapters 1—30). He blesses His people (Chapters 31—57). We should respond to His love by loving Him. Read again Chapters 7 and 24 about the Covenant theme (especially the Covenant theme with marital overtones) to describe man's relationship with God. Read also Chapters 43 and 44, where we discussed love, without which the life of a Christian is unthinkable. We shall discuss now how a free and loving response to God should be conceived by a Christian of the 20th Century.

2b. A loveless code of laws. John says: "This is what loving God is—keeping his commandments" (5:3). If well understood, this is an excellent rule to go by. Unfortunately, it has not always been understood very well. "Keeping the commandments" has often resulted in a kind of legalism which has done much harm to God's people. Too often the law was kept for the law's sake, without paying sufficient attention to people and the situations they had to cope with. We think of the marriage problems of many of God's people! Trespassings of the law (commandments) were neatly registered as mortal and venial sins, punishment was measured accordingly, penance was prescribed, and indulgences distributed. Theologically speaking, this was all right. But the danger was there (and often still is) that the people of God would become totally subservient to a loveless code of laws.

2c. Legalism-minimalism. Moreover, legalism often resulted in a loveless minimalism practiced by God's people. Do nothing more than you "must" do (just the minimum!), avoid mortal sin and save your soul! As if Christianity were just a system to save your soul! This is a far cry of the beautiful child-father relationship which Jesus wants our relationship with God to be. In addition this legalism also brought about a one-sided observance of the law, for example, concerning emphasis on the evils of sex and little or no mention of the law of justice and love for all men regardless of race or creed.

The renewal movement in the Church is a reaction against this legalism. Is God first of all a judge or rather a loving and understanding Father? True, we should love God because He has loved us first. But is "the law" (the Commandments) the only starting point for discussing what a Christian's loving response to God's love should be?

2d. A formed conscience. Since every man is unique (there will never be a second "you"!), man's relationship with his Maker is also unique. Hence, quite a few contemporary theologians suggest that you should take your own unique situation as a starting point when you reflect in all conscience on your response to God's love for you.

However, starting from your own conscience and pondering your own unique situation does not mean that you can just do what you want to do. Your conscience must be formed and guided. First of all your conscience *must* always be guided by love for God and your fellowmen. You must love God because God has loved you first. Furthermore, there are commandments and suggestions for a good life in your Bible and in the rules and regulations of your Church and country.

2e. Codeless love versus loveless code. Today there exists a situation ethics (situation morality) which takes as a starting point man's unique situation and conscience as *guided by love alone*. Those who hold this view accept laws and commandments only as guidelines that do not bind and must be tested in each case against the background of each man's own conscience and situation. This is a situation ethics which is not accepted in the Catholic tradition. The Church's question to these people is: "Can a *codeless* love (love not clarified by laws) be an answer to a loveless code?" (See no. 2b on legalism.)

2f. Catholic situation ethics. But there is a situation ethics which can be accepted by Catholics. You take your own unique situation (for example, *your* marriage) and your own conscience as a starting point for pondering your response to God. You are conscious that genuine love *must* guide you and that there are laws, also absolute norms from which love or justice does not condone exceptions. This situation ethics, acceptable for Catholics, will be explained further in the following chapters. Note, however, that this approach does not undo John's statement: "The love of God consists in this: that we keep his commandments" (1 John 5:3: see no. 2a), just as the first approach (taking the Commandments as a starting point) does not eliminate conscience.

3. Two starting points. As regards your response to God's love, you are free to choose either of the two approaches mentioned above. Either you follow the more traditional way: You observe the law and Commandments conscientiously and let the observance—doing your duty—be your answer to God's love for you. Or, reflecting on your response to God, you take as a starting point your unique situation and your own conscience, guided by love for God and neighbor and taking serious notice of the existing Commandments. This will be explained more extensively in the following chapters. What matters here is that you respond in love to God, Who has loved you first, even before you were even able to think of Him.

4. THINKING IT OVER

Explain two approaches to a Christian response to God's love for man. What are the dangers of the traditional ethics, which starts with the laws that must be observed? Explain the situation ethics which is not accepted in the Catholic tradition. Why does the Church question this situation ethics? Which situation ethics can be accepted by Catholics? What matters first of all, regardless of the approach you choose? When reading Chapter 44, what strikes you most?

5. READ ATTENTIVELY

> We, for our part, love [God]
> because he first loved us.   (1 John 4:19.)

6. PRAY MEDITATIVELY

How great is the goodness, O Lord,
  which you have in store for those who fear you,
And which, toward those who take refuge in you,
  you show in the sight of men.
You hide them in the shelter of your presence
  from the plottings of men;
You screen them within your abode
  from the strife of tongues.
Love the Lord, all you his faithful ones!
  the Lord keeps those who are constant,
  but more than requites those who act proudly. (Psalm 31)

59. An Informed Conscience

1. Fear not, you shall not be put to shame;
   you need not blush, for you shall not be disgraced.
   The shame of your youth you shall forget;
   the reproach of your widowhood no longer remember.
   For he who has become your husband is your Maker;
   his name is the Lord of hosts;
   Your redeemer is the Holy One of Israel,
   called God of all the earth.
   The Lord calls you back,
   like a wife forsaken and grieved in spirit,
   A wife married in youth and then cast off,
   says your God.
   For a brief moment I abandoned you,
   but with great tenderness I will take you back.
   In an outburst of wrath, for a moment
   I hid my face from you;
   But with enduring love I take pity on you,
   says the Lord, your redeemer.
   This is for me like the days of Noah,
   when I swore that the waters of Noah
   should never again deluge the earth;
   So I have sworn not to be angry with you,
   or to rebuke you.
   Though the mountains leave their place
   and the hills be shaken
   My love shall never leave you
   nor my covenant of peace be shaken,
   says the Lord, who has mercy on you (Isaiah 54:4-10).

2a. Conscience as starting point. Like Hosea and Jeremiah, the author of the above passage describes man's relationship with God as a marital one, a relationship of intimate love. Man may be unfaithful; God is willing to forget and "take you back."

Reflecting on a free and loving response to God's love for you, you may take your conscience, guided by love, as a starting point. What does love for God and fellowmen prompt me to do in this concrete situation? (See Chapter 44, no. 2a.)

2b. What is conscience? We speak of a good and a bad conscience, an erroneous conscience, a well educated or poorly educated conscience. What is conscience? Theologians and psychologists quarrel about details, but we may state that every newborn child has a capacity for right moral judgment, just as it has a capacity for speech and interpreting sight and sound. How this capacity will be developed depends on the child's education. Hence, whenever we deal with the conscience of an adolescent or adult, we deal with an already more or less educated conscience. Education from early childhood on and self-education as a lifetime job are of decisive importance.

When a child is brought up and trained in theft, sexual license and murder, we may assume that he considers his behavior as right. His is an erroneous conscience. More or less the same can be stated about people living outside the impact of the Christian outlook on behavior. Their "capacity for moral judgment" is also shaped through the environment they are born into. As long as they honestly follow their conscience, they are good people and we should not judge them when their behavior is different from what we consider as right.

2c. Mature and well informed. A Christian's conscience is formed by a Christian environment: family, parish, school, society. The Christian environment is marked by the presence of Christ. This mysterious presence of our Lord in fellow Christians, the Bible, the signs (Sacraments) He left us, and the guidance of the Church form a Christian conscience. In this environment love for God in Christ develops your capacity for right moral judgment (conscience). From this it becomes clear that a Christian who follows his conscience must know Christ and what He stands for. The more a Christian is mature and well informed, the more he will be guided by real love and the less he needs the many laws that clarify the implications and ramifications of love of God and neighbor.

It is the same as in a family. Children must follow the will of the parent even if they cannot know the reason for that will. But then these children grow up. Love and respect for the parents remain, but gradually obedience can be done away with. If their education was a success, they are behaving well—no longer forced to do so by the parents, but prompted by good sense, love, and justice. Or take a family man who loves his wife and children. He does not need a state law to force him to support the family. He does not ask: "What is the minimum support I must give in order to avoid a lawsuit?" Prompted by love, he provides as well as he can.

3. There are various ways of approaching the question of how to behave as a Christian.

(a) The way of traditional catechisms. Usually, our traditional catechisms take the law as a starting point. You learn the Commandments and just follow them. When you have a problem, you ask your confessor or parish priest and do whatever he tells you is right. This is often the easiest way. It does not require a growth into maturity, and you do not have to inform yourself. "Father told me . . ." is what you go by.

(b) Free for a deeper commitment. Another way is to take as a starting point your unique situation and conscience, guided by love. But then you accept the duty of keeping yourself informed. Growing to Christian adulthood is a lifetime job. Forming your conscience is a lifelong search to discover what God is asking of you in your concrete situation. This way of freedom is not the easier way, since it sets you free only for a deeper commitment. Ever more Christians in the Catholic tradition accept this challenge. They study the charming personality of our Lord, as the early Church presents Him in the New Testament and commit themselves to go by what Jesus of Nazareth stands for.

94

Accepting this challenge does not mean that all Christians must carry a doctor's decree in theology. An average American education and the will to search is enough. Neither does this approach make the Commandments and counseling superfluous, as will be discussed in the next chapter. Rather it is a question of emphasis: first love and entailed in it rules, and not the other way around.

4. THINKING IT OVER

How does Isaiah describe your relationship with Almighty God? How would you describe "conscience"? What about people whose moral behavior is different from ours? How is Christian conscience formed? Why is the traditional approach to moral behavior often the easier one? What are you supposed to do if you follow Christian situation ethics? St. Augustine states: "Love and do as you will." How would you explain this statement? When you have to make a moral decision, do you ever ask yourself: "What is the loving thing to do in this situation?"

5. PRAY MEDITATIVELY

A private act of love for God.

6. THINGS TO DO

Read about Jesus' behavior in any chapter of the Gospels and ask yourself: How should I act in a similar situation?

60. Conscience and the Commandments

1. *Hear, O Israel! The Lord is our God, the Lord alone! Therefore, you shall love the Lord, your God, with all your heart, and with all your soul, and with all your strength. Take to heart these words which I enjoin on you today. Drill them into your children. Speak of them at home and abroad, whether you are busy or at rest. Bind them at your wrist as a sign and let them be as a pendant on your forehead. Write them on the doorposts of your houses and on your gates (Deuteronomy 6:4-9).*

Later on, when your son asks you what these ordinances, statutes and decrees mean which the Lord, our God, has enjoined on you, you shall say to your son, "We were once slaves of Pharaoh in Egypt, but the Lord brought us out of Egypt with his strong hand and wrought before our eyes signs and wonders, great and dire, against Egypt and against Pharaoh and his whole house. He brought us from there to lead us into the land he promised on oath to our fathers, and to give it to us. Therefore, the Lord commanded us to observe all these statutes in fear of the Lord, our God, that we may always have as prosperous and happy a life as we have today; and our justice before the Lord, our God, is to consist in carefully observing all these commandments he has enjoined on us" (Deuteronomy 6:20-25).

2a. Meaning of laws. This is a catechetical instruction such as that which is found in the Jewish home liturgy to this very day. What is the meaning of the laws? Love and gratitude are the background, "that we may always have as prosperous and happy a life as we have today" (Deuteronomy 6:24).

(1) Many commandments as found in the Bible are conditioned by time and culture. These laws do not bind us (e.g.,

Deuteronomy 6:8-9 and 1 Corinthians 7:37-38). Other laws are related to the human condition as such. Those laws are to be paid attention to. (e.g., Deuteronomy 6:4-5 and Exodus 19:12-16).

(2) The example of civil laws. In the jungle it is the strongest animal that prevails. But the human species has outgrown that situation. Man is a social being and the more he unfolded his capacities (Chapter 13, no. 2b), the more he understood that life in society should be organized. There must be laws man goes by, otherwise life in society is like that of the jungle, where the strongest prevails. Some of the civil laws may be outdated, others may be even unjust. But generally speaking we should be law abiding, since these laws explain the ramifications of love for country and fellow citizens in situations which may be ours.

(3) As for Church laws, we accept them by the fact that we are members of the Church. The mere fact that you have responded to God's call to live your dedication to Christ in the Catholic tradition implies that as a rule you go by the laws of the Church. We are acquainted with rules such as attending Mass on Sunday (see Chapter 62), some laws on fasting and abstinence from meat (a minimum as a reminder of our duty to do penance constantly!), and supporting our church. Read again Chapters 27 and 34.

(4) Authority and "laws" in the family. Children owe love, respect, and obedience to their parents. Often children cannot yet see why parents want them to do certain things. Situation ethics requires a certain degree of maturity, which children should grow into. The authority of the family is directed to this mat-

Authority directed to maturation.

uration of the children. Friction between teenagers and parents goes with this process of growing till gradually the time comes when obedience can be done away with and only love and respect remain as a lifetime duty.

2b. The law's aim. How are laws related to the Christian conscience? First of all, the supreme law of love of God and neighbor should guide it. All moral demands (laws) are nothing but expressions and interpretations of the basic demand for love and generosity, though adjusted to various situations of human life. The law's aim is to express and clarify the implications of the great commandment of love for God and fellowman.

2c. Are clarifications needed? The Catholic tradition believes that clarifications of the law are needed. If all men were so mature in Christ that the compass of love would point out the direction unfalteringly, we could do without the laws that explain the ramifications of love in various human situations. But such a maturity of love is rather rare and cannot be considered the usual situation of the average Christian conscience. (See Chapter 50, no. 2b.)

Authentic adulthood also involves humble acknowledgment of what has remained infantile in ourselves, of our bondage to our own past and the fact of concupiscence, egotism, cowardice, etc., which color and distort our picture of reality. Hence, we need laws that reflect the wisdom of fellowmen. They are helpful beacons in our dark and often confused situations. "What is the loving thing to do in this situation?" The laws can help us to find the way, and can be necessary to push us to do "the loving thing" in our situations, whenever we are not as mature in love as we should be!

However, when an adult Christian has to make a decision of conscience, he will not evade his responsibility by depending blindly on the letter of the law; rather he will listen to what the law can provide as a correction of his own views.

3a. Laws in the Bible. If we need the laws, we should be acquainted with them. We should be acquainted first of all with the ethical experience of God's people as related in the Bible. The early Christians meditated on Jesus of Nazareth, His personality, His sayings and most of all His behavior amidst the daily events of life. These reflections on the Christ-event were inspired (guided) by God. You should know the New Testament with its approach to behavioral problems. For example, read Matthew 5.

The Old Testament relates many laws. Actually, the first five books are called "The Law." Figuratively, the Bible relates these laws to Moses and Mount Sinai. Actually, these laws originated gradually in the Hebrew communities. They reflect what the collective Hebrew mind, guided by God, considered as good and evil. When reading laws in the Bible, you should remember what has been mentioned above in no. 2a. Read Exodus 19:16-25 and 20. For the literary form of the Sinai story, read Chapter 67, no. 2a. 98

Since the ethical experience of God's people as related in the Bible was inspired (guided) by God, it is normative also for us. Human situations usually have something in common. This "something in common," found in any passage of Scripture, is called existential understanding. This understanding, related to *your* existence or life-situation, is decisive for faithful Bible reading. 99

3b. Guidelines of the Church. But the Biblical experience of 2,000 years ago does not relate to all the problems of 20th-Century life. Think of the birth control issue, a new understanding of marriage and sexuality (tied solely to procreation and/or as a value of its own—a means of self-realization?), a new outlook on authority, implications of personhood (e.g., the woman a century ago and the working woman now!), euthanasia (mercy killing), 100 sterilization, artificial insemination, abortion (at what stage can the fetus be regarded as a human person with full human rights?), capital punishment, nuclear war, the use of drugs, the ethics of modern business, the race issue, and responsibility for developing countries.

Concerning these ethical issues God's people expects guidelines from the teaching authority of the Church, as embodied in the bishops with their head, the Bishop of Rome. An adult Christian should be acquainted with these rules and guidelines as expressed in papal encyclicals and documents of regional bishops' conferences. (Read again Chapters 27 and 34.)

3c. Civil law. As for civil law, society expects you to be acquainted with the essential laws of your country.

4. THINKING IT OVER

What is the meaning of laws? (See Bible passages!) What about laws in the Bible which are conditioned by time and culture and laws which relate to the human condition as such? Give some examples! What about civil laws, Church laws, and authority in the family? What is the law's aim? Give two reasons why we need laws! How would you relate laws to your conscience? Where do you find the laws which are supposed to help you make your decisions in conscience? What is existential Bible reading?

5. PRAY MEDITATIVELY

With all my heart I seek you;
    let me not stray from your commands.
Within my heart I treasure your promise,
    that I may not sin against you.
Blessed are you, O Lord;
    teach me your statutes.
With my lips I declare
    all the ordinances of your mouth.
In the way of your decrees I rejoice,
    as much as in all riches.
I will meditate on your precepts
    and consider your ways.
In your statutes I will delight;
    I will not forget your words (Psalm 119:10-16).

61. Situation Ethics and Church Guidance

1. *Some men came down to Antioch from Judea and began to teach the brothers, "Unless you are circumcised according to Mosaic practice, you cannot be saved." This created dissension and much controversy between them and Paul and Barnabas. Finally it was decided that Paul, Barnabas, and some others should go up to see the apostles and presbysters in Jerusalem about this question.*

The church saw them off and they made their way through Phoenicia and Samaria telling everyone about the conversion of the Gentiles as they went. Their story caused great joy among the brothers. When they arrived in Jerusalem they were welcomed by that church, as well as by the apostles and the presbysters, to whom they reported all that God had helped them accomplish. Some of the converted Pharisees then got up and demanded that such Gentiles be circumcised and told to keep the Mosaic law.

The apostles and the presbyters accordingly convened to look into the matter. After much discussion, Peter took the floor and said to them: "Brothers, you know well enough that from the early days God selected me from your number to be the one from whose lips the Gentiles would hear the message of the gospel and believe. God, who reads the hearts of men, showed his approval by granting the Holy Spirit to them just as he did to us. He made no distinction between them and us, but purified their hearts by means of faith also. Why, then, do you put God to the test by trying to place on the shoulders of these converts a yoke which neither we nor our fathers were able to bear? Our belief is rather that we are saved by the favor of the Lord Jesus and so are they." At that the whole assembly fell silent. They listened to Barnabas and Paul as the two described all the signs and wonders God had worked among the Gentiles through them (Acts 15:1-12).

2a. Conscience to be followed. Christians who live their dedication to Jesus of Nazareth and what he stands for in the Catholic tradition experience a more detailed guidance concerning their behavior than may be found elsewhere. (See Chapter 34.) What about all these laws? One hears: "What do the priests know about all this? . . . As long as you honestly follow your conscience. . . . I'll decide that for myself." Indeed, guidance and law-making may have been overdone up to the recent past. Often pastoral care was too paternalistic, though many of God's people liked it that way and still do. Whatever your opinion, serious theologians assure us that even the best pastoral theology or textbook morality cannot bridge the gap between "cases" and "life-situations." *Ultimately the decision comes from the personal conscience.* That conscience must be followed and respected, even when, after honestly inquiring and examining the law—in good faith—it errs in its judgment.

2b. Discussion, consulting, study. In order to prevent conflicts in conscience, let us check how lawmaking works in the Catholic tradition. Take the Bible reading of this chapter! The young Church had a problem. The teaching authority made a final decision, but only after the discussion of Apostles and elders (the assembly) had gone on for a long time. (Check verses 6 and 12.) When the Church makes laws, there is discussion, consulting, and study.

(1) The Scriptures. First of all, the Church searches the Scriptures. But as mentioned in the previous chapter (60, no. 3b), the Bible reflects the experience of God's people of 2,000-3,000 years ago. Many of the problems we encounter simply did not exist, hence are not mentioned in the Bible. Circumstances and situations have changed, hence have made many Biblical laws obsolete. (See Chapter 60, no. 2a). The Bible is inspired by God, and should be taken into consideration seriously, but it is just one source of moral behavior and lawmaking.

(2) Tradition. A second source of lawmaking and moral decision is tradition. Throughout the ages, God's people was guided by Him, made moral decisions in situations similar to ours; hence the Church of today should study and consider them seriously. But again, often changed circumstances and a deepened understanding of things have made Church laws of the past obsolete. For example, the medieval Church condemned interest on loans over and over again, till a deepened understanding of what money really is in modern times has abolished these laws. Nowadays the Church only condemns excessive interest or usury.

(3) Reason. A third source of lawmaking is reason. The Church uses it to investigate the world and its problems. But history shows that reason alone can come to very different conclusions about particular issues. All human reason, though guided by God, is limited by the human condition as such. When you pour liquid into a container, it takes the shape of the container! God's wisdom works in all honest reasoning, but necessarily takes its shape with all its human limitations of time and culture; hence later generations may have to correct decisions of the past. See the example in no. 2.

(4) God's people now. A final source of lawmaking by the Church is the experience of God's people now. The teaching Church definitively learns from the experience of the living Church, which means, not from what Christians are doing (many doing wrong does not make it right!), but from what they consider to be right. Popes of the past have condemned religious liberty. [102] Contemporary understanding of the dignity of the human person, especially in this pluralistic country, has led to the "Declaration on Religious Freedom" by the Second Vatican Council.

A deepened understanding of the meaning of marriage and human sexuality (emphasis not just on procreation but more on self-realization in and through sexual love) may bring forth a change of marriage laws in the future, as it has done in the past. See 1 Corinthians 7:36-38. These patriarchal customs do not bind Christians in the changed situation of our time and culture. [103]

Renewed Catholic theology is stressing the fact that the Church is not just "the teaching Church" (the hierarchy) but the whole people of God, which has a part to play in the teaching of the Church. The Spirit can also speak in the lives of the Christian people. The teaching Church must always be attuned to the living word of God no matter where it is found. This does not mean that it functions only by taking a poll of the attitudes of a particular group at a particular time (of what those in the group consider as right); rather the teaching authority of the Church tests the experience of God's people in the light of the living word of God and the tradition of the Church herself. Check again Chapters 27 and 34, no. 2b.

3. Discussion important. Since adult Christians play their role in the teaching of the Church, often there will be a certain tension between personal responsibility and authority. This is inevitable, because there are no ready-made answers for every problem, as soon as modern society brings it up. (See Chapter 60, no. 3b.) We are a pilgrim Church, groping in the semi-darkness of the human condition. That is the reason why, besides studying the above-mentioned sources and taking them seriously, discussion is so important. See the Bible reading in no. 1.

3a. Professional people. Especially professional people, who are directly related to ethical problems of modern life (Chapter 60, no. 3b), should discuss their problems together. Gynecologists, lawyers, politicians, public servants, business managers, professional marriage counselors, psychiatrists should consult not just one priest but many, especially professional theologians, other experts, and last, but not least, fellow members of their profession. Only by patient study of the sources (see no. 2b) and mutual consultation in a prayerful spirit of Faith, can a consensus grow. God's Spirit works through our own efforts to find out what the loving thing is that should be done in a particular situation.

3b. Every Christian. And every Christian should discuss his problems. Ask always: "What is the loving thing to do in this situation?" And as a prudent person, respect opinions and laws which reflect the experience and wisdom of your fellow Christians of both past and present! In situations similar to yours, they too were guided by the Spirit.

You do not have to be a theologian in order to be acquainted with your Bible and to know what is going on in the world of Christianity. Just keep up with the media: television and some solid literature. Without being a professional politician, you have your own political opinions. Why not have them as a member of your Church? But keep yourself informed (see no. 2b) and consult others, whenever feasible. Many adult people consult lawyers, marriage counselors, and psychiatrists. Adult Christians can do the same. Consultation (with more than one priest if you deem it necessary) and open discussion (with groups in your parish!) can result in shedding light on dark situations. And, since prudence is not only naturally acquired but also a gift of the Spirit, pray for guidance!

Catholic situation ethics means that, after you have done all of this, *you* must make up *your* mind and decide what the loving thing is that should be done in *your* situation. "We are to love then, because he [God] loved us first" (1 John 4:19).

And as such, we Christians should be a sign! Why did God reveal Himself in Christ and gather a people for Himself? This people should be a sign, a light on the mountain top, a people that lives and acts and goes by that golden rule: "What is the loving thing to do in this situation?" Indeed, a sign in an often crudely egotistic world!

4. THINKING IT OVER

What about the role of conscience? What about an erroneous conscience—should it be followed? How did the early Church solve a moral problem? (See Bible reading!) Describe the ways the Church proceeds when making laws. Would any of these four ways alone be a sufficient guide to come to a moral decision? Give examples of how deepened understanding of things changed Church laws of the past. Why is discussion of moral problems so important? Asking: "What is the loving thing to do in this situation?," what should you take into consideration? What has prayer to do with all of this? How should Christians be a sign in an often crudely egotistic world?

5. PRAY MEDITATIVELY

Say this prayer, figuratively put into the mouth of King Solomon, applying it to your situation:

> "O Lord, my God, you have made me, your servant, king to succeed my father David; but I am a mere youth, not knowing at all how to act. Give your servant, therefore, an understanding heart to judge your people and to distinguish right from wrong. For who is able to govern this vast people of yours?" (1 Kings 3:7. 9.)

6. THINGS TO DO

On the conscience of a mature Christian, read 1 Corinthians 2:6-16, especially verses 11 and 15. If you take the instructions of this book in a group, select some of the moral issues mentioned in Chapter 60, no. 3b and discuss them, relating the issues to no. 2b:1-4 of this chapter.

62. Community Worship

1. They devoted themselves to the apostles' instruction and the communal life, to the breaking of bread and the prayers. A reverent fear overtook them all, for many wonders and signs were performed by the apostles. Those who believed shared all things in common; they would sell their property and goods, dividing everything on the basis of each one's need. They went to the temple area together every day, while in their homes they broke bread. With exultant and sincere hearts they took their meals in common, praising God and winning the approval of all the people. Day by day the Lord added to their number those who were being saved (Acts 2:42-47).

2a. Direct contact necessary. Studying some of the traditional laws and customs in the Catholic tradition (Chapters 62-64), we should see them as discussed in Chapters 60 and 61. Pondering what loving thing should be done in a particular situation, we may consult fellow Christians and experts, but we can also help ourselves by studying how fellow Christians act and have acted in situations similar to ours.

In this chapter we will discuss man's *direct* relationship with the Ultimate Reality, as seen and practiced in the Catholic tradition. The Hebrews have expressed it by figuratively putting the following commands into the mouth of God: "I am the Lord your God; you shall not have strange gods before me," "You shall not take the name of the Lord your God in vain," and "Remember to keep holy the sabbath day" (See Exodus 20). Loving your wife by providing well is wonderful, but love needs to be expressed directly as well, otherwise it withers. Love for God in your fellowmen is an equally wonderful thing, but direct contact with God is necessary, otherwise this love for fellowmen becomes just a vague humanitarianism.

2b. Worship together. The adoration and "inner" worship you give to God in your heart is the most important of all. (See Chapter 45, no. 2.) But besides this the Church insists on Christian worship *together* at least once a week either on Saturday night or Sunday. Why? Cannot I do it alone in my home? You can, but most probably you do not! There are very few things man can do alone. Perseveringly living up to the high ideals of Christianity is a thing that must be done together. We need one another's inspiration. From the very beginning it has been done this way. Christians form a brotherhood, one body (parts related to one another!) in Christ. (See Bible reading no. 1.) However, this does not mean that today's Christians must practice togetherness in exactly the same way that the early Christians did. Cultural circumstances have changed. But the idea of togetherness has been fostered throughout the ages of Christianity. It seems to be something one does not practice alone. Chapters 47—49 describe how this direct contact with God is established in word and sacred rite. Solidarity with the group of which you are a member requires that you attend the meetings of prayer and worship and contribute to a necessary togetherness, if feasible, also by partaking in parish organizations (parish council, CCD, etc.). [106]

2c. On Sunday. From the very beginning Christians have celebrated the Resurrection of our Lord on the first day of the week, which is thus called "The Lord's Day" (Revelation 1:10). The Romanic languages still use the word. Christians of eastern traditions call it the "Day of the Resurrection." We use the originally pagan word "Sunday," since the old Romans had dedicated this day to Mithras, their god of light (the sun). [107]

Christians could not possibly think of a better way of celebrating our Lord's Resurrection than by celebrating the Eucharist: The risen Lord makes His Sacrifice and Sacred Repast present to us! (See Chapter 47.) But since most of the early Christians came from a Jewish background, they went on observing rest on the Sabbath too. Gradually, by the 4th Century, Sunday became a rest day. When the Roman emperor Constantine became a Christian, he assigned Sunday as a rest day for the army (313) and officials of government (321). In the 6th Century we see that the Church forbade servile work on Sunday in order to guarantee worship by everyone.

3. An expression.

Both private prayer and participation in community worship should be an expression of your inner worship to God. Our Lord condemns people who honor God only with their lips, while their hearts are far away from Him The Christian sacrifice is a symbol of your complete self-surrender to God. But if you outwardly offer the sacrifice to God, while your heart is far away from Him, you are a hypocrite.

"I will worship at Your holy temple and give thanks to Your name" (Ps. 137:2).

4. THINKING IT OVER

On Sunday, pondering conscientiously: "What is the loving thing to do in this situation?", how can the above observations guide you? Why seemingly is community worship so important? Describe the origin of Sunday as the day of community worship! What could be done to promote contemporary togetherness in your congregation?

5. PRAY MEDITATIVELY

And they sang the song of Moses, the servant of God, and the song of the Lamb:

> "Mighty and wonderful are your works,
> Lord God Almighty!
> Righteous and true are your ways,
> O King of the nations!
> Who would dare refuse you honor or the glory
>   due your name, O Lord?
> Since you alone are holy,
> all nations shall come and worship in your presence.
> Your mighty deeds are clearly seen"
>   (Revelation 15:3-4).

6. THINGS TO DO

Read 1 Corinthians 11:17-34 on early Christian worship. Try to come to an existential understanding! (See Chapter 60, no. 3a.) Read James 1:19-27 on true religion. Listen, if possible, to a recording of the "Te Deum" of Bruckner.

63. Situation and Respect for Life

1. [Jesus] left that place and went into their synagogue. A man with a shriveled hand happened to be there, and they put this question to Jesus, hoping to bring accusation against him: "Is it lawful to work a cure on the sabbath?" He said in response: "Suppose one of you has a sheep and it falls into a pit on the sabbath. Will he not take hold of it and pull it out? Well, think how much more precious a human being is than a sheep. Clearly, good deeds may be performed on the sabbath."

To the man he said, "Stretch out your hand." He did so, and it was perfectly restored; it became as sound as the other (Matthew 12:9-13).

2. Every limb. Look at your hands! What do you do with your hands? You use them to hold something; to shake hands in congratulation and condolence. You fold them in prayer; you wring them. You admonish; you show, avert, accept, bless something; you offer a gift or a sacrifice. Every limb of your body is given its own task. The Creator made it so.

You never see simply a body—you see either a living person or mortal remains. Your body tells whether you are male or female. It reveals something about your age, your profession, and even what mood you are in. Your body also makes it possible to disguise yourself. When such is the case, your body then becomes a mask.

The Creator sanctified your body and made it a temple of God. Moreover, the Lord Jesus will give a new form to this lowly body of yours and remake it according to the pattern of His glorified body. (See Philippians 3:21.)

Jesus Himself gives you an example of how to respect your own body and that of your fellowmen, and how to respect life and health. He healed the withered hand, as related in the Gospel story above.

3a. Body and personality. When you see the interest and care the Creator has for your body and its life (how He continues creating you), and when you see Christ's and the Church's concern for human life, you also should have interest in the welfare of your body and that of your fellowman.

Your body shares in the development of your personality toward maturity. By living a soundly Christian life, you grow toward increased maturity in Christ, that is, you continue to become a better Christian.

"Glorify God in your body" (1 Corinthians 6:20).

The young must develop their intellect by study and their mind and heart by seeing and hearing beautiful things. ("A thing of beauty is a joy forever!") Development of mind and heart will enable them to share the joys and sorrows of others. Moreover, the will must be trained in order to be able, with God's grace, to choose good and to avoid evil. Thus you should use your body to develop harmoniously your personality. The Creator expects you to be more and more "in His image!" Parents must guide their children in their growth toward a harmonious personality.

3b. Decency—chastity. Respect for life implies respect for all the functions of the human body, including sex. Read again Chapter 56 on Marriage. Related to sex is a precious value called decency. This value is not to be confused with puritanism or hypocrisy. Man is a sexual being. There is nothing wrong with that and the Creator did not make a mistake! Christians cherish decency. This value is not a good in itself. Decency is a good related to chastity (the right use of sex in marriage or abstinence from it outside marriage).

You may ask whether something (joke, picture, book, dress, behavior, action, kissing, dancing) is decent or not. The answer will depend upon whether or not that particular thing is a danger to your purity or that of others. (You are responsible for others!)

Christian chastity (purity) may be compared to a beautiful rose in a garden. The fence around the garden is decency. If the fence (decency) is strong, the rose (chastity) will not be injured so easily.

God gave you the sense of shame which tells you what is, or is not, decent. You should develop soundly that sense in yourself and, through good example, in your environment. The best thing to do is to adapt yourself to the generally decent, accepted customs of your time and home country.

3c. Body—clothes—sports. You have an obligation to take care of your body: to eat reasonably well, to keep your body clean and healthy, and to dress yourself tastefully. Clothes can tell something about the person wearing them. Both your clothes and the manner in which you wear them reveal what you are.

Clothes tell about your unity with others (sportswear, uniform), about your sympathy with the sorrows and joys of others (mourning and festive wear). Clothes should tell what respect you expect from others. It is possible for a woman to dress herself so that her dress is not an invitation to respect! Clothes tell about your common sense: when and where to use a certain kind of dress (such as sportswear, "lounging" attire, a ballroom dress or tuxedo, etc.). Especially is it important to wear the proper clothes in church.

The aim of sports is to give you the joy of wholesome recreation. Moreover, sports develop not only your body but also the whole person. They develop: fast reaction, concentration, the ability to make decisions, team spirit, fairness (even when you are losing!).

"A sound mind in a sound body."

3d. Fellowman's life.

You are responsible for your fellowman's life. You should help him whenever it is necessary and possible to do so. Respect for your fellowman's life and happiness requires that you are honest and truthful with him. A lie or evil gossip can "kill" a person! Parents have a duty to foster the health of their children: serving them reasonable meals, consulting the physician in case of sickness, and affording them adequate sleep, decent recreation, fresh air and exercise.

3e. Evil. Disrespect for life is considered an evil in both Jewish and Christian tradition. Hence, the Hebrews' commandments "You shall not kill" and "You shall not bear false witness against your neighbor."

4. THINKING IT OVER

Asking: "What is the loving thing to do in this situation, related to life?" how can the above observations guide you? See no. 3a, b, c, d, e. How would law-morality consider these laws? (See Chapter 59, no. 3a.)

5. PRAY MEDITATIVELY

Those who follow you, Lord, will have the light of life (John 8:12).

> Happy the man who follows not
>   the counsel of the wicked
> Nor walks in the way of sinners,
>   nor sits in the company of the insolent,
> But delights in the law of the Lord
>   and meditates on his law day and night.
> He is like a tree
>   planted near running water,
> That yields its fruit in due season,
>   and whose leaves never fade.
>   (What ever he does, prospers).
> Not so the wicked, not so;
>   they are like chaff which the wind drives away.
> For the Lord watches over the way of the just,
>   but the way of the wicked vanishes
>   (Psalm 1:1-2. 4. 6).

6. THINGS TO DO

Read: James 1:26 and 3:2-10; Matthew 7:1-5; Galatians 5:18-25.

64. Situation and Stewardship

1. The case of a man who was going on a journey is similar. He called in his servants and handed his funds over to them according to each man's abilities. To one he disbursed five thousand silver pieces, to a second two thousand, and to a third a thousand. Then he went away. Immediately the man who received the five thousand went to invest it and made another five. In the same way, the man who received the two thousand doubled his figure. The man who received the thousand went off instead and dug a hole in the ground, where he buried his master's money. After a long absence, the master of those servants came home and settled accounts with them. The man who had received the five thousand came forward bringing the additional five. "My lord," he said, "you let me have five thousand. See, I have made five thousand more." His master said to him, "Well done! You are an industrious and reliable servant. Since you were dependable in a small matter I will put you in charge of larger affairs. Come, share your master's joy! The man who had received the two thousand then stepped forward. "My lord," he said, "you entrusted me with two thousand and I have made two thousand more." His master said to him, "Cleverly done! You too are an industrious and reliable servant. Since you were dependable in a small matter I will put you in charge of larger affairs. Come, share your master's joy!"

Finally the man who had received the thousand stepped forward. "My lord," he said, "I knew you were a hard man. You reap where you did not sow and gather where you did not scatter, so out of fear I went off and buried your thousand silver pieces in the ground. Here is your money back." His master exclaimed: "You worthless, lazy lout! You know I reap where I did not sow and gather where I did not scatter. All the more reason to deposit my money with the bankers, so that on my return I could have had it back with interest. You, there! Take the thousand away from him and give it to the man with the ten thousand. Those who have, will get more until they grow rich, while those who have not, will lose even the little they have. Throw this worthless servant into the darkness outside, where he can wail and grind his teeth" (Matthew 25:14-30).

2a. Responsibility. As mentioned (Chapter 31, no. 2d), the people whom Jesus gathered around Him is not the same as the Kingdom (Reign) of God. The Reign of God can be found wherever you find good people. As such the Church should be a sign, a city on a mountaintop, a light, a beacon in the darkness and insecurity of the human condition. The covenant idea (we are God's partners: see Chapters 7 and 24) implies that together with God we are responsible for a better world. The Bible passage reminds us that God is the owner of all things and we are His partners, servants, stewards.

2b. Why private property? God said to the man and woman in Genesis: "Have dominion over the fish of the sea, the birds of the air, the cattle and all the animals that crawl on the earth" (Genesis 1:28). In partnership with God, mankind has the right to use these earthly goods. Therefore, every man must be guaranteed a fair share in their ownership. Historical and sociological considerations indicate that the most practical means of insuring all men's access to these goods is some system of private property.

Some of these considerations are: Private property is a stimulus to personal industry. It encourages greater care in handling goods. It tends to prevent greed and strife, and thus contributes to an ordered community life. It protects the worth and liberty of the individual, the security of the family, the dignity of the working class, and the necessity of providing for the future.

The right of private property is derived, therefore, from the collective right of the human race to use the goods of the earth.

Relying on this principle, the Catholic Church opposes Communism (the doctrine of Marx and Engels) which acknowledges only collective ownership.

Restriction of private property, or even collective ownership by the state, may prevail over private ownership only if the "common good" makes it necessary. Examples would be: laws in some countries to restrict cartel practices in the business world; the army requisitioning cars and buildings in time of war; the state expropriating privately owned land to build a new highway.

2c. To each his own. Everybody, therefore, has a right to own property. But neither collective nor private ownership is sovereign. Only God is the sovereign Owner of all things. Man is only God's caretaker, steward, just as were those servants in the above Bible quotation. The Lord will "settle accounts" also with you.

"You shall eat the fruit of your handiwork" (Psalm 127:2).

You are just when you give *suum cuique,* that is, to each his own according to God's will. All that you gain justly (e.g., by working, buying, changing, selling, as a gift, inheritance, or interest) is your property. All that you obtain unjustly (e.g., by stealing, creating, finding without making a reasonable effort to locate the owner, loafing on your job, paying unjust wages, accepting bribes, practicing graft) is not your property.

2d. Just wages. Everybody has the God-given right to possess or to earn enough earthly goods to permit him and his family to live in decent comfort. Workers are entitled to earn a just wage and to receive human treatment. Of course, they are obligated to do their job as well as possible. This is a question of simple justice: "To each his own!"

If you are a worker, protect your rights by joining your labor union. Be active in seeking Christian social justice. Do not be a party to any labor practices which disregard the God-given rights of man.

Employers are obligated to pay a just wage without distinction of race, as described above, to provide good working conditions, and to consider all their workers as a human beings, members of God's family as well as of their own families. Wages for work are fixed, first of all, by supply and demand, but you may not go below a minimum wage, as described above. Especially if you are a manager of many workers, ask your parish priest for a good book on these questions. Also, employers may join their own union. Both employers and employees must be careful that their unions do not commit collective injustice, which can easily happen in cases of "craze for power." Always bear in mind that you must give to each his due.

2e. Emergency share. If, through circumstances, a person is unable to work and to provide his family with the necessities of life, the collective right of the human race to use the goods of the earth entitles him to take them (assuming there is no other way) rather than to starve. This happened, for example, in occupied countries of Europe during World War II. In our country, it is not necessary to do this. You may ask, if necessary, for an emergency share in the "common earthly goods" by contacting a charitable agency or the Church.

A complete discussion about social questions (Socialism, Communism, the attitude and the duty of the Church, etc.) goes beyond the scope of this book. Read a good book about this subject.

2f. Protecting values. Guided by God, the Hebrews have protected the above mentioned values by putting into God's mouth the commandments: "You shall not steal. You shall not covet your neighbor's goods."

3. Social justice. Christians have the serious duty to promote social justice for all. Check the candidate you are voting for! The ghettos and poverty in rural areas should be also your concern. Speak up in your parish council: What can be done for the poor, especially for constructive programs that make the poor help themselves. Justice is a virtue or habit. As a Christian, you should develop the habit of being fair and just at all times in your contacts with your fellowmen.

4. THINKING IT OVER

What does the covenant idea imply? What are some of the reasons given in Catholic teaching for private property as the best means to guarantee all men a fair share in earthly goods? What teaching directly opposes the Catholic stand on private ownership? To whom are you accountable for the just management of your possessions? When do you act justly? What should be your attitude toward increasing your property? How can you justly enlarge your possessions? What is the Christian teaching on minimum wages? How can both workers and employers protect their rights? What should one do in case of the inability to support oneself and family? What is your opinion on congregations spending huge amounts of money on expensive buildings in comfortable neighborhoods and ignoring poverty in the same area? Are they responsible for those situations? Do you have positive suggestions? Pick out some observations which may guide you, pondering: "What is the loving thing to do in this, my situation?" How would law-morality handle the observations of this chapter? (See Chapter 59, no. 3a.)

5. PRAY MEDITATIVELY

> God arises in the divine assembly;
>   he judges in the midst of the gods.
> "How long will you judge unjustly
>   and favor the cause of the wicked?
> Defend the lowly and the fatherless;
>   render justice to the afflicted and the destitute,
> Rescue the lowly and the poor;
>   from the hand of the wicked deliver them.
> "They know not, neither do they understand;
>   they go about in darkness;
>   all the foundations of the earth are shaken.
> I said: You are gods,
>   all of you sons of the Most High;
> Yet like men you shall die,
>   and fall like any prince."
> Rise, O God, judge the earth,
>   for yours are all the nations (Psalm 82).

6. THINGS TO DO

Read Luke 12:39-48. Read and study the attitude of a religious Israelite toward temporal possessions in the book of Job. Job is the literary character who reflects the ideas of the writer.

Job 1:1-20. For what did the Lord praise Job? Describe his first trial, his sorrow and his answer.

Job 2:1-10. What is the second trial of Job? What does his wife say? What is Job's answer?

Job 3:1-25. How does Job lament his condition?

Job 19:1-19. Job's friends say he is a sinner. What is his answer and how does he express his faith in God?

Job 42:7-17. How is Job's faith and patience rewarded?

Examine these encyclicals: *Rerum Novarum* (Leo XIII) and *Quadragesimo Anno* (Pius XI), on the condition of the working classes; *Mater et Magistra* (Pope John XXIII), Mother and Teacher; *Populorum Progressio* (Pope Paul VI), on the development of peoples, especially no. 23, on property.

THE LAST THINGS

"Lord, for your faithful people life is changed, not ended."

65. Death, Judgment and Good Works

1. *Then he went out and made his way, as was his custom, to the Mount of Olives; his disciples accompanied him. On reaching the place he said to them, "Pray that you may not be put to the test." He withdrew from them about a stone's throw, then went down on his knees and prayed in these words: "Father, if it is your will, take this cup from me; yet not my will but yours be done." An angel then appeared to him from heaven to strengthen him. In his anguish he prayed with all the greater intensity, and his sweat became like drops of blood falling to the ground. Then he rose from prayer and came to his disciples, only to find them asleep, exhausted with grief. He said to them, "Why are you sleeping? Wake up, and pray that you may not be subjected to the trial"* (Luke 22:39-46).

2a. Transformation. Through Adam (The Man) sin entered the world and through sin, death. We, the offspring of Adam, the sinner, should accept death with self-surrender and obedience to God's will. (See Chapter 54, no. 2c, 3.)

Jesus gives us an example to follow. In perfect self-surrender and love He accepted death out of the hands of His Father, as shown in the quotation above and in Luke 23:46: "Jesus uttered a loud cry and said, 'Father, into your hands I commend my spirit.' After he said this, he expired."

Moreover, through His meritorious Death on the Cross, Jesus showed us that death was no longer to be considered as a destruction but as a transformation:

"Lord, for your faithful people life is changed, not ended.
When the body of our earthly dwelling lies in death
we gain an everlasting dwelling place in heaven
(Preface for the Dead).

Death means a freeing from all attachment to material things and to evil, and should be a perfect surrender to love for God. (See Chapter 14, no. 3b.)

2b. Somehow like the resurrection. Thinking of death and judgment, man wants to know: What is the manner of my existence after death? Formerly, the solution was suggested that "the soul" was separated from "the body." The soul goes on existing, while the body decays. The Bible does not speak of such a clear-cut distinction of soul and body. Scripture never thinks of "the soul" as entirely without body. "Soul" means most of all "you."

We have mentioned that your parents did not (and indeed *could* not) want "you." They wanted a "child," a "boy" or a "girl." God wanted "you." Well, "you"—John, James, Mary, Martha—will go on existing after death. "As to the fact that the dead are raised, have you not read what God said to you,

'I am the God of Abraham, the God of Isaac,
the God of Jacob'?

He is the God of the living, not of the dead" (Matthew 22:31-32). And Jesus said to the "good criminal": "I assure you: this day you will be with me in paradise" (Luke 23:43).

We want to know what our existence will be like immediately after death. Jesus speaks of: *"this day you* will be with me," and this "you" is not a "you" entirely without body. We must realize that "body" is not the same as "mortal remains." But Scripture also says: "In Christ all *will* come to life again" (1 Corinthians 15:22). We *will* share in Christ's glorious life, as Mary does already, since she has risen with soul and body.

The only thing we can say is: "Existence after death is already somehow like the resurrection of our new body!" That is all! Scripture does not instruct us as to exactly "how" future life will be.

We must also remember that the Bible does not teach a resurrection from "mortal remains." Resurrection is not reanimation of corpse, but raising to a new spiritual and eternal life. "You" will go on existing and be "at home with the Lord" (2 Corinthians 5:8).

The Church accompanies her children, as they go through the transformation of death, with her Sacraments and prayers (see Chapter 54).

"Go forth from this world, O Christian soul, in the name of God the Father Almighty, who created you; in the name of Jesus Christ, the Son of the living God, who suffered for you; in the name of the Holy Spirit, who has been poured forth upon you.... May peace be your dwelling today, and may your home be in holy Zion. Through Christ our Lord. Amen" (Commendation of the departing soul).

2c. Commendation and farewell. When the Church accompanies your mortal remains to the cemetery, she is really honoring "you" in them. The funeral rites dramatize what happens at the moment of death.

The new Rite of Funerals, issued by the Sacred Congregation for Divine Worship in 1969, expresses clearly the paschal character of Christian death. It commends the dead to God but also supports the Christian hope of the people (see Chapter 43, no. 2c) and gives witness to its faith in the future resurrection of the baptized with Christ.

As a rule, the Christian passover is celebrated with the mortal remains present in church. Prayers and petitions are offered for the deceased. In the communion of all Christ's members, these prayers which bring spiritual help to some may bring to others a consoling hope.

The ceremony in church is completed by the rite called the "final commendation and farewell." This is the last farewell with which the Christian community honors one of its members before the body is buried. The sprinkling with water, which recalls the person's entrance into eternal life through Baptism, and the incensation, which honors the body of the deceased as a temple of the Holy Spirit, may be considered signs of farewell. The priest may say: "Before we part, let us take leave of our brother (sister). May this last farewell express the depth of our love for him (her), ease our sadness, and strengthen our hope. We know that one day we shall joyfully greet him (her) with joy where the love of Christ, which overcomes all things, will destroy even death itself."

At the grave, the priest says:

"Since almighty God has called our brother (sister) N. from this life to himself, we commit his (her) body to the earth from which it was made.

"Christ was the first to rise from the dead, and we know that he will raise up our mortal bodies to be like his in glory.

"We commend our brother (sister) to the Lord: may the Lord receive him (her) into his peace and raise up his (her) body on the last day." (Rite of Funerals.)

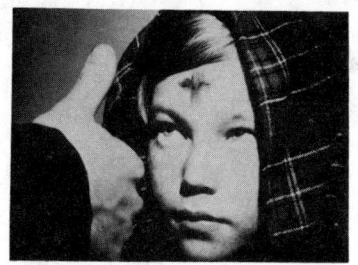

Some symbols used in connection with death are: R.I.P., for *Requiescat in Pace* (May he [she] rest in peace); two palm leaves, which symbolize victory; a cross which also symbolizes victory and hope.

3. Remember, man! At the beginning of Lent, the Church reminds her children of death. On Ash Wednesday the priest places the blessed ashes in the form of a cross on your forehead, saying:

"Remember, man, that you are dust, and into dust you shall return."

You do not know the day or the hour of death. Be prepared always! If you live well, your good works will follow you at the moment of death, and you will get your reward for them in heaven. Christ says that if you do your good works only to be seen and honored by others, you have received your reward already!

4. THINKING IT OVER

How should you, as a Christian, consider death and accept it? How did Christ give you an example to follow? What does the Preface for the Dead (2a) say about death? What are the reasons for penance, pain, and death, as explained in Chapter 14? What happens at the moment of death? How does the Church accompany her children at this decisive moment? What does the funeral rite dramatize and express? Describe the rite of "final commendation and farewell!" What is the meaning of sprinkling with water and incensation at this rite? What are some symbols used in connection with death and funerals? What does the Church teach us at the very beginning of Lent? What about our good works?

5. READ ATTENTIVELY

"I heard a voice from heaven say to me: 'Write this down: Happy now are the dead who die in the Lord!' The Spirit added, 'Yes, they shall find rest from their labors, for their good works accompany them'" (Revelation 14:13).

6. PRAY MEDITATIVELY

Help us, Lord, to receive and understand your gospel,
so that we may find light in this darkness,
faith in our doubts,
and comfort for one another in your saving words.
(Rite of Funerals)

7. THINGS TO DO

Read: 1 Peter 3:13-22.

66. Punishment, Purge and Reward

1. "Once there was a rich man who dressed in purple and linen and feasted splendidly every day. At his gate lay a beggar named Lazarus who was covered with sores. Lazarus longed to eat the scraps that fell from the rich man's table. The dogs even came and licked his sores. Eventually the beggar died. He was carried by angels to the bosom of Abraham. The rich man likewise died and was buried. From the abode of the dead where he was in torment, he raised his eyes and saw Abraham afar off, and Lazarus resting in his bosom.

"He called out, 'Father Abraham, have pity on me. Send Lazarus to dip the tip of his finger in water to refresh my tongue, for I am tortured in these flames.' 'My child,' replied Abraham, 'remember that you were well off in your lifetime, while Lazarus was in misery. Now he has found consolation here, but you have found torment. And that is not all. Between you and us there is fixed a great abyss, so that those who might wish to cross from here to you cannot do so, nor can anyone cross from your side to us.'

"'Father, I ask you, then,' the rich man said, 'send him to my father's house where I have five brothers. Let him be a warning to them so that they may not end in this place of torment.' Abraham answered, 'They have Moses and the prophets. Let them hear them.' 'No, Father Abraham,' replied the rich man. 'But if someone would only go to them from the dead, then they would repent.' Abraham said to him, 'If they do not listen to Moses and the prophets, they will not be convinced even if one should rise from the dead'" (Luke 16:19-31).

> Never again shall they know hunger or thirst,
> nor shall the sun or its heat beat down on them,
> for the Lamb on the throne will shepherd them.
> He will lead them to springs of lifegiving water,
> and God will wipe every tear from their eyes"
> (Revelation 7:16-17).

2a. Judging yourself. In the story about Lazarus and the rich man, Christ teaches you about the punishment of hell. You should believe in hell because you have "Moses and the prophets," that is, God's Revelation brought to you by Christ and the Church. Do not expect someone condemned to hell to come back to tell you about it!

Christ has revealed that "hell" is possible, since man can abuse his freedom. He has never said that there are men who have been condemned or will be condemned for all eternity. Christ's message, inspired by love, warns us of the possibility that a free man can turn away from God deliberately. A condemned person judges himself, since he refuses God's offer of Love. Death simply "permanentizes" that person's adhesion to evil and aversion from God. Scripture uses images of fire, darkness, and gnashing of teeth! Hell means "no God"—"no love."

2b. Purge in death itself? To pray for the deceased is a tradition in the Church. Why do we pray for our dearly beloved who passed away? We do so because there is so much

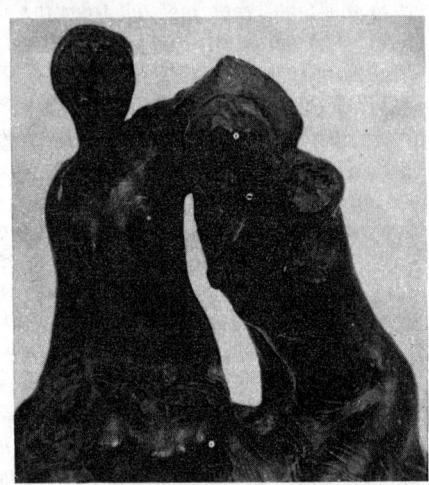

"These will go off to eternal punishment" (Matthew 25:46).
The Condemned. Sculpture by Rodin (1840-1917). France.

ill-will and inclination to evil in a man, even if he dies in grace. There is so much to be purged from man's inborn egotism. This happens through death (see Chapter 14, no. 3b). How long does this "purge" last? Again we must say that this happens outside our concept of time. After death there is no "time" any longer. Formerly, "purgatory" was visualized as a fire. We should go back to the old Christian concept and see this "purge" as belonging to death, as perhaps happening in death itself. This would not make prayer for the dead senseless, since our prayer overlaps time, just as Christ's redemption affects us as well as people of thousands of years ago.

In the Roman canon of the Mass we mention the names of our dearly beloved who have gone before us. We pray:

> "May these, and all who sleep in Christ,
> find in your presence
> light, happiness, and peace."

November 2 is a day of special prayer for our deceased. (See Chapter 38.) You may regard the Masses of "All Souls Day" as a beautiful drama, explaining what possibly takes place at the moment of death.

2c. Generous reward. "Eventually the beggar died. He was carried by angels to the bosom of Abraham." (See Bible quotation above. "Bosom of Abraham" means heaven.)

The happiness of heaven will be greater than anything we can imagine on earth. This happiness will consist, first of all, in seeing God. Moreover, you will see Christ in His humanity, as well as our Blessed Mother, all the saints, your parents and loved ones, and all who died in the Lord. Companionship with those who are in heaven will indeed bring great joy. Further, as stated in the above Bible quotation (Revelation 7:16-17), there will be no hunger, thirst, tears, pain or trouble in heaven. The Lamb (Christ) will guide you to perfect happiness.

Read in your Bible: Matthew 22:2-10. Christ compares heaven to a wedding feast. The King is your Heavenly Father. His Son is Jesus Christ. The "Bride" is the holy people, all of us, united with Christ in love. Heaven is a party. It is a group of people having a really good time.

God has already made you happy in this world through your family, through companionship with friends, listening to good music, seeing beautiful things, such as on a wonderful vacation in the mountains. But God promises to reward you a hundredfold! Hence, your happiness in heaven will be very great, though you cannot now understand all that awaits you in heaven. God is not stingy—He can and will reward generously! Note well, however, that heaven is not just a paycheck for a good life! It will be up to you whatever you make of yourself now, just as your life as an adult is more or less the result of your preparation in youth. (See also Chapter 39, 2b.)

3. Just the beginning. Christianity is a way of life. It furnishes you with special "vision" to guide your life. It teaches you that this life of 60-70-80 years is just the beginning of an everlasting existence. It is a test through which you must go. Try always to see your life in this perspective.

4. THINKING IT OVER

What is the meaning of "God is just"? (See Chapter 13.) What is sin? (See Chapter 13.) Why do you believe there is a hell? How can you help your beloved deceased? Do you know the anniversary of the death of your parents (if they are not living), and do you remember them on that day with a special prayer or holy Mass? What does "Abraham's bosom" mean? (See Bible quotation.) Of what does happiness in heaven consist? Explain Jesus' comparison about happiness in heaven (see Matthew 22:2-10). What does the Book of Revelation tell you about heaven? (See Revelation 7:16-17 above.) What does Christianity teach you about your life on earth?

5. READ ATTENTIVELY

What did Jesus tell you about heaven?

Jesus said: "Be glad and rejoice, for your reward is great in heaven" (Matthew 5:12).

6. PRAY MEDITATIVELY

O God, Who by the Resurrection of your Son, our Lord Jesus Christ, granted joy to the whole world: grant, we beg you, that through the intercession of the Virgin Mary, His Mother, we may lay hold of the joys of eternal life. Through Christ our Lord. Amen. (Prayer from the *Regina Coeli*. See Treasury of Prayers, p. 293.)

67. The Resurrection of the Body and Life Everlasting

1a. "When the Son of Man comes in his glory, escorted by all the angels of heaven, he will sit upon his royal throne, and all the nations will be assembled before him. Then he will separate them into two groups, as a shepherd separates sheep from goats. The sheep he will place on his right hand, the goats on his left. The king will say to those on his right: 'Come. You have my Father's blessing! Inherit the kingdom prepared for you from the creation of the world.'

Resurrection of Body and Life Everlasting

"Then he will say to those on his left: 'Out of my sight, you condemned, into that everlasting fire prepared for the devil and his angels!' These will go off to eternal punishment and the just to eternal life" (Matthew 25:31-34.41.46).

1b. Just as in Adam all die, so in Christ all will come to life again, but each one in proper order: Christ the first fruits and then, at his coming, all those who belong to him. After that will come the end, when, after having destroyed every sovereignty, authority, and power, he will hand over the kingdom to God the Father. When, finally, all has been subjected to the Son, he will then subject himself to the one who made all things subject to him, so that God may be all in all (1 Corinthians 15:22-24.28).

1c. Then I saw new heavens and a new earth. The former heavens and the former earth had passed away, and the sea was no longer. I also saw a new Jerusalem, the holy city, coming down out of heaven from God, beautiful as a bride prepared to meet her husband. I heard a loud voice from the throne cry out: "This is God's dwelling among men. He shall dwell with them and they shall be his people and he shall be their God who is always with them. He shall wipe every tear from their eyes, and there shall be no more death or mourning, crying out or pain, for the former world has passed away" (Revelation 21:1-4).

2a. How will it happen? When the Bible describes a theophany (manifestation of God), it does so with the imagery of clouds, angels, smoke, fire, earthquakes, lightning, war, lies, and persecution. See the theophany on Mount Sinai: Exodus 19:16—20-21. As a Jew who was addressing Jews, Christ adapted Himself to this Biblical way of speaking. The imagery of Matthew 25 (no. 1a above—read the whole Chapter in your Bible) is to be interpreted as symbolical.

"When the Son of Man comes in his glory" (Matthew 25:31).

We are created to be together. That is why Jesus, speaking of the last things, speaks mainly of the last things of all mankind collectively. Exactly how this will happen, we do not know. The calamities of the end describe the suffering, disappointments, pain and distress of all times as well as all God's message: "When these things begin to happen, stand erect and hold your heads high, for your deliverance is near at hand" (Luke 21:28). History is meaningful. God will do with creation (your life) as He has done with the life of Christ: through passion and death to a glorious resurrection!

2b. Fully realized. We believe in the resurrection of the body. (See Chapter 65, no. 2b.) "Arising from the tomb," as related in the Bible, means that it is "you" who will be made to live in Christ. After Christ has made subject all things, including death, He will deliver the Kingdom to God the Father. Then the original blueprint, which God had in mind for man, will be fully realized (see Chapter 12). Man's rebirth through water and the Spirit will be complete (John 3:1-5). All things will have been re-established in Christ. (For God's plan of salvation, see Ephesians 1:3-10.)

2c. As a bride. The Kingdom of God, which has been initiated but not yet perfected, has visible and invisible aspects as well. Its very beauty though is invisible, as a treasure hidden in a field, or a mustard seed in the ground. The Lord is truly with us, though in a hidden way.

On "Judgment Day" the Kingdom of God will be visible, beaming in all its splendor. The "old" world will not be destroyed on that day. God will renew it and make it perfect. The "new" world will then become the abode (residence) of God and man, closely united in love. We will be His people and God Himself will dwell with us.

This is the wedding feast of the Lamb. The author of the Book of Revelation "saw a new Jerusalem, the holy city [that is, the people of God after the resurrection of the body], coming down out of heaven . . . as a bride prepared to meet her husband." The King giving the wedding feast is God the Father, and the feast hall is the "new" world, which becomes heaven because God is visible. The people of God, all of us, are the "bride," who will be united with Christ in intimate love. This wedding feast will be everlasting.

3. Awaiting our blessed hope. Do not think too much about how, when, and where these things will happen. Since these things happen outside our concept of time we cannot speak of "time" in between judgment at our death and "last judgment." We do not know "how" this is or will be. More important is St. Paul's advice to us, as long as we live in this world: "We [must] reject godless ways and worldly desires, and live temperately, justly, and devoutly in this age as we await our blessed hope, the appearing of the glory of the great God and our Savior Christ Jesus" (see Titus 2:12-13).

4. THINKING IT OVER

What imageries does the Bible use to describe manifestations of God? What will Jesus do when all His enemies are made subject to Him? State some qualities of Christ's Kingdom. (See Chapter 9.) With what does Jesus compare the Kingdom of God as it now exists? When will the Kingdom become visible? What will happen to the world on Judgment Day? What does the Book of Revelation tell us about the "new" world? With what does Jesus compare happiness in heaven? (See Chapter 66, no. 2c.) Who is the King? the bride? the Groom? and where is the feast hall? What does St. Paul (in his Epistle to Titus) exhort us to do during our earthly lives?

5. READ ATTENTIVELY

What does St. Paul tell us about the resurrection of the body?

St. Paul says: "Just as in Adam all die, so in Christ all will come to life again" (1 Corinthians 15:22).

6. PRAY MEDITATIVELY

Pour forth, we beseech you, O Lord, your grace into our hearts: that we to whom the Incarnation of Christ your Son was made known by the message of an angel, may by His Passion and Cross be brought to the glory of His Resurrection. Through Christ our Lord. Amen. (See Treasury of Prayers, p. 292: *The Angelus.*)

7. THINGS TO DO

Listen, if possible, to a recording of the last part of Handel's *Messiah.*

Read meditatively Psalm 66: "Shout joyfully to God . . ."; 1 Corinthians 15:29-58; Philippians 3:17-21; Romans 8:18-25.

68. Celebration

1. "Three times a year you shall celebrate a pilgrim feast to me. You shall keep the feast of Unleavened Bread. As I have commanded you, you must eat unleavened bread for seven days at the prescribed time in the month of Abib, for it was then that you came out of Egypt. No one shall appear before me empty-handed. You shall also keep the feast of the grain harvest with the first of the crop that you have sown in the field; and finally, the feast at the fruit harvest at the end of the year, when you gather in the produce from the fields. Thrice a year shall all your men appear before the Lord God" (Exodus 23:14-17).

2a. Growing awareness. In this book, we have studied the growing awareness first of the Hebrews and later on of the early Church of God's loving and revealing presence to His people. It started with the traditions on the legendary patriarch Abraham, who was described as an example for all believers. He is our father in faith. God cares, but man must respond in faith! We studied highlights in that process of growing awareness: Moses, David, the Prophets, Jesus Christ—His Birth, Life, Death, Resurrection, Ascension and Communication of the Spirit.

Guided by God the Hebrews have made history. This history of man's growing awareness of God is called the History of Man's Salvation. And this history goes on. In and through Christ there is a keen awareness of God's saving presence in the Church, till this mysterious history will be completed with Christ's second coming.

2b. The Hebrew way. The Jews celebrated the history of their salvation. They put days apart on which they called forth certain aspects of God's loving presence, as they had experienced it in the past.

The best known Hebrew experience of God's loving care is the Exodus event. This saving event furnishes the background for the Jewish Passover. But note well, "celebration" is not just a memorial, intended to preserve the memory of an event in the past. Celebration means more. It calls forth an experience of the past in order to make this experience ours! Celebrating the Passover, Jews (1) call forth the experience of God's care during the exodus from Egypt, and (2) make it their experience of God saving man from the bondage of evil and leading him into freedom, *now!* (See Chapter 47, no. 2b.)

2c. Rooted in human nature. Our Christian celebrations are not only rooted in Judaism (see Chapter 47, nos. 2b, c, 3), they seem to be rooted in human nature itself. Man wants to celebrate life and its mysteries. Think of our youth festivals. What do those young people want? We see rituals and symbols. Sometimes they seem to be bizarre and eccentric. But it is plain that they want to celebrate life, nature, the mystery of human togetherness.

Christians celebrate different aspects of God's loving presence, especially as experienced in Christ. The early Christians did

"A celebration of life."

so by setting apart four days to celebrate four aspects of the Christ event, as they had experienced it: Christ's Death (Good Friday), the fact that He is alive (Easter—the Resurrection), the fact that He constantly intercedes for us "at God's right hand" (Ascension), and the fact that He communicates the Spirit (Pentecost). The symbolism of numbers, in vogue in the Hebrew culture of that time, made them celebrate these feasts at intervals of three, forty and nine days. (See Chapter 26, no. 2a.)

What do Christians do when they celebrate the feasts of the liturgical year?

(1) We call forth an experience of God's loving presence of the past (e.g., on Easter, the apparitions of our Lord; the joyful experience that He is alive),

(2) and we make this experience ours (e.g., on Easter, our sharing of life with the risen Lord for all eternity; a joyful experience for believers).

Celebration entails two principles:
(1) Calling forth an experience of the past;
(2) Making this experience ours.

These principles should be applied, whenever Christians celebrate their feasts.

2e. Salvation History celebrated. The feasts of the liturgical year are first of all celebrations of our History of Salvation (the highlights of Christian awareness of God's saving presence). These feasts have been arranged around two highlights of our Salvation History, i.e., Christmas and Easter. Hence we have the Christmas and Easter cycles of feasts. When celebrating these feasts, we should apply the two principles of celebration. Let us take Christmas, for example:

(1) We call forth the experience of God's loving presence in the Birth of Jesus, as told in the Infancy narratives of Luke and Matthew: An infant, a mother, tenderness, love. Note also the light and darkness theme in Luke 2:9.13.

(2) We make this experience of God's presence in Christ ours. Note how we use the light and darkness theme at Christmas! Christ is the "Sun of Justice," enlightening us in the darkness of our human condition. Have an open eye for the symbolism of your religion. Make your celebrations meaningful!

2f. Memorials of the saints. Besides the celebrations of our Salvation History (the feasts of the Christmas and Easter cycles), we have the commemorations of the Saints. Christians keep the memory of their heroes alive, just as we do with the great men of our national history. In about the 4th Century a custom arose of honoring the Martyrs by an annual Mass at their tomb. Later on also other Saints, i.e., members, who gave an heroic example of virtue, were honored by a memorial Mass. You will find these Masses in your Daily Missal under "The Proper of the Saints."

3a. Tuning. God is constantly and everywhere present to His people with His loving care. In celebrating our feasts, we should become more aware of that saving presence of God. Prayer and worship may be compared to what happens when we tune a TV set. Tuning merely brings into focus signals that are already present. We must celebrate our feasts with an open heart for that aspect of God's care which is called forth on a particular feast.

3b. Bulletins and Bible reading. You should have a Catholic calendar in your home which reminds you of the feasts of the liturgical year and teaches you their meaning. Often parochial bulletins are very instructive along this line. Read yours every week!

At the end of this course you are supposed to be familiar with both your Bible and your Missal. Keep up the Christian custom of daily Bible reading in the family and use your Missal or Missalette as often as you attend Mass on both Sundays and weekdays. For married couples—if you or your partner cannot go to church on a certain weekday, send one of your children as a representative of the family! There are families who have at least one member attending the Sacrifice of the Mass every day in the name of all. God will bless those families.

4. THINKING IT OVER

What is Salvation History? How did the Hebrews celebrate the History of their Salvation? Explain this from the Jewish Passover celebration: What is called forth and how is it applied? (See quotation of Jewish tradition in Chapter 47, no. 2b.) Recall the roots of our Christian celebration! What do Christians celebrate on their feasts in the first place? Explain this for Easter and Christmas! Mention the two principles of celebration! Could you apply them for the celebration of Pentecost? Why do we have memorials of Saints? How should we celebrate our feasts? (no. 3a.) Do you have a Catholic calendar in your home? Do you read your parochial bulletin? Is there daily Bible reading in your family? Do you attend Mass also on weekdays, when possible?

5. PRAY MEDITATIVELY

> In my heart
> dwells Jesus of Galilee,
> the Man above men,
> the Poet who makes poets of us all,
> the Spirit who knocks at our door that
> we may wake and rise and walk out
> to meet the truth naked and unencumbered.   (Gibran)

TREASURY OF PRAYERS

The Signs of the Cross

In the name of the Father, and of the Son, + and of the Holy Spirit. Amen.

The Lord's Prayer

Our Father, Who art in heaven, hallowed be Thy name; Thy kingdom come; Thy will be done on earth as it is in heaven. Give us this day our daily bread; and forgive us our trespasses as we forgive those who trespass against us; and lead us not into temptation, but deliver us from evil. Amen.

The Hail Mary

Hail Mary, full of grace! the Lord is with thee; blessed art thou among women, and blessed is the fruit of thy womb, Jesus. Holy Mary, Mother of God, pray for us sinners now and at the hour of our death. Amen.

Glory be to the Father

Glory be to the Father, and to the Son, and to the Holy Spirit. As it was in the beginning, is now, and ever shall be, world without end. Amen.

The Apostles' Creed

I believe in God, the Father Almighty, Creator of heaven and earth; and in Jesus Christ, His only Son, our Lord; Who was conceived by the Holy Spirit, born of the Virgin Mary, suffered under Pontius Pilate, was crucified, died and was buried. He descended into hell; the third day He arose again from the dead; He ascended into heaven, sitteth at the right hand of God, the Father Almighty; from thence He shall come to judge the living and the dead. I believe in the Holy Spirit, the Holy Catholic Church, the communion of saints, the forgiveness of sins, the resurrection of the body, and life everlasting. Amen.

Blessing before Meals

Bless us, O Lord, and these Your gifts, which we are about to receive from Your bounty, through Christ our Lord. Amen.

Grace after Meals

We give You thanks for all Your benefits, O Almighty God, Who live and reign forever; and may the souls of the faithful departed, through the mercy of God, rest in peace. Amen.

The Angelus

To be recited at dawn, at noon and at eventide.

V. The angel of the Lord declared to Mary.
R. And she conceived of the Holy Spirit.
Hail Mary, etc.
V. Behold the handmaid of the Lord.
R. Be it done to me according to Your word.
Hail Mary, etc.
V. And the Word was made flesh.
R. And dwelt among us.
Hail Mary, etc.

V. Pray for us, O holy Mother of God.
R. That we may be made worthy of the promises of Christ.

Let us pray

Pour forth, we beg You, O Lord, Your grace into our hearts: that we, to whom the Incarnation of Christ Your Son was made known by the message of an Angel, may by His Passion and Cross be brought to the glory of His Resurrection. Through the same Christ our Lord. Amen.

Regina Coeli

(Said during Paschaltime instead of the Angelus)

Queen of heaven, rejoice. Alleluia.
For He Whom you deserved to bear. Alleluia.
Has risen as He said. Alleluia.
Pray for us to God. Alleluia.

V. Rejoice and be glad, O Virgin Mary. Alleluia.
R. For the Lord is truly risen. Alleluia.

Let us pray

O God, Who by the Resurrection of Your Son, our Lord Jesus Christ, granted joy to the whole world: grant, we beg You, that through the intercession of the Virgin Mary, His Mother, we may lay hold of the joys of eternal life. Through the same Christ our Lord. Amen.

MORNING PRAYERS

Say: *Our Father, Hail Mary, and Apostles' Creed.*

Morning Offering

Most Holy and Adorable Trinity, one God in three Persons, I firmly believe that You are here present; I adore You with the most profound humility; I praise You and give You thanks with all my heart for the favors You have bestowed on me. Your Goodness has brought me safely to the beginning of this day. Behold, O Lord, I offer You my whole being and in particular all my thoughts, words and actions, together with such crosses and contradictions as I may meet with in the course of this day. Give them, O Lord, Your blessing; may Your divine Love animate them and may they tend to the greater honor and glory of Your Sovereign Majesty. Amen.

Prayer to the Holy Spirit

Come, Holy Spirit, fill the hearts of Your faithful and kindle in them the fire of Your love.
V. Send forth Your Spirit, and they shall be created.
R. And You shall renew the face of the earth.

Let us pray

O God, Who taught the hearts of the faithful by the light of the Holy Spirit, grant that, by the gift of the same Spirit, we may be always truly wise, and ever rejoice in His consolation. Through Christ our Lord. R. Amen.

A Prayer to All the Saints

May Holy Mary and all the Saints intercede for us with the Lord, that we may worthily be succoured and preserved by Him. Who lives and reigns, world without end. Amen. *Let us pray*

O Lord God, King of heaven and earth, vouchsafe this day to direct and sanctify, to rule and govern our hearts and bodies, our thoughts, words and deeds, according to Your law and in the works of Your commandments; that here and forever, O Savior of the world, we may be protected and saved, through Your mighty help. Who live an reign forever. R. Amen.

EVENING PRAYERS

Prayer of Thanksgiving

O Almighty and Eternal God! Prostrate before Your Divine Majesty, I adore You with all possible reverence. I believe and hold for certain all You have revealed to Your holy Church. I hope in Your infinite goodness and mercy, and I love You with all my heart.

O Great and Almighty God! I kneel before You to thank You with my whole heart for all the favors which You have bestowed upon me this day; for my food and drink, my health and all my powers of body and soul. I thank You for all Your holy lights and inspirations, for Your care and protection, and for all those other mercies which I do not now recall, or which I do not know how to value as I ought. I thank You for them all, O heavenly Father. Through Jesus Christ, Your Son, our Lord.

Take a short time to examine your conscience. How was your behavior: at home — in church — in school — at work — at play?
Say the Act of Contrition,
Sit down and read one chapter of your Bible.

Prayer for the Dead

O God, the Creator and Redeemer of all the faithful, grant to the souls of Your servants departed full remission of all their sins, that, through our devout prayers, they may obtain the pardon, which they have always desired. Who live and reign, world without end. Amen.

V. Eternal rest grant to them, O Lord. R. And let perpetual light shine upon them. V. May they rest in peace. R. Amen.

The Memorare

Remember, O most gracious Virgin Mary, that never was it known that anyone who fled to your protection, implored your help, or sought your intercession, was left unaided. Inspired with this confidence, I fly to you, O Virgin of virgins, my Mother! To you I come; before you I stand, sinful and sorrowful. O Mother of the Word Incarnate, despise not my petitions, but in your mercy hear and answer me. Amen.

THE ROSARY

The "Apostles' Creed" is said on the Crucifix; the "Our Father" is said on each of the large beads; the "Hail Mary" on each of the small beads; the "Glory be to the Father" after the three Hail Marys at the beginning of the Rosary, and after each decade (i.e. group of ten small beads).

One of the mysteries in the life of Christ and His Blessed Mother, as listed below, is to be mentioned at the beginning of each decade and to be meditated on, while reciting the "Hail Marys."

The Biblical passages indicated below provide many suggestions for meditation.

Joyful Mysteries	Sorrowful Mysteries	Glorious Mysteries
1. The Annunciation (Luke 1:28)	1. Agony in the Garden (Mark 14:35)	1. The Resurrection (Mark 16:6)
2. The Visitation (Luke 1:42)	2. The Scourging (Mark 15:15)	2. The Ascension (Mark 16:39)
3. The Nativity (Luke 2:28)	3. Crowning With Thorns (Mark 15:17)	3. Descent of Holy Ghost on Apostles (Acts 2:4)
4. The Presentation (Luke 2:28)	4. Carrying of Cross (John 19:17)	4. Assumption of Blessed Virgin Mary (Genesis 3:15)
5. Finding of Child in Temple (Luke 2:46)	5. Crucifixion (Luke 23:33)	5. Crowning of Blessed Virgin Mary as Queen of Heaven (Revelation 12:1)

STATIONS OF THE CROSS

The Stations of the Cross remind us of the many things Jesus suffered in order to save us from sin. They help us to understand how much He loved us. When we make the Stations of the Cross, it is like following Jesus from one place to the other and seeing what He suffered.

1. Jesus Is Condemned to Death. God so loved the world that he gave his only Son, that whoever believes in him may not die but may have eternal life (John 3:16).

2. Jesus Bears His Cross. Whoever wishes to be my follower must deny his very self, take up his cross each day, and follow in my steps (Luke 9:23).

3. Jesus Falls the First Time. The Lord laid upon him the guilt of us all (Isaiah 53:6).

4. Jesus Meets His Mother. Come, all you who pass by the way, look and see whether there is any suffering like my suffering (Lamentations 1:12).

5. Jesus Is Helped by Simon. As often as you did it for one of my least brothers, you did it for me (Matthew 25:40).

6. Veronica Wipes the Face of Jesus. Whoever has seen me has seen the Father (John 14:9).

7. Jesus Falls a Second Time. Come to me, all you who are weary and find life burdensome, and I will refresh you (Matthew 11:28).

8. Jesus Speaks to the Women. Daughters of Jerusalem, do not weep for me. Weep for yourselves and for your children (Luke 23:28).

9. Jesus Falls a Third Time. Everyone who exalts himself shall be humbled and he who humbles himself shall be exalted (Luke 14:11).

10. Jesus Is Stripped of His Garments. None of you can be my disciple if he does not renounce all his possessions (Luke 14:33).

11. Jesus Is Nailed to the Cross. It is not to do my own will that I have come down from heaven, but to do the will of him who sent me (John 6:38).

12. Jesus Dies on the Cross. He humbled himself, obediently accepting even death, death on a cross! Because of this God highly exalted him (Philippians 2:8-9).

13. Jesus Is Taken Down from the Cross. Did not the Messiah have to undergo all this so as to enter into his glory? (Luke 24:26).

14. Jesus Is Placed in the Tomb. Unless the grain of wheat falls to the earth and dies, it remains just a grain of wheat. But if it dies, it produces much fruit (John 12:24-25).

HOW TO READ YOUR BIBLE

1. MOST WIDELY DISSEMINATED BOOK

There is no doubt that the Bible is one of the most widely disseminated books. But "most widely disseminated" does not necessarily mean "most read" and "best understood." The Bible is a compilation of many ancient documents stemming from a time and culture which is rather alien to our own. This brings up the question: Why should I read the Bible? It is so old. Why not leave it alone and read contemporary literature, which is more relevant?

2. WHY THE BIBLE?

a. As Americans, we share a rich Judaeo-Christian civilization. Our language, many of our customs and often our outlook on life, love, good and evil are conditioned by the Judaeo-Christian heritage in which we are rooted. You cannot possibly understand them without knowing the Judaeo-Christian classic: the Bible. A few examples will clearly show this. (1) *Customs and practices:* We observe a seven-day week, take an oath with one hand on the Bible, number years as B.C. or A.D., celebrate Christmas and Easter as holidays, print the words "In God we trust" on our money, regard monogamy as a value and accept woman as a companion equal to man. (2) *Sayings of everyday life:* "The patience of Job," "a doubting Thomas," "a Judas," "as old as Methuselah." (3) *Popular songs*: "Tain't Necessarily So" in *Porgy and Bess,* "Miracle of Miracles" in the Broadway musical *Fiddler on the Roof.* (4) *Negro Spirituals and classic Oratoria:* "Let My People Go," and *The Messiah* by Handel. (5) *Classical literature: Paradise Lost* by Milton, *East of Eden* by Steinbeck. (6) *Plastic art:* Paintings and statues by Rembrandt, El Greco, Rubens, Michelangelo, Rodin. (7) *Movies: The Ten Commandments, The Robe, Samson and Delilah.* None of these is really understandable without an acquaintance with the literature of the Bible. From our roots, we should understand ourselves.

b. However, besides being an American, you are a Christian. For Christians, the Bible is inspired by God. God chose that time (2,000-3,000 years ago), that people (the Jews) and that culture (Hebrew) to reveal Himself. Guided by God, the Hebrew genius interpreted history, war and peace, birth and death, famine and abundance, happiness and frustration, success and failure, in the light of God's presence to His people. And Christians, regarding themselves as descendants of God's chosen people of ancient times, share this interpretation of life. The Bible reflects the restless search for life's meaning, as the Hebrews wrestled with it. As believers see it, this search was guided by God, which is the reason why we take note of it. Believers understand that ultimately God Himself speaks to them in and through Scripture.

3. BIBLICAL INSPIRATION

Artists, philosophers and even scientists speak of inspiration, which is the urge to create a work of beauty (artists), a constructive outlook on reality (philosophers) or a solution to a problem (scientists). How to explain this inspiration?

First of all, inspiration is related to a certain sensitivity which exists in a society at a given time. This sensitivity inspires gifted individuals in that society. These individuals in turn heighten that sensitivity in their fellow citizens. For example, we would never have produced our Jazz music, which has captured the whole world, without our Negro communities that are so sensitive to music and rhythm. From such communities we have seen arise such men as Louis Armstrong, Duke Ellington and Ray Charles, who in turn have heightened musical sensitivity in this country and all over the world.

More or less by this same process of mutual influence Hebrew literature came into being. We see in the Hebrew people a highly developed sensitivity for God's presence in their lives. From these pious Hebrew communities we see arise prophets, preachers, writers, who offered their (first spoken) reflections on that shared experience of God's presence with His people. In turn these prophets, preachers and writers heightened that religious sensitivity in their people.

There is a similarity between Hebrew literature and all art. Both are inspired. But Hebrew literature is more than just that. It is inspired (breathed upon) in a very special way by almighty God. This does not mean that God dictated His message as a businessman dictates a letter to a secretary. God takes the author as he is and leaves him free to choose his own means of communication. Isaiah was a great poet and composed beautiful poems to convey his message. Ezekiel was not well-versed in letters and his language is rather poor. Some authors chose existing folktales and even beast fables to bring out their point.

122 *Inspiration is guidance.*

4. INSPIRATION AND REVELATION

123 God Himself guided (inspired) the Hebrew genius in its searching out of the mysteries of the human condition. This guidance is called *inspiration*. When this restless searching for truth and meaning culminates in unfolding one of God's mysteries, we speak of divine *revelation*. This means that God reveals some aspect of Himself or the human condition in and through man's endeavors to find out. Hence, "everything in the Bible is *inspired,* but not everything is *revealed*" (Pierre Benoit). Sometimes inspired searching for meaning leads to conclusions which cannot be qualified as revelation from God. Think of the "holy wars" of total destruction fought by the Hebrews when they invaded Palestine. The search for meaning in those wars centuries later was inspired, but the conclusions which attributed all those atrocities to the command of God were imperfect and provisional. See Judges 1:1-8.

5. A LIBRARY OF BOOKS

Ironically, "The Book" is not just *one* book. It is a library of books, put together in one volume. Look at the contents of your Bible! The authors of these books are mostly unknown. Neither were those books composed at one time. Many centuries elapsed between the oldest traditions and the last book of the Bible. Not even the original language of all these books was the same.

A major disadvantage is that these books are not put together systematically as the books of a modern library. All kinds of literary forms: history, historical novels, parables, allegories, poems, midrash (edifying interpretation of events), and more are often intermingled. Even if you read your Bible in an up-to-date idiomatic American translation, you still need guidance. Therefore read the introductions to the Bible books and pay attention to the footnotes! Know that, if you want to understand what God has to tell you through Scripture, you must first understand what the writer wants to say. The Bible is God's word and man's word. One must understand man's word first in order to understand the word of God.

Since this collection of books is of such great importance as source book for the humanities and religion (see no. 2), it became known in Western civilization as the "Bible," from the Greek word "biblion" (book); hence, "The Book," which is actually a library of books!

6. LITERARY GENRES OR FORMS

It is very important to know what literary form a writer uses to convey his message. Is it a work of history, a poem, a figure of speech, a parable? If you do not know, you may misunderstand the writer's message. That is why we must pay attention to the literary genres (forms) of the Bible. The following are just a few of them.

a. *The Parable:* A short fictitious narrative from which a moral or spiritual truth is drawn. See Isaiah 5:1-7 and the parables of the Gospels! Keep in mind that *the point* of the parable (not the details) is God's message to believers.

b. *The Allegory:* A figurative story with a *veiled* meaning. Read Genesis 2—3; 4:1-16; 6—8; 11:1-9. For centuries these chapters have been misunderstood as inspired lessons in science. The Bible does not teach science; it teaches religious values. It uses these folktales to teach a lesson. Again, *the point* of the allegory (not the details) is God's message to you.

c. *The Beast Fable*: See Genesis 3:1-15 and Numbers 22:22-35. (Understand this from Numbers 22:1-21 and 22:36-38.) The author chose this literary form to convey his message.

d. *The Short Story and the Historical Novel:* See Genesis 37—50; Judges 13—16: 1 Samuel 17; also Genesis 12—36 and Exodus. The core of these stories is historical, but remember that the author did not intend to write history as we find it in our school books; he simply uses *traditions* and fashions them to bring out a religious lesson. Bible scholars call this edifying interpretation of the past "midrash."

e. *The Problem Story*: The best-known problem stories in our contemporary literature are those on the race issue. A Hebrew problem story is the Book of Ruth on intermarriage. The point is a plea for tolerance.

f. *The Speech as a Literary Device*: Read 1 Kings 8:14-21; Acts 17:22-31. It is not important whether or not King Solomon or Paul delivered these speeches verbatim as related here. It is the inspired author who wants to state something by putting these words into the mouth of a person with authority. This literary form is often used in the Acts of the Apostles. (See also no. 13.)

7. CONDITIONED THOUGHT PATTERNS

Though inspired (guided) by God, the Hebrew authors were free to choose their literary genres to convey the message. As a matter of fact, these literary forms were conditioned by time and culture. Read the well-known poem on creation in Genesis 1. The ancient Hebrews saw the earth as a large plate with a huge vault over it. Above the vault is God's palace. This outlook conditioned Genesis 1. Do not be shocked about this! We know that the sun neither rises nor sets, nevertheless we go on speaking of sunset and sunrise, since we did not know better for such a long time.

8. THE BIBLE ON GOD

The sacred writers attribute quite a number of human characteristics to God. In fact the Bible does not offer a philosophy on who the "Ultimate Reality" is in Himself; it is mainly concerned about who God is for us. Speaking of God is necessarily limited by the possibilities of human language and conditioned by time and culture. Read Exodus 19:16-25 and 20:1-21; Exodus 13:20-22; Numbers 9:15-18. Clouds, angels (blasting trumpets!), smoke, fire, earthquake, lightning, thunder, war, calamities, lies and persecution are biblical figures of speech to describe the awe-inspiring greatness of God. As a Jew, who was addressing Jews, Jesus of Nazareth adapted Himself to this biblical way of speaking. Read Matthew 25.

9. POEMS IN THE BIBLE

Poetry, like any other meaningful writing, is a communication from the writer to the reader—usually the communication of a feeling as well as of a thought. The poet wants to pack as much meaning as possible in a few lines. That is why he uses figures of speech, since they involve imaginative comparisons. But Biblical poems in particular can easily be misunderstood. Read them as poems and not as scientific or historical reports, in which one tries to explain every detail as a revelation from God. See no. 4 and read Psalm 137: "Ballad of the Exiles," paying special attention to verses 8 and 9. The feeling, the thought, the total poem is inspired (guided) by God, though it is not necessarily revealed truth! Read some psalms!

10. THE PROPHETS

Like other nations in the Middle East, Israel had its *nabis or* prophets. These were groups of ecstatic persons, somehow related to a sanctuary. Music and dance heightened their exotic and vaguely religious activities. Read 1 Samuel 9:1-10. 16; 1 Kings 22 and 18. From the 8th Century B.C. on, we encounter the classical Prophets, whose oracles and sayings have been preserved in Sacred Scripture. Prophet means "one who speaks for another," especially for God. It does not necessarily mean that he predicts the future!

The classical Prophets' concern focused mainly on such values as *monotheism* (one God, with whom Israel considered itself to live in a sacred partnership or covenant) and *morality as related to religion,* which is seldom found in religions of the ancient world. The "gods" of the ancient world were often anything but morally good, and as such they did not offer any reason to their worshipers to do better. Israel was called to be holy as God Himself!

Another important topic in prophetic preaching is *messianism*. God punishes infidelity to His Covenant (partnership). Israel is humiliated for its sins. But at some future date God's Kingdom on earth will be restored. God's vice-gerent, His Messiah, anointed to royal dignity, will reign in that Kingdom. You should pay attention to this messianic expectation in Hebrew literature. This is necessary to understand the literature of the New Testament, which sees the fulfillment of this messianic expectation in Jesus of Nazareth. (See no. 13a.) Read Matthew 23:33-39; some parts of Amos, Isaiah, Jeremiah.

11. ATONEMENT AND VICARIOUS SUFFERING

In their search for meaning in our human situation, the Hebrews wrestled with the tantalizing problem of evil and guilt, as we see it in and around us. Is there a way out? In the Old Testament we are often confronted with concepts such as atonement-reconciliation and vicarious satisfaction. Read Isaiah 52:13-15 and 53. One person could pray, suffer and make up for others. Symbolically, this could be done by "the scapegoat ritual" and other ritual sin-offerings (sacrifices for sin). Read Leviticus 16.

It is important to keep these Old Testament ideas in mind in order to understand the way early theologians of the Church interpreted Jesus' Death and Resurrection. Who was Jesus of Nazareth? Though innocent, He died a cruel Death, but after his Death, He was seen by witnesses. What does all this mean? Read how Paul (Philippians 2: 6-11) and the authors of the Epistle to the Hebrews (5:1-10; 7; 8; 9; 10:1-18) and the First Epistle of Peter (2:4-8; 3:18-22) tried to explain what Jesus of Nazareth means to the new people of God, the Church.

12. HEBREW PHILOSOPHY

Like all peoples, the Hebrews had their sages or philosophers. In the Bible we find their thoughts mainly in the Wisdom Books. This ancient wisdom is a remarkable mixture of philosophy and poetry. Read it as an inspired search for meaning in life. Do not expect too many ready-made answers. See this literature more as a challenge to a faithful searching for meaning in your own human condition!

13. THE GOSPELS

a. New Testament literature reflects the Christian interpretation of the Hebrew Bible (Old Testament). It is based on the astonishing fact that a Jew of Galilee applied "messianism," as it was known in Hebrew literature (see no. 10), to Himself. Read Luke 4:16-30. Jesus quotes the Prophet Isaiah and states: "This text is fulfilled in your hearing." New Testament literature can only be understood in the light of this "fulfillment" idea. In other words, the New Testament movement is the fulfillment of the Hebrew Bible. Jesus of Nazareth proclaims that He is the promised Messiah (anointed) king to come, to establish the Kingdom (Reign) of God, for which the Old Testament was somehow yearning.

b. *Catechisms*. In no. 6 we mentioned how important it is to know what literary form an author is using. If he chooses to use figurative speech, you should understand it as such. A remarkable fact is that for a long time Christians misunderstood the literary genre of the four Gospels. Until recently they thought that the Gospel writers wanted to present us with a biography of Jesus. After much research, Bible scholars agree now that the Gospel writers wanted to write catechisms or digests of Christian teaching concerning the risen Lord Jesus.

c. *Theological Interpretation of History*. Until recently, Catholics learned their religion from the Baltimore Catechism with its questions and answers. Modern catechisms are different. The Gospels are also catechisms, but composed 1,900 years ago. In that time they had their own way of making catechisms. The Gospel writers often used a typically Hebrew way of teaching by reflecting on events of the past (see no. 6d). What did the authors of the Gospels do? In the congregations, mainly in the cities around the Mediterranean, they found scores of narratives about Jesus, the beloved Founder of the Christian faith. The writers took those narratives and frequently even remolded and refashioned them to bring out the lesson they wanted to teach. 137

d. Read Matthew 1:1-17. What has the sacred writer done? He used a genealogy, probably made available by the family of Joseph, and took it for what it was. Then the writer refashioned this document to a list of three times fourteen ancestors. (The Hebrews loved to play with sacred numbers: 14 equal 2 times 7.) The lesson: The Messiah is firmly rooted in the Jewish people; he is the son of David. 138

e. Reading the Gospels, one should distinguish historical facts from theological elaboration. Take the miracle stories. Catholic Bible scholars accept the fact that Jesus worked miracles. However, the miracle accounts of the Gospel are often more than a record of what actually happened; they also contain theological reflections about what happened in order to bring out its meaning for Christian faith. Moreover, some of these accounts may be adaptations of similar ones in the Old Testament in order to bring out the Christian belief in the importance of Jesus' person and mission. We must keep in mind that the Gospel writers did not intend to write history in the scientific sense; rather they were writing theological reflections on existing traditions (accounts of miracles) in order to teach believing Christians the community's faith in Christ and the Church. 139.

f. *Conflict Stories.* An interesting example of literary form is the conflict story. The author lets his characters debate and thus brings out his lesson. In the conflict stories of the Gospels it is usually Jesus Who is in conflict with his opponents, those Jews who did not believe in Him. Read Luke 10:25-37. One may ask: Was Jesus involved in these conversations? Did He answer exactly as related in the Bible? It is not certain. It is true, Jesus was in conflict with the establishment of His country and this conflict caused His Death. There were controversies which supplied the background material for the conflict stories of the Gospels. But as these accounts now stand, they are literary forms used by the Gospel writers in their catechisms to bring out what they had to tell the opponents of early Christianity. Read Matthew 9, 10-13; Luke 7, 36-50; John 10, 22-39; Matthew 12, 1-8. 140

g. *Infancy Narratives.* The first chapters of Matthew and Luke are dedicated to Jesus' infancy. Both authors have used traditions. How did they handle them? (See no. 13c.) For example, take Matthew 2, 1-23. Bible scholars tell us that a horoscope of the expected King-Messiah circulated during the time of Jesus' birth. Astrologers (wise men from the East) were watching the sky for the appearance of the Messiah's star. King Herod, superstitious and upset by these people, killing children of two years and under, is extremely probable. Kings could make and break people! People, leaving Bethlehem to escape the massacre, is equally acceptable. This would be the historical background of this tradition. The rest is interpretation (no. 13c), elaborated by early Jewish-Christian communities and by the author of Matthew. Its purpose is to show Jesus as the true Israel (God's chosen one!), in whose history the history of the old Israel recapitulated. Note: Israel was in Egypt! God's dealings with Israel in the past are being reproduced in His dealings with Jesus (the new Israel—the new chosen one!). This is a strange literary device, but the ancient writers loved to work with this kind of figurative speech.

h. *On Communication.* Communication is a complicated thing. It is more than just uttering sounds either in English or in Chinese. Often barriers must first be taken away. Emotions, hard feelings, prejudice, ignorance, closed-mindedness must be patiently done away with and only then communication becomes possible. Which means should God use to communicate with man? He is so entirely different and so much greater than we are. He is so incomprehensible that we cannot possibly develop an adequate concept of Him. "In our time, God has spoken to us by His Son" (Hebrews 1:2). God speaks to us through Jesus of Nazareth: a child in a crib, a person, His kindness, goodness, justice, honesty, miracles, parables, death and resurrection. It is this very core of New Testament literature which John tries to explain in the introduction of his Gospel version. He uses figures of speech. He calls Jesus God's *word* to those who are ignorant. He calls Him *light* to people who walk in darkness. Jesus of Nazareth, His charming personality, is God's word to man. Prejudice, lack of interest, closed-mindedness prevent understanding. But could God speak a clearer language than He has done through the appealing personality of Jesus of Nazareth? Read John 1:1-18.

i. *Sayings of Jesus.* Since we do not possess a biography of Jesus (no. 13b), it is difficult to know whether the words or sayings attributed to Him are written exactly as He spoke them. True, the Gospels are based on sound historical facts as related by eye-witnesses, but both deeds and words of Jesus are offered to us in the framework of theological interpretation (no. 13c). The Church was so firmly convinced that the risen Lord Who is the Jesus of history lived in her, and taught through her, that she expressed her teaching in the form of Jesus' sayings. The question is: Can we discover at least some words of Jesus that have escaped such elaboration? Bible scholars point to the very short sayings of Jesus, as for example those put together by Matthew in Chapter 5:1-12. Why? Simply because they are short. Early Christians, who had known Jesus, had His words often on their lips: "The Master used to say . . ." Another question is: Did Jesus sit on a hill and recite this list of sayings on the kingdom of heaven? It is the same question as: Did Moses sit on Mount Sinai writing the law? This composition is figurative. The composer of Matthew, a Jew, wrote his catechism for Christians of Jewish background. He draws a parallel between Moses and Jesus. Moses, the ancient lawmaker, is figuratively related to Mount Sinai. Jesus, the new lawmaker, is figuratively related to a mount in Galilee. 143

j. *Traditions concerning the Resurrection.* There is no doubt that Jesus died and was seen alive by witnesses. All reports are unanimous on that. But again the New Testament writers chose theological interpretation to teach what the risen Lord means to believers. Jesus' Death, His Resurrection, His Ascension and the Communication of the Spirit are actually *one* Christ-event, that of his Glorification. The traditions, 144 told in the Gospels, elucidate the four aspects of the one Christ-event, meaningfully celebrated on four different days. Remember the golden rule: keep historical facts distinct from their theological interpretation.

14. APOCALYPTIC LITERATURE

A real problem for Bible readers is the Book of Revelation. This book is a specimen of a special literary form in vogue just before and in the beginning of the Christian era. It is called apocalyptic literature. In the Old Testament, the Book of Daniel is akin to the Book of Revelation. This literary genre is designated as persecution literature. Its purpose is to console the victims of some crisis by holding out to them the assurance of divine intervention in the near future. The problem for the reader is that apocalyptic literature uses mainly a mysterious or symbolical language, understandable only to one who knows all the ins and outs of the situation. It is in a sense underground literature. The writer wants to console his fellows in suffering in a language understandable to them alone. In our literature we possess this literary form in the Negro spirituals. Take "Let My People Go." The slaves sang it in their wooden plantation churches: "Tell ole Pharaoh, To let my people go." The obvious meaning is a longing for freedom from the bondage of sin, satan, the miseries of life and the hope of a better life hereafter. Obviously genuine Biblical piety! But what about "Ole Pharaoh" as the "boss man" of the plantation? Read Revelation 17:1-8 and 21:1-4 and see the footnotes for the explanations of the symbolic names used in the text.

15. HOW DO YOU KNOW?

Walking into a modern library, you find all the books neatly arranged under fiction and non-fiction. It is not that simple in the library called the Bible. How does one know whether one deals with history or some form of figurative speech?

To begin with, we should always be disposed to follow the teaching authority of the Church. We should also consult renowned Bible scholars who are experts in Hebrew literature. Sometimes, it is secular science which gives Christians the lead to reconsider their Bible understanding. The discoveries of Copernicus and Galileo made Christians aware that Genesis 1 is not a sacred lesson in science but a poem on creation (no. 7). Most scientists hold that the human species has developed somehow from lower forms of life. This knowledge helped Christians to rethink the "how" of God's creative activity and to understand that Genesis 2 and 3 is not a lesson in Anthropology, but an allegory, teaching us the lesson that sin is the root of all evil (no. 6b).

However, one problem remains: You may hear interpreters of the Bible who are literalists or fundamentalists. They explain the Bible according to the letter: Eve really ate from the apple and Jonah was miraculously kept alive in the belly of the whale. Then there are ultra-liberal scholars (outside the Catholic Church!), who qualify the whole Bible as another book of fairy tales. Catholic Bible scholars follow the sound middle of the road, keeping a balance between fundamentalists and scholars who are too liberal. You may make your own choice as long as it is not contrary to the teaching authority of the Church. The signature of a bishop in your Bible assures you that opinions, expressed in footnotes and introductions, reflect what is generally accepted as sound doctrine in the Catholic tradition.

16. UNDERSTANDING THE SITUATION

We have stated: One must understand man's word in order to understand the word of God in the Bible. That is why some knowledge of the Biblical literary forms is necessary. Of great importance also is some knowledge of the situation in which a Bible passage came into being. You understand the Book of Exodus better if you know something about the slavery in Egypt, have seen pictures of monuments, maps and other background material. Jerusalem was threatened by mighty neighbors when Isaiah spoke his oracles. Knowledge of the history of that time will help you to understand Isaiah better. Historical insight of how the Romans colonized other nations contributes highly to the understanding of "messianism" as reflected in the Gospels. Knowing that early Christians mistakenly expected Christ's second coming during their own lifetime, helps you to understand 1 and 2 Thessalonians. Reading introductions and footnotes in your Bible is very important.

17. GOD'S WORD TO YOU, NOW!

Reading your Bible, you must keep in mind that the Bible is God's word to you, now! Reading can only be valuable to you if you grow in truth through reading. This does not come from a grammatical insight or from an understanding of the literary forms, nor does it come from a reconstruction of the situation which prompted the text (no. 16).

The past is dead. *We* do not expect Christ's second coming to happen tonight; *we* are not an occupied country (no. 16) nor can we artificially recreate this situation of 2,000 years ago. Yet there is *something in common,* namely, *we* are captives in our odd and sorry human situation (as the Hebrews in Egypt, in Palestine during the Roman occupation); *we* know about God's coming in Christ and wait for a brighter future through Christ's coming (as the early Christians of 1 and 2 Thessalonians have done it in their way). This *something in common,* found in any passage of Scripture, is called *existential understanding.* This understanding, related to *your* existence or life-situation, is aided by faithful Bible reading. It is the very reason why a Christian can read the same Bible time and again, since it is *his* book! The Hebrews were restless searchers for meaning in our human condition. Reading their inspired literature should challenge you to go on with a faithful search for meaning in your own situation.

EXPLANATION

of the Chronological and Synoptic Chart showing the Growth of God's Promise in the Old Covenant (opposite page)

The heavy line indicates where God's Chosen People happened to be sojourning in the various epochs. The arrows indicate the direction of the People's wanderings.

The chart reads from the upper right-hand corner. Thus: Abraham departs about the year 2000 B.C. (by some accounts, about 1700 B.C.) from Chaldea for the Promised Land, which by its geographic situation forms the crossroads of three continents. There he and his descendants Isaac and Jacob dwell about 300 years; then Jacob (about 1700, or 1400 according to some) journeys with his sons in time of famine to Egypt, to which his son Joseph had been sold into bondage by his brethren. Jacob's family increases in the course of more than 300 years to a numerous people, and is sorely oppressed by the Egyptians until Moses, called by God, leads them back to their homeland in forty years of nomadic wanderings in the wilderness (about 1449, by some accounts, about 1250 B.C.)

After the period of the Judges, the People, under Kings Saul (1030-1010), David (1010-971) and Solomon (971-929), reach their peak of political and religious (building of the Temple) development. In 929, the Kingdom is divided by economic pressures and dissensions into a Northern Kingdom (of Israel), conquered in 722 by the Assyrians, and a Southern Kingdom (of Judea), conquered in 586 by the Babylonians. In 538 Cyrus the King of the Persians conquers Babylon and allows the captives and deportees to return home, enabling them to recognize their community and rebuild the destroyed Temple. Influence of foreign powers thenceforward becomes dominant (Persians, Macedonians, Egyptians, Syrians), until in 63 B.C. political independence is lost to the power of Rome and the "Fullness of Time" (Christ) is at hand.

THE GROWTH OF GOD'S PROMISE

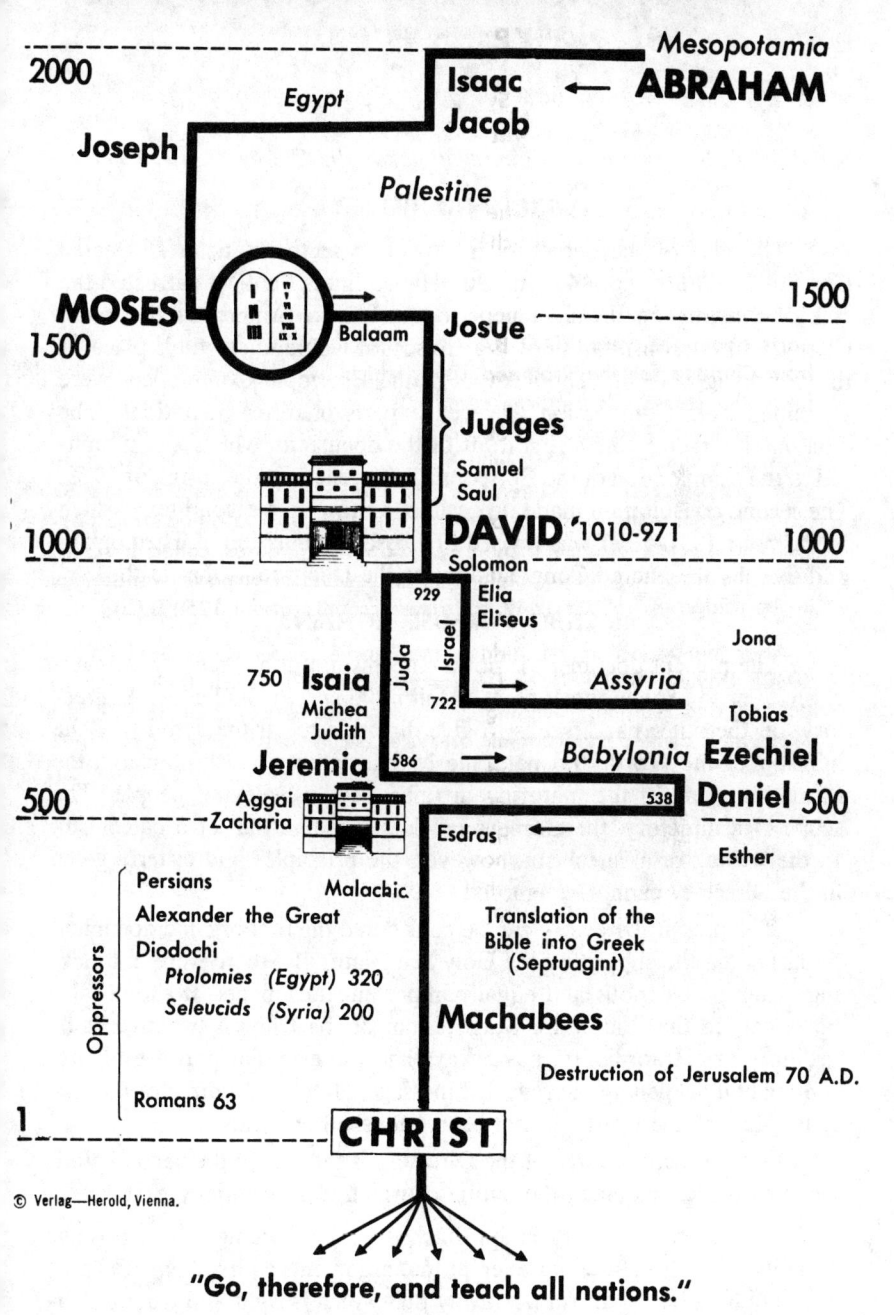

2000

Mesopotamia ← **ABRAHAM**

Egypt — Isaac / Jacob

Joseph

Palestine

MOSES 1500 — Balaam → Josue — 1500

Judges

Samuel
Saul

1000 — **DAVID** '1010-971 — 1000

Solomon

929 — Elia / Eliseus

Juda | Israel

Jona

750 **Isaia**
Michea
Judith

722 → Assyria

Tobias

Jeremia 586 → Babylonia **Ezechiel**

500 — Aggai / Zacharia — 538 — **Daniel** 500

Esdras

Esther

Malachic

Oppressors:
- Persians
- Alexander the Great
- Diodochi
  - Ptolomies (Egypt) 320
  - Seleucids (Syria) 200

Translation of the Bible into Greek (Septuagint)

Machabees

Destruction of Jerusalem 70 A.D.

Romans 63

1 — **CHRIST**

© Verlag—Herold, Vienna.

"Go, therefore, and teach all nations."

THE GENERAL CATECHETICAL DIRECTORY

Published by the Sacred Congregation for the Clergy, April, 1971

ORIGIN AND HISTORY

The idea of the Directory is expressed in the Vatican II Decree *Christus Dominus* (no. 44). In 1967 His Holiness Paul VI entrusted the task of drawing up the document to the Sacred Congregation for the Clergy. A first consultation of the Episcopal Conferences took place at the beginning of 1968. The answers of the Episcopal Conferences were examined by a Commission of seven experts of different nations. The Commission then wrote a first draft of the document, which was submitted to the examination of the Episcopal Conferences in the spring of 1969. The second consultation made it possible to draw up a second text, which in the years 1970-1971 was revised first by a Commission of Theologians and then by the Sacred Congregation for the Doctrine of the Faith.

NATURE, PURPOSE, CONTENT

The present document is not a catechism, but a directory. A catechism aims to explain the content of faith to a specific audience. A directory, on the other hand, seeks to give direction to all the activity of the ministry of the Word, and particularly that activity which concerns the formation, that is, the maturing in faith, of the believing people. The scope of a directory, therefore, is much wider than that of a catechism. In the writing of a catechism, however, the principles and criteria given in the Directory cannot be ignored.

The present Directory can be considered the first organic document published on the subject by the Holy See. Naturally, there were not lacking in the past various and equally important documents. It should also be remarked that the entire Magisterium of the Church, whether it be ordinary or extraordinary, has always had the essential purpose of presenting and deepening the revealed message. However, a directory, in the strict sense of the word, has not been published until now.

The principal source of the Directory is the acts of the Second Vatican Ecumenical Council, the nature of which was essentially pastoral.

Catechetical activity is approached in the document in a positive fashion. There is no attempt to enter into arguments with anyone, the purpose being rather to affirm positively that which is right and true. Nevertheless, some deviations and exaggeration, which, as is known, are found in catechetics, today are taken into consideration. Precisely because of its positive tone, it can appear that the theoretical aspect of the Directory prevails over the practical and normative. It is true, in fact, that much importance has been given to the analysis of the act of catechizing and to its purpose, to the relationship, between catechetics and the deposit of revelation, to the statement of the basic content to be transmitted. However, practical and normative aspects are not lacking as is shown in particular by the chapter on criteria for content, the sixth part on pastoral plans, as well as the Appendix, which treats of the initiation of young children in the Sacraments.

In a general document like this it has not been possible to take into account what might be called the overall situation of the Church. For that reason the document does not pretend to be exhaustive but to stimulate further research and to guide the preparation of local directories and of national catechisms.

SUMMARY

Part I: Today's problem. Some indications are given concerning the present situation of the world and of the Church. Only general observations are made concerning a few vast cultural areas. The purpose here is to suggest to national directors the necessity of an attentive analysis of their own situations, in such a way that catechetical activity can operate effectively in the concrete human, social and cultural context.

Part II: The ministry of the Word. Above all, there is considered the relationship that should exist between the minister of the Word and the deposit of revelation. The minister of the Word must announce that which God has revealed. In the light of this message, transmitted faithfully by Tradition and taught infallibly by the Magisterium, he interprets human demands and realities. This is followed by an analysis, within the frame of the various forms of the ministry of the Word, of catechetical activity strictly understood, that is, that activity which seeks the complete and harmonious formation of the Christian.

Part III: The Christian message. Catechetics does not proclaim a human word but a divine Word. The first chapter of this part III lays down the fundamental criteria that must be followed in the selection and the exposition of the contents of catechetics. They are criteria that are particularly important for compiling catechisms The second chapter offers a brief presentation of the essential elements that constitute the contents of Christian faith and it points out that the unavoidable purpose of catechetics is the faithful and integral communication to men of that which God has revealed.

Part IV: Methodology. A short treatment of general methodology is presented since it is valid and even necessary in every form of catechetics. The Directory, however, does not choose one method over another nor does it enter into an analysis of the various methods. The selection of the proper methodology depends, in fact, on those who write the catechism expected to be produced.

Part V: Catechetics for different age groups. Catechetics can take different ways in the fulfillment of its mission. Catechetics taught according to age groups is, in practice, the most important of these ways and the most dependable. For this reason the Directory gives this catechetical approach more attention in regards to methods, pedagogy and content. Catechetics for adults, because of the possibility it offers to present the Christian message in a more complete way, and because it affords a basis for work with children and youth, is considered the most important form of catechetics by the Directory.

Part VI: Pastoral plan. It presents some suggestions concerning what Episcopal Conferences, and other groups charged with catechesis, can do to extend the faithful and efficacious preaching of the Word of God. It is a high level plan, which, given the diversity of conditions and possibilities in the various local Churches, will be able to be carried out only gradually by certain Episcopal Conferences.

Appendix: Initiation of young to the Sacraments. The delicate and difficult problem is faced of whether, as is occurring in some parts of the Church, it is possible to admit young children to First Communion without their first receiving the Sacrament of Penance. After analyzing the arguments pro and con regarding the experiment, the Directory reaffirms the value of the traditional practice, that is, to make a First Confession before First Communion, although permitting the Episcopal Conferences to continue in some cases—as an experiment—the new practice, but provided that all is done in communion and in agreement with the Apostolic See, which has the final decision on the matter.

General Catechetical Directory

EXCERPTS

(The following excerpts are a private translation from the Latin text)

1. Destinataries and Aim

This Directory has been composed mainly for Bishops, Episcopal Conferences and generally for all who under their guidance carry responsibility in the field of catechetics. Its direct aim is to offer help for composing catechetical directories and catechisms. (p. 1)

2. The World of Today in Constant Evolution

Believers of our time are certainly not the same as believers of former ages. Hence the necessity arises both to confirm the continuity of the Faith and to offer the message of salvation in a new fashion. (2 b)

3. The Situation of Religious Understanding

In former ages, devious opinions and errors in both Faith and the Christian way of life usually affected relatively few people and were the more than today confined to intellectual circles. But in our time, human progress and the means of communication cause such opinions to spread rapidly and to have an ever greater impact on believers, especially the youth, who undergo graver crises and are often led to accept a way of thinking and acting which is contrary to religion. In this situation, apt pastoral remedies are requested. (5)

4. Traditional Faith

In spite of the progress of secularization, a strong religious sense continues to flower in many parts of the Church. Nobody can ignore it, since it is sincerely and authentically expressed in the daily lives of very many people. This popular religious sense constitutes an occasion or starting point for the proclamation of the Faith. It is simply a question, obviously, of purifying this popular faith and evaluating its valid elements so that one may not be content with pastoral methods which are outdated, less apt, and perhaps do not concern the heart of the matter at all. (6)

5. Faith and Different Cultures

Many Christians with an excellent education experience difficulty concerning the language in which the Faith is discussed. They believe that this language is too restricted to an outdated and obsolete terminology or too closely linked to Western culture. Hence, they seek a new way of expressing religious truth, a way that is geared to the present human condition, permitting their Faith to shed light on the realities wich concern people today, so that the Gospel can be transmitted to all cultures. It is certainly the duty of the Church to give the greatest consideration to their aspiration of man. (8)

6. The Work of Renewal

In order to offer efficient help to preachers of the Gospel, the catechetical renewal must use the aids which can be provided by the sacred sciences, theology, biblical studies, pastoral reflection, and the human sciences as well as other means by which ideas and opinion are spread nowadays, especially the mass media of communication. (9)

7. The Ministry of the Word: Act of Living Tradition

"This tradition which comes from the apostles develops in the Church with the help of the Holy Spirit. For there is a growth in the understanding of the realities and the words which have been handed down. This happens through the contemplation and study made by believers, who treasure these things in their hearts, through a penetrating understanding of the spiritual realities which they experience, and through the preaching of those who have received through episcopal succession the sure gift of truth" (*Constitution on Divine Revelation,* no. 8).

Hence, it is necessary that the ministry of the word transmit divine revelation as it is taught by the teaching authority of the Church and as it expresses itself—under the guidance of this teaching authority—in the living conscience and Faith of God's people. In this way, the ministry of the word is not the mere repetition of an ancient doctrine, but its faithful reproduction adapted to new problems and rendered ever more understandable. (13)

8. Sacred Scripture

Under special inspiration of the Holy Spirit, divine revelation is presented in the sacred books of both the Old and the New Testaments, which contain and present to view divinely revealed truth.

The Church, custodian and interpreter of Sacred Scripture, learns ings. Faithful to tradition, the ministry of the word finds nourishment and guidance in Sacred Scripture. For in the sacred books, the Father Who is in heaven meets His children with great love and speaks with them. It is from Sacred Scripture that the Church, prompted by the Spirit, takes her pattern of thinking and interprets herself. (14)

Indeed, while the Church takes the norm of her thought from Sacred Scripture, she can also interpret it in virtue of the Spirit by whom she is animated: "the sacred writings themselves are more profoundly understood and unceasingly made active in her" (*Constitution on Divine Revelation,* no. 8).

9. Efficiency of God's Word in Catechesis

The following words from Sacred Scripture apply also to catechesis: "Indeed, God's word is living and effective" (Hebrews 4, 12).

The word of God becomes present in catechesis through the word of man. In order to bear fruit in man and to inspire in him sentiments that will expel indifference and doubt and lead him to accept the Faith, catechesis must faithfully express and intelligently present the word of God. Most of all, it is the living testimony of catechist and congregation which contributes exceedingly to the efficiency of catechesis.

Hence, catechesis must translate the word of God, as it is present by the Church, into the language of the people to whom it is directed. When God revealed Himself to the human race, He entrusted His word to human words, expressing it in a language that was related to a particular culture. The Church, to whom Christ entrusted the deposit of divine revelation, must transmit, explain and interpret it in an up-to-date fashion to people of whatever culture and condition. (32)

10. Fidelity to God and Fidelity to Man

Drawing the truth from God's word and faithfully adhering to a correct expression of that word, catechesis is to teach that word of God with dedicated fidelity; however, its task cannot be restricted to the mere repetition of traditional formulas. It is an essential prerequisite that these formulas be understood and, when necessary, that they be faithfully presented also in a new fashion, using a terminology adapted to the intellectual capacity of the audience. This terminology differs according to different age groups, social situations of peoples, and cultures and structures of civilizations. (34)

11. The Content of Catechesis Related to Various Forms in Church life, Different Cultures, and Diverse Ways of Speaking

The first and absolutely necessary task of the prophetical ministry of the Church is to make the message intelligible to people of all times, so that through Christ they may be converted to God, interpret life in the light of their Faith, considering the particular condition of time and circumstances they live in, and live according to that dignity which the message of salvation presents and Faith reveals.

In order to achieve this aim, catechesis, as the "most acceptable time" of the Church's prophetical ministry, must not only cultivate an intimate association with the various life styles of the ecclesial community, but also strive to establish closer relations between the possible formulations of the divine message and various cultures as well as modes of speaking. (37)

12. The Sources of Catechesis

The content of catechesis is found in God's word, both written and handed down; it is more profoundly understood and explained by the believing community under the guidance of the Teaching Authority which alone teaches with authority; it is celebrated in the Liturgy; it shines forth in the life of the Church, especially in the just and the Saints; and, in a certain sense, it is evident in those genuine moral values which through God's providence exist in human society.

All of these constitute the principal or subsidiary sources of catechesis. But they should not be considered as all having the same value. In using these sources, the catechist must first of all respectfully pay attention to the indisputable preeminence of both written and handed down revelation, as well as to the Church's Teaching Authority in matters related to the Faith. (45)

13. Theological, Anthropological and Methodological Training of Catechists

a. *Doctrine*. There is a self-evident need to acquire a valid doctrinal patrimony, which must always include an adequate understanding of Catholic doctrine and must attain the level of scientific theology in the higher institutes of catechetics. This entire formation must have Sacred Scripture as its soul.

In any case, this doctrine must become so much a part of the catechist that he will be able not only to set forth the Gospel message with exactness but also to render those being catechized capable of receiving that message in an active way and of discerning on their spiritual journey whatever conforms to the faith.

b. *The human sciences.* Our age is characterized by the phenomenal development of the anthropological sciences. These sciences are no longer reserved solely to specialists; they pervade the very consciousness that modern man has of himself. They touch upon social relations and constitute a kind of cultural context which is common even to those with less education.

The task of teaching the human sciences poses difficult problems of selection and methodology because of the enormous extension and diversity of this discipline. Since it is a question of forming catechists rather than specialists in psychology, the criterion to be followed is one of distinguishing and selecting whatever can directly aid them in acquiring the ability to communicate.

c. *Methodological formation.* In itself methodology is simply the reflection on the means that have proved themselves in actual practice. Hence greater emphasis must be placed on practical exercises rather than on the theoretical instructions of pedagogy. Nevertheless, theoretical instruction is necessary to aid the catechist to adapt himself to various situations, to avoid empirical forms of teaching, to take advantage of the changes that take place in the field of education, and to direct future labors in a correct way. (112)

14. Textbooks

Textbook are subsidiaries offered to the Christian community involved in catechetics. No textbook can replace the living communication of the Christian message. However, textbooks do have great importance, since they provide a wider explanation of the documents of Christian tradition and of other elements which foster catechetical activities. Editing these textbooks however requires the combined effort of several specialists in the field of catechetics, as well as the advice of other specialists. (120)

15. Mass Media

The task of catechesis is to educate the faithful to discern the nature and value of whatever is presented by the "Mass Media." (123)

16. The Necessity of Promoting Scientific Research

There can be topics of research which are of universal importance: e.g., the relation between catechetics and contemporary exegesis, catechesis and anthropology, catechesis and the "mass media," etc. The nature and difficulties of this kind of research often require combined international effort. (131)

ANALYTICAL INDEX

Abraham, appearance of God to, 15-17; election by God of, 11-14; history of, 11-19; offering of his son Isaac to God by, 18-19; as our father in faith, 13-14; trial by God of, 18-19

Adam and Eve, disobedience of, 51-52

Advent, meaning of, 62

Allegories, in the Bible, 299

Ancestors, significance of, 48

Angels, the Bible on the subject of, 44-46

Animals, sacrifice of, 32, 34, 90-92, 204

Anointing, of the senses, 225-6

Anointing of the Sick, Sacrament of, 222-226

Anthropomorphism, definition of, 42

Apocalyptic Literature, 305-306

Apostles, commission of, 113, 115-116, 122-123, 129-130, 215

Apostolicity of the Church, 130-131

Ascension of Christ, 102-104

Ash Wednesday, significance of, 277-278

Assumption of Mary, as infallible doctrine, 137

Atheists and the meaning of death, 225

Baptism, of children, 166-167; of Christ, 64, 67, 115, 162; in the early Church, 162-166, 170; Sacrament of, 159-169; symbols in the ceremony of, 167-168; water in the Sacrament of, 160-161

Beast Fables in the Bible, 299

Benoit, Pierre, on the subject of the Bible, 298

Bible, allegories in the, 299; apocalyptic literature in the, 305-306; atonement and vicarious suffering in the, 301-302; on the subject of angels, 44-46; beast fables in the, 299; depiction of God in the, 300; devils in the, 45-46; Hebrew philosophy in the, 302; inspiration in the, 297-298; laws in the, 254-255; as a library of books, 298-299; literary genres in the, 299-300; the need for a correct understanding of the, 56-57; as a non-scientific book, 12, 56-57; poems in the, 300-301; the Prophets in the, 39-62, 301; reading of the, 296-307; as a techer of religion, 12-13

Bishops, authority of the, 107

Blind Man, cure by Christ of the, 241

Bloch, Ernest, on the subject of hope, 174

Body, resurrection of the, 282-285

Buber, Martin, on the subject of prayer, 182-183

Burning Bush, God's revelation to Moses in the, 22-25

Catechesis, the content of, 315-316; God's Word in, 315; the sources of, 316

Catechetics, textbooks in, 317

"Catechism of the Council of Trent," on the death of Christ, 86

Catechisms, the Gospels as, 81-82, 302

Catechists, training of, 316-317

Celebrations, Christian, 287-9; in the "Constitution on the Sacred Liturgy," 205; Jewish, 286-287

Celibacy, of priests of the Latin Rite, 230; sign value of marriage and, 187-192

Chastity, and respect for life, 266-267

Children, Baptism of, 166-167; love, sex, and, 237

Christ, and the Agony in the Garden, 274; the arrest of, 87; the Ascension of, 102-104; the Baptism of, 64, 67, 115, 162; the Church of, 122-134; the conception of, 71-74; the Crucifixion and Death of, 88, 91-92, 96, 275; the cure of the leper by, 241; and the cure of the man born blind, 241; the cure of a paralytic by, 215; the denial by Peter of, 212-213; on the subject of divorce, 187-188; on the subject of the Final Judgment, 282-283; Herod and the birth of, 80-82; the introduction by John the Baptizer of, 63-65; the life of, 67-104; as a light of revelation to the Gentiles, 79-83; marriage and, 232-240; the meaning of the Death of, 88, 92, 96; the miracles of, 215, 241, 275; the Mystical Body of, 126-129; the New Covenant in the Blood of, 94-97; as a non-political Messiah, 84-85, 208; the office of, 228; and the Parable of the Good Samaritan, 177-178; and the Parable of Lazarus and the Rich Man, 279; as the Passover Lamb, 196; as the priest-mediator, 228; as priest and victim, 63-65; the priesthood of, 144-146; the Real Presence in the Eucharist of, 197-199; as redeemer, priest, and victim, 63-65; the rejection of, 84-86; the relations between John the Baptizer and, 76-77; the responsibility for the Death of, 85-86; and the restoration to life of a young girl, 241; the Resurrection of, 98-101; on the subject of the Sabbath, 265; the sayings of, 304-305; as the Son of God, 75-78; as the Suffering Servant, 87-89; the task of, 65; the tempta-

318

Analytical Index 319

tion of, 207; as true man, 71-72; turning points in the life of, 76-77; the unity of life with, 126-128

Christian, the meaning of being a, 98

Christianity, divisions within, 140-141

Church, apostolicity of the, 130-131; authority in the, 130-134; and the authority to forgive sins, 215-219; Baptism in the early, 162-166, 170; Christ's priesthood as continued by the, 144-146; and the commission to preach, 135; in the "Constitution on the Church," 107; as the custodian of divine Tradition, 139-143; as the custodian and interpreter of Sacred Scripture, 314-315; in the "Decree on Ecumenism," 148; the ecclesiastical office of the, 129-134; infallibility of the, 136; of Jesus Christ, 122-134; laws and the, 253-256; liturgy as the public worship of the, 34-35; the missionary nature of the, 83; as the new people of God, 122-125; organization of the, 132-133; as a sign, 83; and situation ethics, 257-261; teaching authority of the, 104, 135-137

Church Councils, infallibility of, 136

Commandments, conscience and the, 252-256

Communion, under both signs, 205

Communion of Saints, explanation of, 150-155

Community Worship, necessity of, 262-264

Confession, rite of, 221; of sin, 219-221

Confirmation, Sacrament of, 170-172; symbols in the ceremony of, 171-172

Conflict Stories in the Gospels, 303

Conscience, and the Commandments, 252-256; erroneous, 250; formed, 247; informed, 249-251; theology of, 247-251

"Constitution on the Church," on the Church, 107; on the evangelical counsels, 191; on the guidance of the Holy Spirit, 73; on the lay apostolate, 128; on Mary, 154

"Constitution on Divine Revelation," on the Ministry of the Word, 314; on Sacred Scripture, 315

"Constitution on the Sacred Liturgy," on liturgical celebrations, 205; on public worship, 35

Contrition, guilt, forgiveness, and, 212-214

Council of Trent, Catechism of the, 86

Covenant, see New Covenant, Old Covenant

David, as king of Israel, 36-38;

Death, atheistic view of, 225

Death, of Christ, 88, 91-92, 96, 275; judgment, good works, and, 274-278

Decency, and respect for life, 266-267

"Declaration on the Relationship on the Church to Non-Christian Religions," on the Jews, 85

"Decree on Ecumenism," on the Catholic Church, 148; on the separated brethren, 148-149; on worship in common, 149

Demons, power of, 223

Devils in the Bible, 45-46

Diaconate, restoration of the office of, 133, 229-230

Dialogue and prayer, 182-183

Divorce, Christ on the subject of, 187-188

Earth, God as Creator of the, 39-43

Easter, two mysteries of, 100-101

Easter Lamb, as prefigured by the Passover Lamb, 28

Easter Vigil, rite of the, 100-101

Ecclesiastical Office, twofold dimension of the, 131

Ecumenism, need for, 146-149

Egypt, departure of Israel from, 26-29; flight of the Holy Family from, 81

Elizabeth, visit of Mary to, 152

Enemies, love of, 178

Episcopal Authority, exercise of, 107

Eucharist, meal aspect of the, 201-202; Real Presence of Christ in the, 197-199; Sacrament of the, 193-206; sacrificial aspect of the, 201-202

Evangelical Counsels, in the "Constitution on the Church," 191

Evil, collectivity in, 54

Evolution, Catholic viewpoint on, 49-50; God in the process of, 42-43

Exodus, story of the, 26-29

Extreme Unction, see Anointing of the Sick

Faith, Abraham as our father in, 13-14; and different cultures, 313-314; as a gift of God, 14, 69; traditional, 313; virtue of, 174

Final Judgment, Christ on the subject of, 282-283

Forgiveness, contrition, guilt, and, 212-214

Funerals, rite of, 276-277

"General Catechetical Directory," background and summary, 310-311; excerpts concerning (312-317): content of catechesis related to various

Analytical Index

forms of Church life and various cultures, 315; destinataries and aim, 313; efficacy of God's Word in catechetics, 315; faith and different cultures, 313; fidelity to God and man, 315; mass media, 317; ministry of the Word, 314; priestly scientific research, 317; Sacred Scripture, 314; situation and religious understanding, 313; source of Catechesis, 316; textbooks, 317; traditional faith, 313; training of Catechists, 316; work of renewal, 313; world in constant evolution, 313

Gentiles, Christ as a light of revelation to the, 79-83

God, Adam and Eve's disobedience of, 51-52; animal sacrifices to, 32, 34, 90-92, 204; the appearances to Abraham by, 11-19; in the Bible, 300; Christ as the Son of, 75-78; the communication with man by, 45; as the Creator of heaven and earth, 39-43; as the Creator of man, 47-50; the descent of the Spirit of, 105-108; the election of Abraham by, 11-14; fidelity to, 315; the identity of, 23-25; the immanence in all creation of, 24; the Kingdom of, 67-70; the knowledge and justice of, 51-52; man as the co-worker of, 43; Mary as the Mother of, 72-73; the mercy of, 57-62; Moses protected by, 20-22; and the process of evolution, 42-43; the promise of a redeemer by, 57-62; the self-comunication of, 110; the self-revelation to Moses by, 22-25; the trial of Abraham by, 18-19

Good Samaritan, Parable of the, 177-178

Good Works, death, judgment, and, 274-278

Gospels, background of the, 302-305; as catechisms, 81-82, 302; conflict stories in the, 303; infancy narratives in the, 304

Grace, actual, 114; as God's self-communication, 109-111; and the Sacraments, 242-243; sanctifying, 114

Guilt, contrition, forgiveness, and, 212-214

Haring, Bernhard, on the subject of sexual intercourse, 239-240

Healing, oil as a symbol of, 225

Heaven, God as the Creator of, 39-43; happiness of, 281

Hebrew Philosophy in the Bible, 302

Hell, reality of, 279-280

Herod, and the birth of Jesus, 80-82, 304

History, theological interpretation of, 302-303

Holy Family, flight from Egypt of the, 81

Holy Innocents, massacre of the, 81-82

Holy Orders, Sacrament of, 227-231

Holy Spirit, in the "Constitution on the Church," 73; the descent upon the Apostles of the, 105-108; gift of the, 109-112; help of the, 113-114; seven gifts of the, 173-174; work of the, 105-118

Hope, virtue of, 174

Human Race, consequences of sin for the, 53-55

Immaculate Conception, as infallible doctrine, 137

Immersion, in the Sacrament of Baptism, 163

Imprimatur, meaning of the, 135, 141-142

Infallibility, of the Church, the Pope, and Church Councils, 136-137

Infancy Narratives, in the Gospels, 304

Inspiration, in the Bible, 297-298; and revelation, 298

Isaac, the offering to God by Abraham of, 18

Israel, departure from Egypt of the people of, 26-29; the Messiah-expectation in, 61

Jesus, **see** Christ

Jews, and the consecration of priests, 161; in the "Declaration on the Relationship of the Church to Non-Christian Religions," 85; and the rite of initiation, 161; and responsibility for the death of Christ, 85-86

John the Baptizer, and the Baptism of Jesus, 64, 67, 115, 162; introduction of Christ by, 63-65; imprisonment and death of, 76-77; relations of Jesus with, 76-77; task of, 64

Joseph, St., role of, 73-74

Judas, betrayal of Christ by, 87; suicide of, 213

Judgment, death, good works, and, 274-278; final, 282-285

Justice, of God, 51-52; social, 272

Just Wages, the right to, 271

Kingdom of God, as proclaimed by Christ, 67-70

Knowledge, as an attribute of God, 51-52

Last Supper, narrative of the, 194

Last Things, theology of the, 274-289

Laws, in the Bible, 254-255; and the Church, 253-256; civil, 253, 256; the meaning of, 252-254

Lay Apostolate, in the "Constitution of the Church," 128

Lazarus, Parable of the Rich Man and, 279

Analytical Index   321

Legalism, danger of, 246-247
Leper, cure by Christ of the, 241
Life, after death, 276; disrespect for, 268; respect for, 265-268
Life Everlasting, and the resurrection of the body, 282-285
Literary Genres, in the Bible, 299-300
Literature, apocalyptic, 306
Liturgical Celebrations, in the "Constitution on the Sacred Liturgy," 205
Liturgy, as the public worship of the Church, 34-35; sacrifice in the, 35
Love, in the Epistles of St. John, 245-246; of God for men, 245-248; of neighbor, 177-180; sex, children, and, 237; the virtue of, 175
Magi, journey of the, 80-82, 304
Man, Christ as, 71-72; communication of God with, 45; as the co-worker with God, 43; creation by God of, 47-50
Marcel, Gabriel, on the subject of hope, 174-175
Marriage, and law, 234; mixed, 235-237; rite of, 234; Sacrament of, 232-240; sign value of celibacy and, 187-192
Mary, in the "Constitution on the Church," 154; the Immaculate Conception of, 54; as the Mother of all Christians, 152-155; as the Mother of God, 72-73; purification of, 80; virginity of, 72-73; visit to Elizabeth by, 152
Mass, and the Passover, 196, 199-202
Mercy, of God, 57-62
Messiah, Christ as a non-political, 84-85, 208; expectation in Israel of a, 61
Midrash, definition of, 69
Ministry of the Word, as an act of living tradition, 314; in the "Constitution on Divine Revelation," 314
Miracles, of Christ, 215, 241, 275; the significance of, 123; as symbols, 69
Mortal Sin, theology of, 208-209
Moses, the birth of, 20-21; the education of, 21; the history of, 20-35; the protection by God of, 20-22; the revelation of God to, 22-23
Mount Sinai, ratification of the Covenant on, 29-30, 32
Mystical Body, theology of the, 126-129
Neighbor, love of, 177-180
New Covenant, as the legacy of Christ, 96
Oil, as a symbol of healing, 223, 225
Old Covenant, based on love, 31; establishment of the, 29-32; mediator and blood as aspects of the, 32; public worship in the, 33-35; the theme of the, 31
Old Testament, Prophets of the, 39-62; worship in the, 34
Original Sin, meaning of, 54
Parable, of the Good Samaritan, 177-178; of Lazarus and the Rich Man, 219
Parables, in the Bible, 299
Paralytic, the cure by Christ of the, 275
Parenthood, the responsibilities of, 238-239
Passover, the feast of, 28; the Mass and the, 196, 199-202; the meal aspect of, 201; the sacrificial aspect of, 200-201
Passover Lamb, the Easter Lamb prefigured by the, 28
Penance, Sacrament of, 207-221; various rites of, 216-217
People of God, the Church as the new, 122-124
Peter, St., the denial of Christ by, 212-213; the office of, 133
Poems, in the Bible, 300-301
Pope, the infallibility of the, 136-137; the role of the, 133; the task of the, 136
Prayer, as dialogue, 182-183; need for, 183-184; and sacrifice, 184-185; theology of, 181-186
Prayers, treasury of, 290-295
Priest, role of the, 229
Priesthood, of Christ, 144-146
Private Property, the right to, 270-271
Prodigal Son, Parable of the, 219-220
Prophets, of the Old Testament, 39-62, 301; role of, 39
Public Worship, in the "Constitution on the Sacred Liturgy," 35
Punishment, and reward, 279-281
Purgatory, reality of, 280
Purification, of Mary, 80
Real Presence, of Christ in the Eucharist, 197-199
Reason, as a source of Church law, 258
Redeemer, as priest and victim, 63-65; as promised by God, 57-62
Red Sea, the crossing by the Israelites of the, 26-27
Religion, the Bible as a teacher of, 12-13
Religious Understanding, situation of, 313
Renewal, work of, 314
Resurrection, of the body, 282-285; of Christ, 98-101; Gospel traditions on the, 98-100; traditions concerning the, 305
Revelation, and inspiration, 298; private, 137; public, 137

Analytical Index

Reward, and punishment, 279-281

Sabbath, Christ on the subject of the, 265

Sacramentals, and Sacraments, 145

Sacraments, and grace, 242-243; and sacramentals, 145; as sacred signs, 144-145

Sacrifice, of animals to God, 32, 34, 90-92; 204; in the liturgy, 35; and prayer, 184-185

Saints, the communion of, 150-155; memorials of the, 288-289

Salvation History, celebration of, 288

Schillebeekx, Edward, on the subject of prayer, 184

Science, and evolution, 49-50

Scientific Research, the necessity of promoting, 317

Scripture, the apostolic nature of, 140; the Church as the custodian and interpreter of, 314-315; in the "Constitution on Divine Revelation," 315; as a source of Church law, 258

Senses, anointing of the, 225-226

Separated Brethren, in the "Decree on Ecumenism," 148-49

Sex, love, children, and, 237

Sexual Intercourse, proper use of, 239-240

Simeon, and Jesus in the temple, 80

Sin, all disasters caused by, 48-49; the authority to forgive, 215-219; the confession of, 219-221; the consequences of, 53-55; mortal, 208-209; and temptation, 51-52, 207-211; venial, 208-210, 220

Sin Offering, in the Bible, 91-93

Situation Ethics, a Catholic view of, 247; and Church guidance, 257-261

Social Justice, the Christian requirement of, 272

Suffering, the Christian meaning of, 54-55; as a mystery, 21-22

Suffering Servant, as depicted in Isaiah, 87-89

Sunday, as a day of worship, 263

Suzerainty Treaty, explanation of a, 31

Symbols, in the ceremony of Baptism, 167-168; in the ceremony of Confirmation, 171-172; the language of, 242

Temptation, and sin, 51-52, 207-211

Three Wise Men, see Magi

Tradition, the Church as the custodian of, 139-143; as a source of Church law, 258

Trinity, mystery of the, 115-118

Unity, Christianity's need for, 146-149

Unleavened Bread, symbolism of eating, 204-205

Vatican Council II, on the Church, 107, 148; on the evangelical counsels, 191; on the guidance of the Holy Spirit, 73; on the Jews, 85; on the lay apostolate, 128; on liturgical celebrations, 205; on Mary, 154; on the Ministry of the Word, 314; on public worship, 35; on Sacred Scripture, 315; on the separated brethren, 148-149; on worship in common, 149

Venial Sin, theology of, 208-210, 220

Virginity, of Mary, 72-73

Virtues, of Faith, Hope, and Love, 173-176

Vows, taken by religious, 132, 190-191

Water, in the Sacrament of Baptism, 160-161

Word of God, in catechesis, 315

Worship, in common, 149; of the community, 262-264; in the "Constitution on the Sacred Liturgy," 35; as a duty of Christians, 262-263; in the Old Testament, 34

BIBLIOGRAPHICAL NOTES

1. "The Interpretation of Dogma", E. Schillebeeckx, O.P. in "Tijdschrift voor Theologie", 1968. nr. 3. (Albertinum. Nijmegen, Netherlands.)

"Historicity and the Interpretation of Dogma", P. Schoonenberg, S.J. in "Theology Digest", Summer 1970. nr. 2.

"The Survival of Dogma", Avery Dulles, S.J. (Doubleday), Chapters 11 "The Hermeneutics of Dogmatic Statements", 12 "The 'Irreformability' of Dogma."

"Relation Catechesis, Magisterium and Theology", Discussions at the International Catechetical Congress, Sept. 20-25, 1971 (Rome) in "Verbum", Jan. 1972, p. 25-26. (Hoger Katechetisch Instituut, Nijmegen, Netherlands.)

2. "Israel's Concept of the Beginning", H. Renckens, S.J. (New York, 1964).

"The Hebrew Patriarchs and History", Roland de Vaux, O.P. in "Theology Digest", Winter, 1964.

"The Truth of the Bible and Historicity", Norbert Lohfink, S.J. in "Theology Digest", Spring, 1967.

3. "The Godsdienst van Israel" (The Religion of Israel), H. Renckens, S.J., Ch. II "Israel's Patriarchs". (Romen en Zonen, Roermond, Netherlands.)

4. "Psychological Conditions of Adult Faith", Antoine Vergrote in "Lumen Vitae", 1960. nr. 4. (International Centre for Studies in Religious Education, Brussels, Belgium.)

5. "De Godsdienst van Israel" (The Religion of Israel), H. Renckens, S.J.

"Worship in Ancient Israel", H. H. Rowley (London, England, S.P.C.K. 1967), Ch. 1 "Worship in the Patriarchal Age".

6. "Record of the Promise", The Old Testament, Wilfrid J. Harrington, O.P. (The Priory Press, Chicago, Illinois), The Exodus and Conquest. p. 44 ss.

7. Ibid. Literary Criticism of the Pentateuch, p. 105 ss.

"The Bible and the Ancient Near East", Roland de Vaux, O.P. (Doubleday), Reflections on the Present State of Pentateuchal Criticism on p. 31 ss.

8. "God — talk", John Macquarrie (Harper and Row, New York). —An Examination of the Language and Logic of Theology.

"Language, Logic and God", Frederic Ferré (Harper and Row, New York).

"Taalanalytische Perspectieven op Godsdienst en Kunst" (Language-analytical Perspectives on Religion and Art), W.A. de Pater. (De Nederlandse Boekhandel, Antwerp, Belgium.)

"Rahner's Argument for God", Joseph Doncel in "America", Oct. 31, 1970.

"God" — Commonwealth papers.

"The Language of Faith and Theology", J.P. de Rudder in "Tijdschrift voor Theologie", 1968. nr. 3. (publ. above).

"Silence and Speaking about God in a Secularized World", E. Schillebeeckx, O.P. in "Tijdschrift voor Theologie", 1967. nr. 4. (publ. above).

"Prayer in a Secularized Society", Fons D. Hoog in Concilium 49, p. 42 ss. (Paulist Press).

"The Vertical and Horizontal Dimensions In Symbolic Language about God", Antoine Vergrote in "Lumen Vitae", 1970. nr. 2.

9. "Striking a Covenant", Leonard Bushinski in "The Bible Today", February, 1963 (The Liturgical Press, Collegeville, Minnesota).

"Theology and Covenant in the Old Testament", Dennis J. McCarthy, S.J. Ibid. April, 1969.

"Covenant Theology in 1 Peter 1:1 - 2:10", Eugene A. La Verdiere. S.S.S. Ibid. April, 1969.

10. "Sacrifice in the Old Testament", Kevin G. O'Connel, S.J. Ibid. March, 1969.

"De Godsdienst van Israel", H. Renckens. Ch. IV "Israel's Worship." (publ. above.)

"Worship in Ancient Israel", H. H. Rowley (publ. above.), Ch. 4 "The Forms and the Meaning of Sacrifice."

"The Bible and the Ancient Near East", Roland de Vaux (publ. above.), "Is it possible to write a Theology of the Old Testament?" p. 49 ss.

11. "Record of the Promise" The Old Testament, Wilfrid J. Harrington (publ. above.), The Books of Samuel — The Books of Kings, p. 160 ss.

12. "Israel's Concept of the Beginning" H. Renckens, S.J. (publ. above.)

"The Creation Accounts in the Old Testament and in Ancient Egypt", J. Murtagh, S.M.A. in "The Bible Today", Oct. 1971, p. 447 ss.

"Vreemde Verleiding" (Strange Temptation) H.A.M. Fiolet, "Victory of the God-is-dead Crisis by discovering the Earthly Reality as Place for the Encounter with God." (Lemniscaat, Rotterdam, Netherlands.)

13. "Demonology and Diabolical Temptation", H.A. Kelly in "Theology Digest", Summer, 1966, p. 136.

"Angels and Devils", John Quinlan in "Tijdschrift voor Theologie", 1967. nr. 1.

"Maechte und Gewalten im Neuen Testament", Heinrich Schlier, in "Quaestiones Disputatae" 3, p. 63. (Herder, Basel, Freiburg, Wien.)

"Wijsgerige en Theologische Opmerkingen over Engelen en Duivelen" (Philosophical and Theological Observations on Angels and Devils), P. Schoonenberg, in "Annalen v.h. Thymgenootschap" 55 (1968) p. 66-90.

14. "The Book of our Faith", H. Renckens, S.J. "Verbum", June 1960.

"God's Creation" — Creation, Sin and Redemption in an Evolutionary World Concept", A. Hulsbosch, O.S.A. (De Schepping Gods — publ. Romen en Zonen, Roermond, Netherlands.)

"Primeval Man" Claus Westermann, in "Theology Digest", Spring 1969.

Literature indicated at Abraham Cycle, ch 1-3.

15. "The Phenomenon of Man", Teilhard de Chardin. p. 159.

"The Wisdom of Evolution", Raymond J. Nogar, O.P. in "Theology Digest", Winter 1965.

See "How to Read Your Bible" on p. 306 nr. 15 and footnote 146.

Bibliographical Notes

16. "God's Worden de Wereld" — (God's World Becoming) P. Schoonenberg. Evolution and Creation. esp. p. 36. (publ. Lannoo, Tielt, Belgium).

17. "The One and the Many: Corporate Personality", Philip Kaufman, O.S.B. in "Worship" Nov. 1968.

18. "Toward a Theology of Original Sin", Alfred Vanneste in "Theology Digest", Autumn 1967.
"Evolution of the Doctrine of Original Sin", S. Trooster, S.J. (Newman Press) p. 26 and p. 89-90.
"An Evolutionary View of Original Sin", Zoltan Alszeghy, S.J. and Maurizio Flick, S.J. in "Theology Digest", Autumn 1967.
"Sin of the World and Original Sin", P. Schoonenberg, S.J. in "Verbum", 1961, p. 50.
"Original Sin and Man's Situation", P. Schoonenberg, S.J. in "Theology Digest", Autumn 1967.
"Is Original Sin in Scripture?", Herbert Haag (Sheed and Ward).
"The Survival of Dogma", Avery Dulles, S.J. p. 192. publ. above).

19. "The Bible and the Ancient Near East", Roland de Vaux, p. 167 and 181. (publ. above).
"The Great Archeologists", Thomas Aquinas Collins, in "The Bible Today" Feb. 1965.
"Archeology and Genesis 1-11", John L. McKenzie, Ibid.
"Keeping up to Date on Biblical Excavations", Robert North, S.J. Ibid.

20. "Record of the Promise" The Old Testament, Wilfrid J. Harrington, O.P. p. 67-97. (publ. above).

21. "The Bible and the Ancient Near East", Roland de Vaux, O.P. p. 178.

22. "Christ the Sacrament of the Encounter with God", E. Schillebeeckx, O.P. — Christ, Sacrament of God. p. 7 ss.

23. See "How to Read Your Bible" on p. 302 13a and indicated literature.

24. "The Mystery of Faith in a Catechetical Perspective", Francois Coudreau in "The Living Light", Fall 1966.
"The Fabric of Modern Faith", Vincent Ryan Ruggerio in "Guide" May 1969 (Paulist Press).
"The Survival of Dogma", Avery Dulles, S.J. — Faith and Inquiry in Ch. 1-4. (publ. above).

25. See "How to Read Your Bible" on p. 303, nr. 13 e. and literature in footnote.

26. "Options", Pierre Babin, — The Kingdom on p. 19 ss.

27. "Discussion on the Virgin Birth of Christ", P. Schoonenberg, S.J. in "Verbum", May 1967 p. 188 ss.
"The Literary Genre of Matthew 1-2", David Ashbeck, O.F.M. cap. in "The Bible Today", Dec. 1971, p. 572 ss.
"Mary the Virginal Wife and the Married Virgin", John F. Craghan in "The Bible Today", April 1968.

28. "Marie, Nouvelle Eve: Le Contexte de la Foi dans la Virginité de Marie", A.J. Brekelmans, M.S.F. in "Tijdschrift voor Theologie" 1970. nr. 2.

29. "Jezus van Nazareth en Zijn Zending" (Jesus of Nazareth and His Mission), G. Schreiner, S.J. in "Verbum", Oct. 1960, p. 299 ss.
"De Evolutie van Jezus Zendings bewustzijn" (The Evolution of Jesus' Mission Awareness), G. Schreiner, S.J. in "Verbum", 1965, p. 395 ss.
"How much did Jesus Know?", Raymond E. Brown in "Theology Digest", Spring 1969.
"Hij is een God van Mensen" (He is a God of Men)), P. Schoonenberg, S.J. — De Mens die God's Zoon is (The Man, Who is the Son of God). p. 66 ss. (Malmberg. 'S-Hertogenbosch, 1969, Netherlands.)

30. "Christ the Sacrament of the Encounter with God", E. Schillebeeckx, O.P. — The Church Sacrament of the Risen Christ. p. 47.

31. "Torah and Gospel", ed. by Philip Scharper, "Evaluating the Past in Christian Jewish Relations" by Rabbi Solomon Grayzel and Rev. John B. Sheerin, C.S.P. p. 5-34. (Sheed and Ward, 1966.)

32. "New Testament Development of Old Testament Themes", F.F. Bruce. Ch VII The Servant Messiah. (Wm. B. Eerdmans Publ. Co. Grand Rapids, Mich.)

33. "Worship in Ancient Israel", H. H. Rowley — The Sin offering and the Guilt offering. (publ. above), p. 126 ss.
Ch. 8 of this book with indicated literature.

34. "New Testament Development of Old Testament Themes", F.F. Bruce (publ. above), Ch. VIII The Shepherd King.

35. "De Godsdienst van Israel" (The Religion of Israel), H. Renckens, S.J. p. 130 ss. (publ. above).
—See also Ch. 8 of this book, footnote 10.

36. "The Reality of the Risen One", P. Schoonenberg, S.J., Special Issue of "Verbum", June, 1966.
"Reflections on the Synoptic Gospels", Forbes J. Monaghan, S.J. p. 3 ss. (Alba House).
"Gospel Traditions about Christ's Resurrection", Joseph Ponthot in "Lumen Vitae" 1966. nr. 1, p. 66 ss. and 1966 nr. 2, p. 205 ss. (esp. p. 211).

37. See literature indicated at Ch. 25.

38. "The Survival of Dogma", Avery Dulles, S.J. (publ. above) — The Permanence of Prophecy in the Church, p. 125 ss.
"Kerkelijk Ambt als Prophetisme" (Church Ministry as Prophecy), F. Haarsma in "Tijdschrift voor Theologie" 1970. nr. 2.
"Charism: A relational Concept", William Koupal in "Worship", November 1968.
"The Charismatic Dimension of the Church", Cardinal Leon Suenens — Speech at Vatican II in "Council Speeches of Vatican II, p. 29 ss., ed. by H. Kueng, Congar, O'Hanlon (Paulist Press).

39. See Ch. 33 and 34 of this book and indicated literature.

40. "Person and Grace", Juan Alfaro, S.J. in "Theology Digest", Spring 1966.
"The Holy Spirit and Catechesis", in "Lumen Vitae" 1962. nr. 2. The whole issue!
"Sacramental Grace", James E. Griffiss, Jr. in "Worship", Oct. 1968.

Bibliographical Notes

"The Holy Spirit and Catechetics", Wilfrid Tuninck, O.S.B. in "The Living Light", Spring 1965.

41. See Ch. 28 and 57 of this book and indicated literature.

42. "God for Us Men", Development in the Theology of the Blessed Trinity — by S. Trooster, S.J. (Gottmer, Haarlem, Netherlands).

"Trinity", K. Rahner in "Sacramentum Mundi" p. 301. (Herder and Herder).

"The Survival of Dogma", Avery Dulles, S.J. (publ. above) — Ch. 11 The Hermeneutics of Dogmatic Statements. Also p. 147 and p. 196.

These theologians work with the concepts "three modes of being or existence in God." It is just an approach, which does not yet have the approval of the Church!

43. "Lumen Gentium", Vat. II, nr. 9.

44. See "How to Read Your Bible" 13. e. on p. 303 and indicated literature.

45. In "Tijdschrift voor Theologie", 1969. nr. 3; Special Issue "Christian Freedom and Church Authority":

"The Varying Role of Peter's Successors", T.M. Schoof, O.P.

"Foi et Moeurs", P. Fransen.

"Exercise of Authority in the Church", F. Haarsma.

"Christian Liberty according to Paul", W. Grossauw.

"Priest and Bishop", Biblical Reflections, Raymond E. Brown, S.S. (Paulist Press).

"The Contemporary Magisterium", Avery Dulles, S.J. in "Theology Digest.", Winter 1969

"The Survival of Dogma", Avery Dulles, S.J. — II Teachers in the Church.

"Authority in the Church", John L. McKenzie. (Sheed & Ward).

"The State of the Priesthood", Andrew M. Greeley's Comments to the Ad Hoc Committee on the Implementation of the Priesthood Study. February 1972.

"Episcopal Collegiality according to "Lumen Gentium", G. Dejaive, S.J. in "Lumen Vitae" 1965. nr. 4.

46. "Episkopat und Primat", K. Rahner in "Quaestiones Disputatae" 1961, nr. 11, p. 91, esp. footnote 23 on p. 93. (Herder, Basel, Freiburg, Wien).

"Coresponsibility in the Church", Cardinal Suenens. Ch. III The Responsibility of the Papacy.

"How can we evaluate Collegiality vis-a-vis Papal Primacy?" in the New Concilium 64, p. 89. — ref. Lumen Gentium 22.

47. "Réflexions théologiques sur la crise des Prêtres", E. Schillebeeckx, O.P. in "Tijdschrift voor Theologie" 1968, nr. 4. esp. p. 414-415.

48. "Lumen Gentium", Vat. II, nr. 12.

"Authority in the Church", John L. McKenzie, p. 58. (Sheed & Ward).

"Primacy and Episcopacy", J. Ratzinger in "Theology Digest", Autumn, 1971, p. 206-207.

"The Magisterium in a Changing Church", Gregory Baum in Concilium 21, esp. p. 72-75 and p. 83.

"The Dogmatic Constitution on Divine Revelation", Peter van Leeuwen in Concilium 21, esp. p. 15.

"Recent Catholic Views on the Development of Dogma", H. Hanmans in Concilium 21, p. 130.

49. "Die Entstehung der Christliche Bibel", Hans Freiherr von Campenhausen. Ch. IV Die Enstehung des Neuen Testamentes, p. 173 ss. (Mohr, Tuebingen, Germany).

"Record of Revelation", The Bible by Wilfrid J. Harrington, O.P. The Criterion of Canonicity, p. 72.

50. "Christ the Sacrament of the Encounter with God", E. Schillebeeckx, O.P. — The Infallible Working of Grace in the Sacraments. p. 68 ss. (publ. above).

51. "The Ecumenist" — A Journal for Promoting Christian Unity. 1962 - 1972 ss. (Paulist Press).

"Ecumenical Experiences", ed. by Louis V. Romeu. (The Newman Press).

Decree on Ecumenism, Vat. II.

52. "The Virgin Mary in the Constitution on the Church", René Laurentin. in Concilium 8.

"Eschatology and the Assumption", Donal Flanagan, Concilium 41, p. 135 ss.

"The Present Position in Mariology", Stanislav Napiorkowski, in Concilium 29, p. 133 ss.

53. "Who Spoke the 'Magnificat'?, Richard H. McGrath in "The Bible Today", Dec. 1967.

54. "De Dooppraktijk in de Jonge Kerk" (Baptism in the Early Church), Ambrose Verheul, O.S.B. Special Issue on the Baptism of Infants of "Tijdschrift voor Liturgie", 1968, nr. 3 (Abbey of Affligem, Belgium).

"Baptism in the Name of the Lord Jesus", P. Pas.

"Questions on the Baptism of Infants", G. Danneels. both in "Tijdschrift vor Liturgie, 1969, nr. 1.

"We Profess One Baptism for the Forgiveness of Sins", Raymond E. Brown, S.S. in "Worship", May 1966.

"Infant Baptism", Christophor Klesling in "Worship", Dec. 1968.

55. "Baptism and the New Covenant", Sister M. Rosalle Ryan, C.S.J. in "Worship", Oct. 1963.

56. "Infant Baptism" in "Evolution and the Doctrine of Original Sin", S. Trooster, S.J. (publ. above).

"Why Baptists do not baptize Infants", James McClendon in Concilium 24, p. 7 ss.

"L'Interprétation Chrétienne du Baptême et du Baptême des Enfants", B.A. Willems in "Tijdschrift voor Theologie", 1967, nr. 4.

See Ch. 40 and indicated literature.

57. "Who Belongs to the Church", Bonifact Williams, O.P. in Concilium 1, esp. on p. 150.

58. "The New Rite of Infant Baptism", Richard H. Guerette in "Worship", April 1969.

Chapter 14 with footnotes-literature on Original Sin.

59. "Public Worship", Joseph A. Jungmann, S.J. —Reception into the Church: Baptism and Confirmation, p. 72 ss.

"Confirmation: Being and Becoming Christian", Mary Charles Bryce, O.S.B. in "Worship" May 1967.

"Baptism and Confirmation", Wilhelm Breuning in Concilium 22.

60. "Les Saint Paiens de l'Ancient Testament", Jean Daniélou. (Editions du Seuil, France).

Bibliographical Notes

"The Survival of Dogma", Avery Dulles, S.J. — Ch. 4 Toward an Apologetics of Hope. (publ. above).

61. "Teaching Prayer Today", Daniel O'Rourke, O.F.M. in "The Living Light", Fall 1970.

"Prayer and Contempory Man", Jane Marie Richardson in "Worship", March 1971.

"Prayer in a Secularized Society", Fons D'Hoogh in Concilium 49, p. 37 ss.

"Why is Prayer so Difficult Nowadays?", A. Leenhouwers. O. cap. in "Tijdschrift voor Liturgie", 1971, nr. 2.

"Prayer Horizontal or Vertical", Robert Sargent, S.M. in "The Bible Today". Oct. 1969.

62. "Recherche sur le Sens de la Vie Religieuse", Alain Durand in "Tijdschrift voor Theologie" 1970, nr. 3.

"Human Couple in Scripture", Pierre Grelot in "Theology Digest", Summer 1966, esp. p. 141.

"Zending van de Kerk — Theologische Peilingen (Mission of the Church — Theological Soundings). Ch. III Religious Life, E. Schillebeeckx, O.P. (Nelissen, Bilthoven, Netherlands).

63. "De Mis als Gratiarum Actio" (The Mass as Gratiarum Actio), G. Claeys, c.i.c.m. in "Tijdschrift voor Liturgie" 1966, nr. 6.

"The Eucharistic Prayer and the Gifts over Which It is Spoken", Robert J. Ledogar in "Worship", Dec. 1967.

"Het Eucharistisch Gebed" (The Eucharistic Prayer), Dr. H. Manders, C.ss.R. in "Tijdschrift voor Liturgie" 1967, nr. 1.

64. "Reflections on the Title and Function of the Lamb of God", William J. Tobin In "The Bible Today", Feb. 1968, p. 2367 ss.

65. "The Real Presence of Christ in the Eucharist", E. Schillebeeckx In "Tijdschrift voor Theologie" 1965, nr. 2.

"La Modalité Eucharistique de l'unique Présence réele du Christ", E. Schillebeeckx In "Tijdschrift voor Theologie", 1966, nr. 4.

"Transsubstantiation", R. Sonnen, S.J. In "Verbum", June 1965. p. 223 ss.

"Presence", P. Schoonenberg, S.J. In "Verbum", Dec. 1962, nr. 12.

"The Real Presence In Contemporary Discussion", P. Schoonenberg, S.J. in "Theology Digest", Spring, 1967.

"The Survival of Dogma", Avery Dulles, S.J. (publ. above)—Ch. 11. esp. p. 178, 183 and Ch. 12, p. 192.

"The Presence of the Lord Jesus", Paul de Haes In "Lumen Vitae", 1965, nr. 3.

"Mysterium Fidei and the Theology of the Eucharist", Joseph M. Powers, S.J. in "Worship", January 1966.

"Transsubstantiation, Transfinalization, Transsignification", E. Schillebeeckx in "Worship", June 1966.

"Questions on the Doctrine of the Eucharist in Holland", Leo van Hout in "Theology Digest", Spring 1968.

"Trans-substantiation: How far Is this Doctrine Historically Determined?" — (Related to "Mysterium Fidei"), P. Schoonenberg, S.J. In Concilium 24, esp. p. 26.

66. "Passover in the Old Testament", John H. O'Rourke.

"The Eucharist — The New Passover Meal", Goffrey Wood, S.A.

"The Eucharist: A Covenant Meal", William E. Lynch, C.M.

All in "The Bible Today", March 1963.

"Public Worship", J.A. Jungmann, S.J. — Holy Mass, p. 89.

"Missarum Solemnia", J.A. Jungmann, S.J.

67. Chapter 7 of this book and indicated literature.

68. "The Bible and the Liturgy", Jean Daniélou, S.J. p. 128. (Notre Dame).

"Is the Eucharist a Sacrifce?", Joseph Ratzinger in Concilium 24, p. 66 ss.

69. "Biblical Joy in the Lucan Eucharist", Paul J. Bernadican, S.J. in "The Bible Today", Dec. 1970, p. 162.

70. "Mortal Sin—Sin unto Death?", Bruno Shueller, S.J. in "Theology Digest", Autumn 1968.

71. "Sin and Community in the New Testament", Jerome Murphy — O'Connor, O.P. in "Theology Digest", Summer 1968.

72. "Sin and Conversion", Joseph Fuchs, S.J. in "Theology Digest", Autumn 1966.

"Anxiety, Guilt, and Shame in the Atonement.", Paul W. Pruyser in "Theology Digest", Autumn 1966.

73. "Penance in the Eastern Church", David Kirk in "Worship", March 1966.

74. "Public Worship", Joseph A. Jungmann, S.J. (publ. above).—The Sacrament of Penance p. 77 ss.

75. "Communal Penance", Gabriel-M. Nissln, O.P. in "Theology Digest", Spring 1968.

76. "The Sacrament of Penance"—Special Issue with four Articles on Penance in "Tijdschrift voor Liturgie" 1971, nr. 5.

77. "De Ziekenzalving" (Anointing of the Sick), L. Bortier, O. Praem. in "Tijdschrift voor Liturgie" 1971, nr. 3.

"Public Worship", J.A. Jungmann, S.J.—The Anointing of the Sick. p. 81 ss. (publ. above).

"Het Sacrament van de Stervenden" (The Sacrament of the Dying), H. Grond, in "Tijdschrift voor Liturgie", 1969, nr. 3.

78. "Priestly Character and Ministry", Joseph Moingt, S.J. in "Theology Digest", Autumn 1969.

"Réflexions théologiques sur la Crise des Prêtres", E. Schillebeeckx in "Tijdschrift voor Theologie" 1968, nr. 4. — Digest of this article: "Towards a more adequate theology of the priesthood" in "Theology Digest", Summer 1970.

"L'Homme Prêtre", R. Coste (Publ. Desclée). Ch. III Fondements Scripturaires p. 49 ss.

"A New Approach to the Validity of Church Orders", Daniel J. O'Hanlon in "Worship", Aug.-Sept. 1967.

"Public Worship", J.A. Jungmann. — Holy Orders, p. 83 ss.

79. "De Huidige Situatie van de Priester" (Today's Situation of the Priest), Special Issue of

"Tijdschrift voor Theologie", 1965, nr. 3.
"The Root of Priestly Office", Karl Lehmann in "Theology Digest", Autumn 1970.
"Office and Unity of the Church", Joseph Ratzinger in "Theology Digest", Summer 1966.
"The Priest in Crisis"—A Study in Role Change, David O'Neill. Being a Man of many Faces p. 16; New Tasks for the Priest p. 111. (Pflaum Press, Dayton, Ohio).

80. USA Bishops Study on the Priesthood—Comments to the Ad Hoc Committee by Andrew Greeley, N.C.R., February 28, 1972.

81. "Public Worship", Joseph A. Jungmann, p. 87.

"Het Huwelijk, Aardse Werkelijkheid en Heilsmysterie" (Marriage. Earthly Reality and Mystery of Salvation), Vol. I, E. Schillebeeckx, 1963 (Nelissen, Bilthoven, Netherlands), p. 169: "The first centuries . . . Christians married as the pagans did . . ." p. 180: "From the fourth to the eleventh century: Marriage remains a **secular** concern, but Church concern, though without obligation for juridical validity, is underlined by surrounding **secular marrage** with liturgical celebrations."

82. "The Indissolubility of Marriage and Church Order", P. Huizinga, S.J. in Concilium 38, esp. p. 48.

"When the Courts Don't Work", Rev. John T. Catoir, J.C.D. in "America", Oct. 9, 1971.

"Rethinking the Marriage Bond", Paul F. Palmer, S.J. in "America", Jan. 17, 1970.

"Dissolubilité du Lien du Mariage: Une Tradition Unanime?", Th. van Eupen in "Tijdschrift voor Theologie", 1970, nr. 3.

83. Speech of Archbishop of Luxor (Egypt) in Council Daybook Vol. III, Session IV, p. 92.

"Divorce and Remarriage East and West", Olivier Rousseau, O.S.B. in Concilium 24.

84. "Régulations des Naisances. Dix Annees de Réflexions Théologiques", A. Valsechi, esp. note added to the French edition of 1970, in which the author describes the various interpretations of national bishops conferences on "Humanae Vitae", Pope Paul's encyclical on responsible parenthood.

"How does God Teach us Morals?". Joseph E. Kerns (Paulist Press) esp. p. 50: "No Pope in the history of the Church has ever spoken ex cathedra (infallibly) on moral questions." — Hence, the different interpretations of national bishops conferences:

a. Unconditional obedience: Australia, Spain, East Germany, USA, Italy, Ireland.—These bishops treat the encyclical as a **de facto** "ex cathedra" (infallible) statement, though some admit it is not.

b. Encyclical is not infallible, hence, no obligation for unconditional and absolute obedience: Belgium, West-Germany, England and Wales, France, Canada. — Noting that the encyclical is not infallible or unchangeable, the Belgian bishops say that a Catholic may "after a serious examination before God, come to other conclusions on certain points. In such a case, he has the right to follow his conviction."

For the same reason, the French bishops observe that this is a case in which one may appeal to "the following established moral teaching: When there is an alternative of duties in which no matter what decision is made one cannot avoid a disorder (either obeying the Pope's ruling on contraception or practicing responsible parenthood without dangerously interrupting the sexual dialogue), traditional wisdom tells us to inquire before God as to which duty, under the circumstances, is greater. After mutual discussion, the spouses should make their decision with all the care they owe to the greatness of their conjugal vocation."

c. Possibility for further study: Respect for the authority of the Pope, the duty not to neglect this encyclical when forming one's conscience. "No duty **for all** to accept the encyclical as to contraception" (Swiss). "Possibility open for later correction" (Scandinavia, Netherlands, Indonesia.)

See F. Haarsma, "Tijdschrift voor Theologie", 1969, "Remarks on the Authentic Pronouncements of the Magisterium", Bruno Schueller, S.J. in "Theology Digest", Winter 1968.

85. "Christ the Sacrament of the Encounter with God", E. Schillebeekx (publ. above) — The Sacraments as Ecclesial Manifestation of Christ's Divine Love for Men, p. 63 ss. Also "Sevenfold Ecclesial Realization of the One Mystery of Redemption" p. 73-79.

"Teaching the Sacraments", Charles J. Keating in "The Living Light", Winter 1965.

"Sacramental Symbolism and the Mysterion of the Early Church", Herbert Musurillo, S.J. in "Worship", May 1965.

"Signs, Symbols and Mysteries", J.D. Chrichton in "Worship", Nov. 1965.

"Symbol and Sacrament", John R. Sheets, S.J. in "Worship", April 1967.

86. "How Many Sacraments", Christophor Kiesling in "Worship", May 1970.

"Paradigms of Sacramentality", Christophor Kiesling in "Worship" Aug./Sept. 1970.

"Sacramental Grace", James E. Giffis, in "Worship" Oct. 1968.

87. "The Moral Teaching of Jesus in the Synoptics", John P. Keating, S.J. in "The Bible Today", Dec. 1969.

"Sin, Liberty and Law", Louis Monden, S.J. Ch. 3 Legal Ethics or Situation Ethics? p. 73 ss., esp. p. 105 on textbook morality. Also p. 119-120. (Sheed and Ward).

Archbishop Zoghbi's plea for the innocent party at Vat. II. See Council Daybook III p. 91, nr. 1-4 (publ. above).

"Farewell to the Tribunal", Leo M. Croghan In "America", Oct. 3, 1970.

"Marriage Law and Real Life", Leo M. Croghan In "America", Oct. 5, 1969.

"Canon Law: Justice by Variety", Martin J. McManus in "America", Oct. 9, 1971.

"A New Look at Christian Morality", Charles E. Curran — Dialogue with Joseph Fletcher, p. 60. (Fides, Notre Dame).

"The New Morality in Focus", Daniel C. Maguire in "The Living Light", Winter '67-68.

"The Modern Catechist and the New Approach to Christian Morality", James A. O'Donohoe In "The Living Light", Winter 1965-66.

88. "Sin, Liberty and Law", L. Monden (Sheed and Ward), p. 116.

89. The author refers to "Situation Ethics" and "Moral Responsibility", Joseph Fletcher (Westminster) and "Hello Lovers", Joseph Fletcher and Thomas A. Wassmer (Corpus Books). Situation ethics as explained in these books is not accepted in the Catholic tradition.
"Norm and Content in Christian Ethics", ed. by Gene H. Outka and Paul Ramsey (Scribners). — See 'Love, Situations, and Rules" by Donald Evans on p. 367 ss. and "Absolute Norms in Moral Theology", Charles E. Curran on p. 139 ss.
"A New Look at Christan Morality", Charles E. Curran, — Dialogue with Joseph Fletcher. (publ. above).

90. "Sin, Liberty and Law", Louis Monden (publ. above) — Situation Ethics within Catholicism. p. 83 ss.
"Rahner's Christian Ethics", J.F. Breshahan in "America", Oct. 31, 1970: "Rahner has successfully demythologized an older form of ethical reasoning", p. 351.
"Christian Morals", Richard McCormick in "America", Jan. 10, 1970, esp. last par. "to a value ethics".

91. "Sin, Liberty and Law" — above. p. 104.

92. Ibid.—The Christian Conscience before the Law. p. 102 ss.
"A New Catholic Morality", John G. Milhaven, S.J. in "The Critic", June/July 1968.
"A New Look at Christian Morality", Charles E. Curran (publ. above) — "The Moral Theology of Bernard Haering", esp. p. 151, par. 3 on "kairos".
"How do I know I'm doing right?", G.S. Sloyan, p. 102-103. (Pflaum).
"Dynamics and Continuity in a Personalistic Approach to Natural Law"—V. The Biblical Ethics of Vigilance toward the Kairos; VII The True Countenance of Love, B. Haering in "Norm and Context in Christian Ethics", See above!
"Het Degelijk Gevormd Geweten'" (Well informed Conscience), J. Ghoos in "Tijdschrift voor Theologie", 1969, nr. 3.
"Let Your Conscience be Your Guide", C.J. van der Poel, C.S.Sp in "The Living Light", Spring 1971.
"Law and Conscience", Franz Boeckle, — Norm and Situation in Catholic Moral Theology (Sheed and Ward).
"The New Morality"—Continuity and Discontinuity, ed. by William Dunphy. (Herder and Herder).
"Conscience in Today's World", ed. Jeremy Harrington, O.F.M. — "Conscience is my capacity to read my situation in the light of faith and how I ought to act to be responsible", p. 34. See also p. 20, 27, 110-111. (St. Anthony Messenger Press).
"Morality is for Persons", Bernard Haering. publ. Farrar, Straus and Giroux.
"Catholic Moral Theology in Dialogue", Charles E. Curran, Fides, Notre Dame, Ind.

93. "How do I know I'm doing right?", Sloyan (above) — What is Conscience? p. 96 ss.

94. "Sin, Liberty and Law" (above), p. 116-117.

95. "Law and Conscience" (above) —"Existential ethics can lead pure essential ethics out of the danger of legalizing", p. 113.

96. "Human Significance and Christian Significance", Richard A. McCormick in "Norm and Context in Christian Ethics" (above),—"The Primacy of Charity (agape)"—"The essential interiority of Law in the New Covenant", p. 234-237.
"Biblical Revelation of the Primacy of Charity", G. Gilleman, S.J. in "Lumen Vitae", 1961, nr. 1.
"General Catechetical Directory", Sacred Congregation for the Clergy (U.S. Catholic Conference), nr. 23 "Catechesis, therefore, must foster and illumine the increase of theological charity ... and also the **manifestation of that same virtue in connection with the duties. . .**"

97. "Sin, Liberty and Law" (above), p. 102-105.
"God en Mens" (God and Man), E. Schillebeeckx in "Theologische Peilingen" (Theological Soundings), Vol. IV. (Nelissen, Bilthoven, Netherlands).

98. "Bibel Auslegung im Wandel", Norbert Lohfink, S.J. — Die Zehn Gebote ohne den Berg Sinai. (The Ten Commandments without Mount Sinai), p. 129 ss.

99. The author avoids the term "Natural Law", though the "res" is there. E.g. See this book: p. 250 (top), p. 250 (bottom), 258 (3) and (4). The reason is the theological confusion around the traditional concept of "Natural Law". See "A New Look at Christian Morality", Charles E. Curran (publ. above) — The Natural Law in Catholic Theology, p. 74 ss. — Critique of Natural Law, p. 162 ss.
"What is Happening to Morality?", Nicholas Lohkamp, S.T.D. — Natural Law, p. 68-70. (St. Anthony Messenger Press).
"How do I know I'm doing right?" (above) p. 77.
"What Ethical Principals are Universally Valid?", Bruno Schueller, S.J. in "Theology Digest", Spring 1971.
'Divine Law and Church Structure", Peter Huizinga, S.J. in "Theology Digest", Summer 1970.—Mutable Natural Law, on p. 145.
"Human Significance and Christian Significance" (above) — Natural Law on p. 239. See also p. 241 last par.
The Pastoral Constitution on the Church in the Modern World, the longest document of the Vatican II Council, uses the term "natural law" only three times!

100. "Recent Developments in the Theology of Marriage", W. van der Marck in "Tijdschrift voor Theologie" 1967, nr. 2.

101. "Absolute Norms in Moral Theology" (above) p. 152.

102. "Human Significance and Christian Significance" (above). The existence of the Natural Law. p. 237 ss. Religious Freedom: Introduction by J.M. Murray. The Documents of Vatican II ed. W.M. Abbott, p. 673.

103. See 102 "Human . . ." p. 249.

104. "A New Catholic Morality", J.G. Milhaven (above), last par. on p. 45.

105. "Prudence and Moral Change", Franz Furger in Concilium 35. — Rahner's Existential Ethics as a Possible Synthesis, esp. on p. 129 (bottom)

"... how the concern of situation ethics can be actually worked out in Catholic moral theology through a deepened understanding of the traditional teaching on prudence."

106. See also Ch. 31, nr. 3 of this book.

107. "Sunday, the Day of the Lord", Karl Rahner, "Verbum", May 1965, p. 163.

"The Bible and the Liturgy", J. Danielou — The Lord's Day on p. 242 ss.

"Public Worship", J. Jungmann, Ch. 2. History.

"From the Sabbath to the Day of the Lord", Ambrose Verheul, O.S.B. in "Theology Digest", Spring 1971.

108. "The Modern Sexual Revolution", Guenter Struck, in Concilium 35.

109. "Man's Right over His Body and the Principle of Totality", Alonzo M. Hamelin in Concilium 15.

110. "Survey on Warfare, Peace and Pacifism" in Concilium 15, p. 105-141.

111. "Empirical Social Study and Ethics", Wilhelm Korff in Concilium 35.

"Property" by Franz Klueber in Sacramentum Mundi nr. 5 (Herder and Herder).

112. "The Theological Structure of Marxist Atheism", Gaston Fessard, S.J. in Concilium 16. On private property, p. 14 ss.

113. "How can the Church Provide Guidelines in Social Ethics?", Philip Herder-Dornesch in Concilium 35.

114. "De Derde Nachtwake", G. Bouwman, SVD. —The Death of the Christian on p. 48 ss. (Lannoo, Tielt, Belgium).

"Eschatology and Catechesis" — "Lumen Vitae", 1963, nr. 3. (The whole issue).

"Leven ondanks de Dood" (Life regardless Death), Special issue of "Tijdschrift voor Theologie", 1970, nr. 4. Five articles!

115. "How to Read Your Bible", nr. 8 on p. 300 of this book and indicated literature.

116. "The Bible on Life Everlasting", Franz Schreibmayer in "Verbum", Oct. 1961, p. 355 ss.

"The New Heaven and the New Earth", P. Schoonenberg, S.J. in "Verbum", Oct. 1961, p. 372 ss.

"The Final Completion", P. Schoonenberg, S.J. in "Verbum", Nov. 1963, p. 362 ss.

117. "Das Leben der Toten", K. Rahner in "Schriften zur Theologie" IV, 1960, p. 430.

"Questions about Death and Life in the New Testament", B. van Iersel in "Verbum", May 1966, p. 185 ss.

118. "De Godsdienst van Israel" (The Religion of Israel), H. Renckens, S.J.—The Great Feasts, p. 138 ss.

"The Mystery of Christian Worship", Odo Casel, O.S.B.

119. "Worship and the Celebration of Life", David P. O'Neil in "The Living Light", Spring 1970.

"Public Worship", J.A. Jungmann, S.J.—The Church Year, p. 178 ss.

120. Reprint of the author's article in the New American Bible, publ. Catholic Book Publ. Co.

121. "Sprache Gottes und Sprache der Menschen" — Literarische und Sprachpsychologische Beobachtungen zur Heiligen Schrift. (Language of God and Man — Literary and language-psychological Observations on Sacred Scripture), Luis Alonso Schoekel (Patmos, Duesseldorf), esp. Psychologie der Inspiration (Psychology of Inspiration) p. 128, 149, 154 ss. The original book is "The Inspired Word", publ. Herder and Herder, N.Y. The author knows the German translation only.

122. "Inspiration and Revelation", Pierre Benoit, O.P. in Concilium 10, p. 10 ss.

123. Ibid. p. 18 and 21.

"Understanding the Bible", Ignatius Hunt, O.S.B. p. 9-10. (Sheed and Ward).

124. Dogmatic Constitution on Divine Revelation. Vat. II, nr. 12.

"The Bible and Literary Forms", Francis Seper, M.S.C. in "The Bible Today," April 1963.

"De Historiciteit van de Synoptische Evangelien", A. Bea. (Historicity of the Synoptic Gospels). (Nelissen, Bilthoven, Netherlands).

"Understanding the Bible (above), p. 41 ss., also p. 49 ss.

"Bibel Auslegung im Wandel", Norbert Lohfink, S.J. (Joseph Knecht, Frankfurt am Main, Germany) p. 76 ss.

"A Lesson by Satire", William G. Heidt, O.S.B. in "The Bible Today", Oct. 1967, p. 2191 ss.

125. "Reading a Parable", Hamish J.G. Swanston, in "The Bible Today", Nov. 1967 and Dec. 1968.

"The Point of a Parable", Charles J. Galloway, S.J. in "The Bible Today" p. 1952.

126. "Record of the Promise", The Old Testament, Wilfrid J. Harrington, O.P. p. 115-117 (publ. above).

127. Ibid. p. 353-354 — Literary Form and Message of "Ruth".

128. "Understanding the Bible", Ignatius Hunt, p. 42 ss. (publ. above).

"Israel's Concept of the Beginning", H. Renckens. (publ. above).

"The Creation Accounts in the Old Testament and in Ancient Egypt", J. Murtagh in "The Bible Today", Oct. 1971.

"De Schepping God's (God's Creation) — Creation, Sin and Redemption in an Evolutionary World Concept, A. Hulsbosch, O.S.A. (Romen en Zonen, Roermond, Netherlands).

"Genesis and the Secret of Creation", Carrol Stuhlmueller, C.P. in "The Bible Today" Oct. 1962.

"Archeology and Genesis 1-11", John L. McKenzie in "The Bible Today", Feb. 1965.

129. "The Godsdienst van Israel" (The Religion of Israel), H. Renckens. SJ. Ch. II, Israel's God, p. 82 ss.

130. Jerusalem Bible: Matt. 24. footnote 24.a. on theophanies.

Jersalem Bible: Ex. 19. footnote 19,j. and Ex. 13. footnote 13, f.

"Bibel Auslegung im Wandel", Norbert Lohfink, S.J. —Die Zehn Gebote ohne den Berg Sinai (Ten Commandments without Mount Sinai), p. 129 ss. (publ. above).

"Symbolism and the Eschatological Discourses", William J. Rewak, S.J. n "The Bible Today", Nov. 1964, esp. p. 934.

131. "Record of the Promise", The Old Testament, Wilfrid H. Harrington — The Psalms. p. 281 ss.

132. "The Conscience of Israel", Bruce Vawter (Sheed and Ward).

"The Prophets as Social Reformers", John A. Lucal, S.J. in "The Bible Today", Nov. 1967.

"De Godsdienst van Israel" (The Religion of Israel), H. Renckens (publ. above) — Ch. VI. Israel's Prophets.

"Introduction aux Livres Saints", P. Grelot — Ch. VI Le Message des Prophètes on p. 76 ss. (Eugène Belin, Paris, France).

"Heilsmittler im Alten Testament und im Alten Orient", Josef Scharbert. — Die Propheten als Mittler (The Prophets as Mediators), p. 280. (Quaestiones Disputatae 23/24, Herder, Freiburg, Basel, Wien).

133. "Worship in Ancient Israel", H.H. Rowley. — The Sin Offering and the Guilt Offering, on p. 126 ss. (London, S.P.C.K. 1967).

134. "Seven Books of Wisdom", Roland E. Murphy, O. Carm. (Bruce, Milwaukee).

135. Dogmatic Constitution on Divine Revelation, Vat. II nr. 12.

"New Testament Development of Old Testament Themes", F.F. Bruce, Ch. 1 "Organizing Old Testament Theology" and Ch. 2 "The Rule of God".

"God's Rule and Kingdom", R. Schnackenburg, p. 77 ss. (Herder and Herder).

136. "The Power and the Wisdom", John L. McKenzie, p. 27 ss. esp. "The Literary Forms of the Gospels" on p. 35. (Bruce, Milwaukee).

"New Testament Theology Today", R. Schnackenburg, p. 19; 37. (Herder and Herder).

"The Method of Form Criticism in Gospel Research", R. Schnackenburg in "Theology Digest", Autumn 1964.

"Reflections on the Synoptic Gospels", Forbes J. Monghan, S.J. p. 100 (Alba House).

137. "The Infancy Narratives", J. Danielou, p. 8 ss. (Herder and Herder).

138. Ibid. p. 11 ss.

139. "The Place of Gospel Miracles in the Teaching of Christology", B.L. Marthaler, O.F.M. in "The Living Light", Winter 1966-67.

"The Presence of God's Love in the Power of Jesus' Works", John Crossan, in Concilium 50. esp. p. 68.

"Dismemberment or Renewal of Fundamental Theology", Rene Latourelle, S.J. in Concilium 50, p. 38 ss.

"The Four Gospels", Bruce Vawter, p. 101-102; p. 107; p. 176. (Doubleday).

"The Miracles of Jesus", Leopold Sabourin, S.J. in "Biblical Theology Bulletin", February 1971, p. 59 ss. (Piazza del Gesù 45 - 00186 Rome).

"Nieuwe Kijk op het Oude Boek" (New Look to the Old Book), Luc. H. Grollenberg, O.P. Ch. VIII De Vier Evangelien (The Four Gospels). (Elsevier, Amsterdam/Brussels).

"The Miracles of the Gospels", Donald A. Youngblood in "The Bible Today", Dec. 1968.

"Miracles and Science, a linguistic Approach", W.A. de Pater in "Tijdschrift voor Theologie", 1969, nr. 1.

"Jesus and His Miracles", William Braude in "The Bible Today", Feb. 1972.

"De Bijbel over het Wonder" (The Bible on Miracles), A. de Groot, SVD. (Romen en Zonen, Roermond, Netherlands, 1961).

"Preaching the Miracles", Francis Murray in "Worship", June/July 1968.

140. "De Derde Nachtwake" — The Genesis of Luke's Gospel, G. Bouwman, SVD. p. 25.

141. "The Infancy Narratives", Cardinal Jean Danielou, esp. p. 71 ss. (publ. above).

142. "Theology of Revelation", Gabriel Moran, Ch. III — Christ as Revelatory Communion, p. 57 ss.

143. "Discover the Bible", The Bible Center of the Archdiocese of Montreal. Weekly Bulletin, nrs. 266; 270.

"The Location of the Mount of Beatitudes", M. Schoenberg, O.S.C. in "The Bible Today", February 1963.

"The Power and the Wisdom", John L. McKenzie, p. 42. (publ. above).

144. "Gospel Traditions about Christ's Resurrection", Joseph Ponthot in "Lumen Vitae", 1966, nr. 1 p. 66 ss. and 1966 nr. 2 p. 205 ss. (esp. p. 211).

"The Celebration of Pentecost", J. Hoogma, S.J. in "Verbum", May 1961, p. 186.

145. "Introduction to the Apocalyptic", Michael J. Cantley in "The Bible Today", Nov. 1963.

146. "The Phenomenon of Man", Teilhard de Chardin, p. 159.

"Evolution and the Doctrine of Original Sin", S. Trooster, S.J., (Newman Press).

"Das Problem der Hominisation", Paul Overhage/Karl Rahner in "Quaestiones Disputatae", 12/13 (Herder, Freiburg, Basel, Wien).

"Um das Ercheinungsbild der Menschen", Paul Overhage, "Quaestiones Disputatae", 7. (publ. above).

147. "The Bible and the Ancient Near East", Roland de Vaux, O.P. (Doubleday).

"Atlas of the Bible", L. Grollenberg, O.P. (Nelson).

"Atlas of Mesopotamia", H.H. Rowley. (Nelson, 1962).

148. "Can We Base our Spiritual Life Today on the Bible?", Gijs Bouwman, SVD in Concilium, 49, p. 19 ss.